Children's Engagement in the World

This volume describes children's development in its cultural context. It stresses that children's development in diverse cultures follows different paths, depending on the opportunities provided by their cultures. It illustrates that the everyday work, school, and play activities provided for children vary from one culture to another depending on the social and economical structure of children's cultures and adult beliefs about what is valuable for children's participation to secure optimal development.

Thus, *Children's Engagement in the World: Sociocultural Perspectives* considers children's development and education within its social as well as cultural context. This book brings together the most recent theoretical advances in cultural psychology in order to establish a framework for the studies reported in it. The book also draws from the cross-cultural tradition in Developmental Psychology and from Vygotsky and Activity Theory.

Artin Göncü is Associate Professor of Education and Coordinator of the Master's Program in Early Childhood Education at the University of Illinois, Chicago.

Children's Engagement in the World

Sociocultural Perspectives

Edited By

ARTİN GÖNCÜ

CAMBRIDGE
UNIVERSITY PRESS

PUBLISHED BY THE PRESS SYNDICATE OF THE UNIVERSITY OF CAMBRIDGE
The Pitt Building, Trumpington Street, Cambridge, United Kingdom

CAMBRIDGE UNIVERSITY PRESS
The Edinburgh Building, Cambridge CB2 2RU, UK   http://www.cup.cam.ac.uk
40 West 20th Street, New York, NY 10011-4211, USA   http://www.cup.org
10 Stamford Road, Oakleigh, Melbourne 3166, Australia

First published 1999

Printed in the United States of America

Typeface Times Roman 10.5/13   *System* DeskTopPro$_{/UX}$® [BV]

A catalog record for this book is available from the British Library

Library of Congress Cataloging-in-Publication Data
Children's engagement in the world : sociocultural perspectives /
edited by Artin Göncü.
p.   cm.
Includes bibliographical references and index.
ISBN 0-521-58324-1. – ISBN 0-521-58722-0 (pbk.)
1. Child development – Cross-cultural studies.   2. Child
psychology – Cross-cultural studies.   I. Göncü, Artin.
HQ767.9.C4558   1999
305.231 – dc21   98-33945
                                                      CIP
ISBN 0 521 58324 1 hardback
ISBN 0 521 58722 0 paperback

Contents

v

Contributors

Jo Ann M. Farver
University of Southern California,
Los Angeles, CA, USA

Suzanne Gaskins
Northeastern Illinois University
Chicago, IL, USA

Mary Gauvain
University of California
Riverside, CA, USA

Artin Göncü
University of Illinois
Chicago, IL, USA

Steven R. Guberman
University of Colorado
Boulder, CO, USA

Wendy L. Haight
University of Illinois
Urbana-Champaign, IL, USA

Diane Hogan
The Children's Research Centre
Trinity College
Dublin, Ireland

Jyoti Jain
University of Illinois
Chicago, IL, USA

Danielle Johnson
University of Illinois
Chicago, IL, USA

Natalya Kulakova
Institute of Ethnology and
Anthropology
Moscow, Russia

Soeun Lee
Chungbuk National University
Cheongju, Korea

Marika Meltsas
University of Tartu Estonia

Christine C. Pappas
University of Illinois
Chicago, IL, USA

Sarah Putnam
The University of North Carolina
Greensboro, NC, USA

Irina Snezhkova
Institute of Ethnology and
Anthropology
Moscow, Russia

Peeter Tammeveski
Pennsylvania State University
College Park, PA, USA

Jonathan Tudge
The University of North Carolina
Greensboro, NC, USA

Ute Tuermer
University of Illinois
Chicago, IL, USA

Foreword

Robert A. LeVine

At the end of the twentieth century, serious cultural and ecological studies are still rarities in child development research, although cultural context and ecological validity have been explicit concerns in the literature since at least the 1950s. The field as a whole as embodied in the Society for Research in Child Development and its organ *Child Development*, though officially interdisciplinary and with a distinguished sociologist as its president, includes little sophisticated social research and few proposals to rebuild its decrepit bridges to the social sciences. The present volume suggests what the study of childhood might look like as a social science, beginning with a critique of mainstream child development research and moving on to lay the theoretical and empirical groundwork for a systematic understanding of children as actors in complex social worlds.

The contributors to this volume demonstrate a variety of directions for social research on child development, unified by common aims, sources, and strategies. They share the desire to focus the study of childhood on the actual conditions in which children grow up and on the activities and practices in which children participate. Their real-world or naturalistic focus is based on the conviction that useful knowledge of child development must accurately represent the social features and forces that influence learning during the early years. These social influences deserve to be studied in themselves rather than treated simply as independent variables in a statistical model. The authors also share theoretical models of psychologically salient childhood environments derived from the concepts of Vygotsky, Leont'ev, Bronfenbrenner, and the Whitings – models in which concepts such as interaction, activity, and setting guide the investigator to focus attention on certain aspects of environment rather than others. These aspects, as the chapters point out, are related to the social relationships and processes and cultural meanings and practices that constitute the wider environments of children and their parents.

The contributors concern themselves – directly and at length – with

ix

how the interactions, activities, and settings of childhood vary across a wide range of cultures, as well as subcultures defined by ethnicity and social class. They take this comparative perspective to be central to the task of understanding any developmental phenomenon in the human species. Finally, they share an interest in play as a category of childhood activity that, though universal in a broad sense, is highly variable in form and frequency across the childhood environments of different cultures and different segments of a single society. There is more interesting information about play in the chapters of this book than in any other source of which I am aware.

With these common aims, sources, and interests, the contributors to this volume examine not only play but also children's work and cognitive skills in various domains. Their methods vary widely and exemplify the methodological flexibility needed for investigating the divergent conditions and directions of children's development. Rather than clinging to the standard measures favored in conventional psychological research, these seasoned investigators devised measures adjusted to the activities and settings on which they were working. All contributors approach their topics with theoretical sophistication, and some dared to explore environments without a priori hypotheses in order to describe their features and distributions – an investigative style closer to that of Darwin or Piaget than that of the experimental psychologist. The results are informative and provocative, pointing the way to new and significant arenas of research.

The comparative study of childhood learning has a long history – it could be said to have started with the early ethnographies of Mead (1930), Fortes (1938), and Whiting (1941). I believe that the new thinking and research represented here by Artin Göncü and his colleagues will give this field a new vitality and help to integrate it at last within a social science of child development.

References

Fortes, Meyer. (1938). *Social and psychological aspects of education in Taleland.* London: Oxford University Press.
Mead, Margaret. (1930). *Growing up in New Guinea.* New York: William Morrow.
Whiting, John W. M. (1941). *Becoming a Kwoma.* New Haven, CT: Yale University Press.

PART ONE

Introduction

1 Children's and Researchers' Engagement in the World

Artin Göncü

This book emerged from conversations occurring among the contributors over the last decade. Some conversations occurred in a formal fashion in the meetings of the Society of Research in Child Development (Beizer & Miller, 1991; Göncü & Nicolopoulou, 1995) and Piaget Society (Gauvain, 1997; Lucy, 1988). Others occurred in informal gatherings or in study groups. These conversations focused primarily on two related questions of shared interest: How do children's culture and their development mutually constitute one another? How does understanding the relation between culture and child development require an extension of mainstream theory and research? This book brings together the major points at which we converged in developing our sociocultural perspectives. The first of the three sections of this introduction offers a characterization of children found in mainstream research, which we extend in our effort to provide sociocultural descriptions of children's development. The second section provides a summary of how previous work in the sociocultural tradition has guided us in developing our descriptions. The third section is a characterization of the unique contribution of this book – namely, the examinations of the cultural activities through which children engage in the making of their development. The contributors document cultural

I am deeply indebted to many people for their generous support during my effort to bring this book together. Credit goes to Julia Hough, my editor at Cambridge University Press, for her support throughout this project as well as for offering the innovative title of this book. The contributors of this book have proven to be the most cooperative colleagues in obliging with my deadlines and requests for revisions. Most of this book was prepared during my sabbatical leave supported by the University of Illinois at Chicago. During the preparation of this book, my work was also supported by the Spencer Foundation. The proposal for the work reported in this book had gone through the inspection of three anonymous reviewers who should be acknowledged for generously engaging in this effort with us. Finally, I acknowledge Joe Becker for providing critical comments on earlier versions of this introductory chapter.

3

variations and similarities in the activities available for children's participation, how children participate in them, and how they develop as a result of participating in those activities. This collective effort emphasizes the cultural situatedness of children's development and illustrates that understanding it requires an interdisciplinary stance. Finally, the fourth section is an overview of the book with a brief summary of how each chapter contributes to *Children's Engagement in the World*, highlighting the specific research questions of each contribution.

Challenges to Mainstream Psychology's Universal Child

Most of us in our profession are socialized into the mainstream research tradition of psychology and education in Europe and North America. We continue to work within this tradition as we formulate our research questions and develop appropriate methodology to address them. As part of this effort, we must also point out the limitations of mainstream research tradition and its needs for expansion. It is in this self-critical spirit that I characterize some features of the child in contemporary developmental psychology as follows.

The child described in our journals is a generic child. This description is supposed to be a representation of all children in the world, capturing what Shweder (1990) referred to as the "psychic unity" that is hidden behind children of different cultures. In the effort to identify the universal features of children, the mainstream research adopted certain scientific values that promoted a decontextualized description of children. For the purposes of this book, four of those values are worth noting. First, the mainstream research tradition values standardized universal descriptions through variables such as age and gender that hold for all children of the world. When more information about children is considered, it does not go beyond a standard global measure of family, ethnicity, and income. Even locale of children often remains unidentified as if the investigations occurred in a vacuum. Indeed, mainstream research tradition gives the impression that a complete scientific understanding of childhood is achieved through these variables. As this book illustrates, these categories so valued by mainstream research prove insufficient to penetrate into local knowledge about children's development in their own cultures. The contributors of this book argue that to understand children's development in a given culture we need to understand that culture's particular definitions and goals of development for its children. I shall return to this in the second section.

Second, unless the research takes children's relationships as its explicit and specific focus of inquiry, mainstream research values a description of children as individuals without reference to their relationships. This is most evident in cognitive development research. Although there are notable exceptions (e.g., Wertsch, McNamee, McLane, & Budwig, 1980; Yowell, 1997), until recently the social origins of cognition have not been explicitly acknowledged. Despite the emphasis of psychological theory on the significance of relationships (e.g., G. H. Mead, 1934; Piaget, 1965; Vygotksy, 1978), even some of the most immediate and possibly relevant social interactions of children have not become a part of our descriptions. For example, in reports of experimental work on children's performance on cognitive tasks, little, if any, information is supplied on the children's interactions with the researchers, which may have a bearing on children's performance. Furthermore, information provided is not made an integral part of the new understanding offered by the research.

Our field has officially acknowledged the contribution of children's interactions to their cognitive development only recently (Rogoff, 1998). As Guberman (this volume) discusses, however, most of the research still focuses on dyadic relationships. In this book, we argue that in order to present meaningful descriptions, psychological research should consider children's development as inherently situated in their system of social relationships. Even when children are observed alone, we need to be aware of how their solitary activities are shaped by the system of relationships that constitute the context of their development. This book provides examples of the intricate connections between children's social context and their functioning in diverse activities such as play (Gaskins; Tudge et al.; Farver; Haight; and Göncü et al.), school work (Farver; Tudge et al.), economic work and maintenance work (Farver; Gaskins; Tudge et al.), planning (Gauvain), solving math problems (Guberman), and literacy (Pappas).

Third, mainstream research in developmental psychology values work that illustrates cause-and-effect relationships between variables. The advantage of this honorable tradition is evidenced in textbooks summarizing the causes of children's development in many areas of psychological functioning. However, establishing cause-and-effect relationships often requires designing confound-free laboratory experiments using tasks created by the researchers. As many scholars have argued (e.g., Bronfenbrenner, 1986; Bronfenbrenner & Morris, 1998), children do not encounter these tasks in their day-to-day living. Thus, unless we show that cause–effect relationships obtained in the psychological laboratories also hold in children's daily activities, the value of these relationships remains ambiguous at best. As Gauvain (this volume) argues and illustrates, a student of culture and development seeks to validate the findings coming from the laboratories in children's natural environments, and moreover seeks to explain the simultaneous functioning of a complex of variables in such environments. Furthermore, as Gaskins (this volume) argues, understanding the working of variables in situ results in interpretations of children's-development-in-context rather than an interpretation of development as a collection of relationships among isolated variables.

Fourth, in keeping with its goal of describing the universal child, mainstream psychology values inferential statistics that aim to make generalizations from samples to populations. When cultural differences are believed to be a matter of degree on a given measure, data analyses relying on inferential statistics are appropriate. For example, once we prove that pretend play occurs in all cultures included in a project, use of inferential statistics to reach generalizations from the comparisons is appropriate. Much of the work summarized in the present book makes use of inferential statistics.

However, reliance on the statistical analyses has not been without problems. The present book notes three of these problems and makes proposals to advance the interpretation of research data. The first two problems and the related solutions emerge from within the mainstream research tradition. First, in light of the previous illustrations that mean difference approaches to comparison of groups consider the group as a more or less homogeneous entity and minimize within-group variability (LeVine, 1970; Rogoff, 1982), we make an effort to understand within-group variability. The statistical and conceptual arguments provided in this book all emphasize that understanding within-group variability is crucial in cultural research. Understanding that members of every culture may vary in the extent to which they share a trait prevents us from making stereotypical statements about any group. Such variability can be documented in many ways including making the individual data points available (e.g., Gaskins, this volume) and creating groups that may differ from one another within the same culture such as fathers and mothers without assuming that this difference holds cross-culturally (e.g., Haight; Tudge et al., this volume).

A second advance put forth in this book relates to the purpose of the statistical analyses. As Tudge et al. (this volume) illustrate, when two or more cultures are compared by means of statistical analyses, unless such comparison carries the purpose of determining whether the findings are generalizable to other cultures in the quantitative forms, inferential statistics are not appropriate. Rather, statistical techniques other than inferential statistics should be used as a descriptive language to communicate the significance of difference obtained in the analyses.

The third advance discussed in this book comes from outside of the mainstream research tradition in developmental psychology and early education. Our proposal is that variations within and across cultures can be a matter of kind as well as degree. When difference is a matter of kind, generalizability theory and inferential statistics are not appropriate tools to interpret the data. For example, statistical analyses do not take us far enough in our efforts to understand why some cultures rely on child labor while other cultures don't. Cultural differences in such phenomena such as child labor shift the level of comparison from quantitative to qualitative. In such cases, our analysis should focus on understanding the unique features of each culture through ethnographic methods. The subsequent cultural comparisons are based on our interpretation of each culture.

In my view, psychology prefers to focus on understanding the degree of difference in common traits across groups using what Allport (1937) referred to as the nomothetic method, ignoring the idiographic method (i.e., study of the unique features of an individual person or an individual culture) (also see Kagitcibasi, 1996). As evidenced in the work reported in this book by Gaskins, Haight, and Pappas, the cultural approach needs the idiographic method as well as the nomothetic method – sometimes to focus on the individual child within a given culture, and sometimes to focus on the individual culture. Consistent with this emphasis, this book espouses a variety of views of what constitutes scientific evidence and how such evidence is treated. We need to keep ourselves aware of our knowledge that our values and theories influence what we consider to be legitimate data.

To summarize, research activity in developmental psychology in the Western world has had a culture of its own with specific scientific values. This culture has the goal of identifying features of childhood that are universally true. The product of this culture is knowledge about decontextualized and average abilities of often unidentified children. This knowledge may partially describe children in a given culture, capturing what is deemed relevant and meaningful for the advancement of psychological theory by the developmental scientist. However, it leaves out what is important for children's development from the viewpoint of their cultures. Our additional effort to understand children's development as situated in their culture led us to examine it from the perspective of their own cultures. In pursuit of this, we were guided by the following theory and research.

The Child of the Sociocultural Tradition

The contributors to this book drew from many different theoretical frameworks. However, despite the theoretical and methodological variations across the chapters, a review reveals that three particular approaches have influenced and guided most of the work reported in this book. The rest of this section is an overview of these approaches.

The Cross-cultural Tradition in Developmental Psychology

In earlier efforts to illustrate the relationship between child development and culture, culture was treated as an independent variable, like age and gender, which shaped children's development. For example, in the first volume of *A Handbook of Child Psychology*, Margaret Mead (1931) argued that studying children of different cultures enables us to understand how different social environments result in differences in children's development. Mead used this argument to help justify the study of what she called the "primitive child." She stated that "the primitive child starts life with the same innate capacities as the child of civilized parents" and, therefore, "the startling differences in habit, emotional development, and mental outlook between primitive and civilized man must be laid at the door of difference in social environment" (pp. 669–70). Thus, Mead likened cross-cultural research to experimental research treating variations across cultures as natural manipulations of the independent variable whose effect can be observed on dependent variables such as habit and emotion.

J. Whiting (1954) argued for what he called a "cross-cultural method" in the *Handbook of Social Psychology*, seeing it as essential for understanding both similarities and differences across cultures. On the one hand, he believed that the cross-cultural approach is necessary to find out what is universal about child development. In the second edition of the *Handbook*, Whiting (1968) concluded that the cross-cultural method "is one of the methods by which the scientific laws governing humans and their behavior can be established" (p. 720). Whiting stated that unless they are validated cross-culturally, theories of child development remain ethnocentric.

On the other hand, Whiting proposed that the cross-cultural method was a way of understanding difference. He stated that the cross-cultural method "provides one more way in which our presumptions and prejudices may be put in jeopardy" (p. 720). By implication, Whiting invited Western researchers not to judge other cultures if their children's development follows a path that is not Western. Cultural differences in child development must be understood and not judged, because there may not be one right way in which children develop (Gaskins & Göncü, 1992).

Seeking similarities and differences in child development across different cultures of the world situated on the same platform of legitimacy is exemplified in Whiting and Whiting (1975) and in Whiting and Edwards (1988). They took functions such as nurturing the young as universals in human development and revealed cultural differences in how these functions were achieved. Whiting and Edwards (1988) stated that in all cultures included in their study, infants received nurturance from their older companions, although how children received nurturance varied from culture to culture. In addition, Whiting and Edwards (1988) emphasized that the unique influence of each culture becomes increasingly evident with increasing age from infancy to school years. Children's biological need to rely on adults in maintaining their survival lessens, leading to greater engagement in a variety of cultural activities that shape the development of young members in each culture in unique ways.

The influence of the cross-cultural approach becomes evident in many ways throughout this book. In those studies where the focus is on quantitative differences across cultures in a given variable, our work clearly draws from the cross-cultural tradition. Furthermore, the influence of the cross-cultural tradition is seen in the comparative way in which we interpret our data. As will be evident to the reader, even if in a given chapter the empirical data derive from a single culture, the interpretation of the data goes beyond that culture to point to similarities and differences across a variety of cultures. The specific purpose of these comparisons varies across chapters, however. Finally, the influence of the cross-cultural tradition is seen in the ways in which we transfrom the idea of culture-as-an-independent-variable to culture-as-a-system-of-meanings. To do so, we draw from B. Whiting (1976), LeVine (1970), and Laboratory of Comparative Human Cognition (1983), among others, who made a pioneering effort to unpack the meaning of culture, leading the way to cultural psychology.

Cultural Psychology

Several efforts have already been made to provide a history of cultural psychology as well as to define its meaning, boundaries, and priorities (e.g., Brunner, 1996; Cahan & White, 1992; Cole, 1996; Shweder, 1990; Shweder, Goodnow, Hatano, LeVine, Markus, & Miller, 1998; Shweder & Sullivan, 1993). A shared conviction among the contributors of this book, developed on the basis of previous work, is that culture should be conceptualized as a system of meanings that provides the context for children's development as one of its constituents rather than as a variable that exerts an influence on children's development. In this view, then, culture cannot be separated from children's development.

The conceptualization of culture-as-a-system-of-meanings has important implications for scientific activity: First of all, this approach calls for determination of what development means, and how it occurs, on the basis of local theories within each culture (cf. Harkness & Super, 1996). When we see each culture as having its own telos for its children's development, then our focus becomes one of providing descriptions of how children are guided to reach culturally varied developmental goals established for them. Illustrations of this can be found in language socialization research where scholars have shown that cultural variations in children's development of language are related to cultural variations in acceptable ways of communication (Brice-Heath, 1983; Miller, 1982; Ochs, 1988; Ochs & Shieffelin, 1984).

The effort to understand children's development on the basis of local theories does not preclude cultural comparisons. Remaining within the boundaries of cultural psychology, it is still possible to make such comparisons. What we need to understand in comparing specific meanings coming from different cultures is that we ought not to take it for granted that cultural meanings are commensurate. Only after the meanings are determined to be commensurate should we explore the degree of similarity or difference between different cultures.

A second important implication of conceptualizing culture as a system of meanings is that a culture need not be defined in terms of national boundaries but as groups of people with shared meanings. When understood in this way, cultural psychology allows the social scientist to identify different cultures within a given nation. As Goodnow (in press) notes, and as we witness during our day-to-day living within the United States, cultures defining themselves on the basis of ethnicity, race, sexual orientation, and professional affiliation, among others, live next to, or in an overlapping manner, with one another. Cultural psychology also recognizes the fact that certain cultures cross national boundaries. For example, as one Turkish mother's response to my interview question brought to my attention, at a certain economic and educational level, parents in different parts of the world may belong to the same culture (i.e., parents who read books about child rearing in making decisions about how to interact with their children [cf. Rogoff, Mistry, Göncü, & Mosier, 1993]).

The influence of cultural psychology on this book is evident in the elaborations of the concept of culture as a system of meaning. Common to all the scholars participating in this volume is the view that each culture, when unpacked, presents itself as a unique network of variables, or meanings, that demand an understanding as a whole. Furthermore, Gauvain, Guberman, and Pappas discuss how children attain certain specific meanings such as planning, mathematics, and literacy, respectively, through varied cultural activities.

Vygotsky and Activity Theory

Vygotsky influenced the work reported in this book both as a theorist who conceptualized development as a process of socialization into the existing system of cultural meanings and, more importantly, as a theorist who proposed a specific social mechanism by which cultural meanings become children's means of functioning as they "internalize" those meanings (Moll, 1993; Rogoff, 1998; Wertsch, 1985). The contributors borrow from Vygotsky his now-famous thesis that children internalize cultural meanings in the *zone of proximal development* in their effort to become independently functioning members of their society. Children's internalization of meanings occurs through two different kinds of engagement: through children's collaboration with other more competent members of the society in problem solving, or through children's play (Gaskins & Göncü, 1988). Children's collaboration with competent members of the society help children decide what meanings are worth engaging in as well as how to engage in those meanings. Children's play, on the other hand, enables children to internalize the meanings that children consider on their own as worth engaging in (Göncü & Becker, 1992).

We extend Vygotksy's theory in three interrelated ways in this book. One extension relates to how children and other members of their community determine what meanings are considered worthwhile to engage in as opposed to others. To address this issue, we draw from Leont'ev's theory of activity. Leont'ev (1981) defines activity as a unit of life in which an individual engages to satisfy a need. The appropriation of cultural meaning occurs in the process of satisfying the need (cf. Farver; Gaskins; Gauvain; Göncü et al., Guberman; this volume).

Second, as Göncü et al. (this volume) discuss, Leont'ev proposed certain types of activities as leading activities that result in the satisfaction of a need and that also give way to other activities. Leont'ev considered mastery of physical objects, play, schoolwork, and income-producing work as leading activities for infants, preschool children, school-age children, and adults, respectively. This conceptualization of Leont'ev influenced the participants of this volume in their choice of activities as units of analysis through which they can explore child development. Also, Leont'ev's theory brings to our attention that the economic, social, and physical conditions of a culture determine the activities that are available to children. In order to understand why some activities are valued more than others, we need to pay attention to the survival value of activities for children.

A third extension of Vygotksy's theory relates to the kind of participation of children in cultural activity. Previous research in the sociocultural tradition (e.g., Greenfield & Cocking, 1994; Lancy, 1996; Rogoff & Lave, 1984) brought to our attention that children of the world may participate in and learn from activities in more ways than was originally conceived by Western researchers and educators. Following this tradition, we illustrate that variations in participation occur in how many people participate in the activities, in who participates, in the institutional context of the activities, and in whether or not the activities are defined explicitly as activities of teaching and learning.

In summary, then, once we define children's development as a process of socialization into the existing system of meanings in their culture, the goal for research becomes one of understanding how children attain those meanings. We make an effort to achieve that understanding by considering the social and economic structure of each culture along with its goals for children's development, and the mechanisms by which children attain such goals. This requires identification of a unit of analysis for research that corresponds to a unit of meaning in children's lives as determined by members of the children's cultures. For us, cultural activity as a unit of life comprises the unit of meaning that children are expected to attain and therefore should be the unit of analysis for research.

Cultural Activity and Children's Engagement

This book presents conceptualizations of children's development as a process of socialization into cultural activity. Against the theoretical background already established, the book proposes three specific questions to guide research: (1) What are the activities that are available for children in their communities? (2) How do children engage in those activities? (3) What do children learn as a result of their engagement?

Adopting these questions to guide research has important consequences. One such consequence is the necessity of an interdisciplinary stance to the study of child development in terms of substance and method. With regard to substance, the effort to understand the availability of activities and children's engagement in them requires integrating psychological approaches to the study of activity with sociological, anthropological, and educational approaches to child development. This is necessary because children's activities occur always in the economic, institutional, attitudinal, and interactional contexts of their community, which traditionally have not been a part of research in psychology. The interdisciplinary approach is evident throughout this book. For example, Gaskins, Tudge et al., Farver, Haight, and Göncü et al. illustrate that to understand the variations in children's play, we need to go beyond psychological theory and explore how economics and the value system of children's communities prepare opportunities for play. In a similar vein, Gauvain, Guberman, and Pappas illustrate that we need to draw from other relevant disciplines to determine whether or how the opportunities necessary for the development of planning (Gauvain), solving math problems (Guberman), and becoming literate (Pappas) are afforded to children. Finally, the contributors make recommendations for more integral social and educational policy than we presently have, taking into account knowledge emerging from an interdisciplinary approach to the study of child development.

As for the need for interdisciplinary methodology, our goal of understanding children's development from the perspective of their own cultures in conjunction with our goal of providing cultural comparisons of children's development required integrating psychological methods with those from other disciplines. To understand children's development from the perspective of their own communities, many of the contributors in this book integrated an emic approach into their works. Our need to identify the local developmental goals and activities led us to engage in observations and dialogue with the participants. Depending on the research question, the authors' involvement in the communities in which they worked varied, although all the researchers engaged in dialogue with the adults who participated in their projects. These dialogues addressed what adults considered as valuable goals for children's growth, why they thought so, and how children reached the goals.

When our works included cultural comparisons, we assured commensurability of meaning across cultures on the foci of inquiry by collaborating with people from each of the communities in which the research was carried out. In fact, in some cases the collaborators belonged to both the scientific community at large and the local community in which the research was carried out. Examples include Tudge et al. and Pappas and teacher/researchers as well as many others mentioned in individual chapters.

The contributors made use of sociological literature in an effort to examine the social and economic structure of children's communities. This has been done through census data where available. Otherwise, contributors relied on information obtained from the participants on such aspects of their lives as income and formal education. As is evident in the work of all the contributors, there is a strong methodological effort to establish connections between community structure, adult values, and children's activities. Finally, the contributors observed children and their partners as they engaged in activities in their own communities. This approach, well known in ecological psychology (Barker & Wright, 1955) and ethnography (Brice-Heath, 1983; Corsaro, 1985; Miller, 1982), provides direct information about children's engagement and also serves as a validity check for the information reported in the dialogues.

The emic approach led contributors to the discovery of categories of children's engagement that presented cultural variability in kind, as well as in the frequency of occurrence. For example, Göncü et al. illustrate that when children's play is approached from the communities' perspective, new categories of play emerge that have not been identified in the extant literature. In a similar vein, Gaskins, Tudge et al., and Farver illustrate that in some communities the life of a young child may include work activities either to bring in money for the family or to contribute to the maintenance of daily life (e.g., cleaning the living quarters), whereas this is not common in other communities.

Equally important, this book illustrates that children may engage in the same meaning through different activities. To this end, Haight illustrates that children's caregivers socialize the young into the world of symbolic functioning through differing forms of participation in symbolic play depending on what is deemed to be culturally appropriate. Gauvain illustrates that children in all cultures develop the ability to plan their lives although they may have different opportunities to do so depending on the developmental priorities of their communities. Guberman provides examples of how children's specific cultural activities in the communities outside of school enable them to engage in math problems. Finally, Pappas illustrates how young children learn to be literate through different activities.

Along with the variability in the kind and frequency of occurrence of children's activities, the ways in which children participate in and appropriate from their activities present cultural variations also. Contributors to this volume identify as participation in a cultural activity cases where children learn by observation. This takes place in activities that are part of day-to-day living, necessary for children's and their families' survival, but not organized as activities of teaching and learning. For example, as Gaskins discusses, children's learning can occur through observation of adults' activities that have the purpose of accomplishing the daily chores. Guberman illustrates that children learn to solve complex problems of number by merely participating in daily shopping activities without being instructed on how to solve such problems. Gauvain provides other descriptions of children's participation in cultural activity through which children develop the ability to plan without being explicitly instructed.

Another type of participation occurs in activities defined as activities of teaching and learning. These activities can occur in the family as well as in school. In sharp contrast to the community activities of children, these activities can be decontextualized from children's day-to-day living. Farver provides examples of this type of teaching and learning in preschool settings. The variability in children's participation in these activities is vast. For example, Farver and Tudge et al. state that these activities can take the form of imparting or receiving knowledge in a didactic manner where the adult determines the course of action. However, as shown in the work of Pappas, literacy activities in school can be presented to children as part of their community life by integrating community and school activities and by engaging children in determining the curriculum of their own schooling.

Finally, this book presents variations in children's participation in their play activities. Farver, Haight, and Göncü et al. show that in communities where adults consider play as a valuable activity, provide children with the resources for play materials, and interact with children as their conversational partners, adults engage in play with children, and the children enjoy the play for its own sake. However, as Haight and Tudge et al. illustrate, parents may value play as an educational medium in which they provide academic and etiquette lessons. Examples of both types of activities can be seen in different settings such as home and school. In some contrast, Farver and Gaskins show that in communities where parents do not have the time or resources to engage in play with children and do not see themselves as conversational partners to their children, they simply do not play with them. In such communities, children's siblings and peers often serve as their play partners.

Overview of the Book

This volume presents programs of research. Chapters often include more than one study conducted to address an evolving string of questions. When a chapter reports one study, reference is made to the relevant previous research to provide the reader with appropriate background information.

The volume consists of three sections on children's engagement. Part Two presents works that focus on cultural variations in the availability of different everyday activities to children. In Chapter 2, Gaskins provides an ethnography of Mayan children's cultural engagement in the Yucatan based on many years of work in a remote village. To explicate children's socialization into their community, Gaskins proffers three principles of cultural engagement: the primacy of adult work, parental beliefs, and child motivation. She illustrates the connection between these principles and children's activities of self-maintenance, social orientation (observations and conversations), play, and work. After discussing children's engagement, Gaskins concludes her chapter with a discussion of children's learning.

In Chapter 3, Tudge et al. shift our attention to within-culture heterogeneity by comparing middle- and working-class communities in the United States, South Korea, Russia, and Estonia as well as examining similarities and differences of middle- and working-class communities across these societies. Tudge et al. find categories of activity available for children's participation that are similar to those reported by Gaskins. These are play, work, and conversation. In addition, however, Tudge et al. report academic lessons as another category of activity in which children participate in urban communities, where schooling is an inevitable part of their lives. Like Gaskins, Tudge et al. elaborate their picture of children's socialization by establishing relationships among children's activities, parental beliefs, and children's developing competence.

Part Three includes work conducted to understand whether or how children's play varies across cultures. In our view, since the publication of the fourth edition of the *Handbook of Child Psychology*, the most important advances in play research have been in the illustration of cultural variations in this important childhood activity. Because the fifth edition of the *Handbook* did not include a review chapter on play, we made an effort to cover important new trends that have emerged in play research. One common goal of the research programs in this section is to describe cultural variations in pretend play and to offer explanations for those variations. As Farver, Haight, and Göncü et al. discuss, this goal emerged from a developing belief in the literature that when pretend play does not occur in the same way as Western researchers expected, it may be an indication of children's deficit.

In Chapter 4, Farver examines cultural differences in her work on the pretend play of toddlers in communities in the United States, Mexico, and Indonesia as well as in work on the pretend play of Korean-American and European-American preschool children. Farver adopts activity setting as the unit of analysis. Selecting and analyzing an activity setting requires identification of the purpose of the activities, the participants, the specific tasks being performed, the scripts and plans for the activity, and the cultural goals of the activity. Farver's work illustrates that when children's play is observed in terms of such an activity setting, judgments made about the frequency of pretend play in isolation are transformed to meaningful cultural interpretations.

In Chapter 5, Haight focuses on the role of culture in caregiver–child play. By interpreting the detailed examples of parent–child play in Chinese and U.S. families from the perspective of their cultures, Haight claims that cultural variations in parent–child pretend play derive from variations in parental beliefs about play. Through this connection, Haight explores the concepts of "socialization" and "acquisition," the relationship between parents' ideas about child development and children's responses to them. Haight shows that when socialization practices are observed in light of parental beliefs, intracultural constancy and variation as well as intercultural constancy and variation emerge as dimensions of interpretation of the empirical data.

In Chapter 6, Göncü et al. include a study on cultural variations in the play of toddlers in communities in Guatemala, Turkey, India, and the

United States as well as a study of cultural variations in the play of preschool-age children from African-American, European-American, and Turkish communities. Taking into account community features such as economic structure, adult value system, intersubjectivity between adults and children, and the content of children's play, Göncü et al. offer a model to guide the understanding of cultural variations in children's play. They emphasize that when children's play is examined from their communities' perspective, new types of play emerge that were not previously recognized by researchers.

Part Four brings together works conducted to understand whether or how the same ability develops through different activities in diverse cultures of the world. The work included in this section addresses the role of schooling and of the children's community in how children learn to plan their activities, how they solve mathematics problems, and how they become literate. In Chapter 7, Gauvain examines the development of planning. She first reviews experimental work conducted in the laboratory settings in the Western world. Afterward, she reviews the limited ethnographic literature on children's planning and weaves both literatures in her discussion of the development of planning. Gauvain proposes to expand planning research by going beyond how children plan specific tasks and activities. She conceptualizes planning as a process in which children and their parents establish goals for their future. Within this framework, Gauvain reports her findings of how U.S. children from different ethnic backgrounds plan their day-to-day living. Taking together this work and the work of others, Gauvain draws inferences relevant to social policy suggesting that young children are rushed by adults whereas adolescents are lacking direction to guide their lives.

In Chapter 8, Guberman addresses how children learn to solve number problems outside of school in what he calls "supportive contexts." As an example for such contexts, Guberman first summarizes his work with middle-class U.S. mothers and their young children on how mothers support children's counting activities. Afterward, he shows that supportive contexts occur in children's communities outside of home, and he takes examples from his work in Recife, Brazil. Finally, Guberman shows that children create supportive contexts of learning for one another in games such as MONOPOLY without adults being present. Guberman concludes that to understand how children learn to function in the world of numbers, we need to look at their development of numerical concepts in relation to cultural activities.

In Chapter 9, Pappas explores how urban kindergarten and first-grade U.S. children from diverse linguistic backgrounds become literate. Pappas addresses this question at two critical levels. The first is a description of activities of literacy in the classroom. This description shows how the participating teachers provide literacy activities that are meaningful for young children by negotiating the curriculum with children rather than determining it on their own. Examples include Sonia White Soltero's geography lessons with bilingual kindergarten children, Ann Barry's use of first-grade ABC books, and Pamela Wolfer's first-grade writing lessons. The second level of Pappas's discussion examines how we can produce a description of children's and teachers' activities that is meaningful and acceptable to both the university researcher and the participants. This motivates Pappas to collaborate with teacher/researchers in a mutually constructed research agenda, an approach consistent with that of other contributors to this volume (e.g., Tudge et al.).

References

Allport, G. (1937). *Personality: A psychological interpretation*. New York: Holt.

Barker, R. G., & Wright, H. F. (1955). *Midwest and its children*. New York: Harper & Row.

Beizer, L., & Miller, P. (Chairs). (1991). Cultural dimensions of pretend play in infancy and early childhood. Symposium conducted at the meeting of the Society for Research in Child Development, Seattle, WA.

Brice-Heath, S. (1983). *Ways with words: Language, life, and work in communities and classrooms*. New York: Cambridge University Press.

Bronfenbrenner, U. (1986). Recent advances in research on the ecology of human development. In R. K. Silbereisen, K. Eyferth, & G. Rudinger (Eds.), *Development as action in context: Problem behavior and normal youth development* (pp. 286–309). New York: Springer Verlag.

Bronfenbrenner, U., & Morris, P. A. (1998). The ecology of developmental processes. In W. Damon (Series Ed.) & R. Learner (Vol. Ed.), *Handbook of child psychology: Vol. 1. Theoretical models of human development* (pp. 993–1028). New York: Wiley.

Bruner, J. (1996). *The culture of education*. Cambridge, MA: Harvard University Press.

Cahan, E., & White, S. (1992). Proposals for a second psychology. The special issue: The history of American psychology. *American Psychologist, 47* (2), 224–35.

Cole, M. (1996). *Cultural psychology: A once and future discipline*. Cambridge, MA: Harvard University Press.

Corsaro, W. A. (1985). *Friendship and peer culture in the early years.* Norwood, NJ: Ablex.

Gaskins, S., & Göncü, A. (1988). Children's play as representation and imagination: The case of Piaget and Vygotksy. *The Quarterly Newsletter of the Laboratory of Comparative Human Cognition, 10,* 104–107.

Gaskins, S., & Göncü, A. (1992). Cultural variation in play: A challenge to Piaget and Vygotsky. *The Quarterly Newsletter of the Laboratory of Comparative Human Cognition, 14,* 31–35.

Gauvain, M. (Chair). (1997). Children's everyday activities: Cultural opportunities for cognitive development. Symposium conducted at the meeting of the Piaget Society, Santa Monica, CA.

Göncü, A., & Becker, J. (1992). Some contributions of a Vygotskyan approach to early education. *International Journal of Cognitive Education and Mediated Learning, 2,* 2, 147–53.

Göncü, A., & Nicolopoulou, A. (Chairs). (1995). The pretend play of cultures: Cultures of pretend play. Symposium conducted at the meeting of the Society for Research in Child Development, Indianapolis, IN.

Goodnow, J. (in press). Parenting and the "tranmission" and "internalization" of values: From social-cultural perspectives to within-family analyses. In J. Grusec & L. Kuczynski (Eds.), *Parenting strategies and children's internalization of values: A handbook of theoretical and research proposals.* New York: Wiley.

Greenfield, P., & Cocking, R. (1994). *Cross-cultural roots of minority child development.* Hillsdale, NJ: Erlbaum.

Harkness, S., & Super, C. (1996). *Parents' cultural beliefs systems: Their origins, expressions, and consequences.* New York: Guilford.

Kagitcibasi, C. (1996). *Family and human development across cultures: A view from the other side.* Mahwah, NJ: Erlbaum.

Laboratory of Comparative Human Cognition (1983). Culture and cognitive development. In P. Mussen (Series Ed.) & W. Kessen (Vol. Ed.), *Handbook of child psychology: Vol. 1. History, theory, and methods* (pp. 296–356). New York: Wiley.

Lancy, D. F. (1996). Playing on the mother ground: Cultural routines for children's development. New York: Guilford.

Leont'ev, A. N. (1981). *Problems of the development of the mind.* Moscow: Progress Publishers.

LeVine, R. A. (1970). Cross-cultural study in child psychology. In P. Mussen (Ed.), *Carmichael's manual of child psychology* (3rd ed.) (pp. 559–612). New York: Wiley.

Lucy, J. (Chair). (1988). Representation and imagination in the theories of Piaget and Vygotksy. Symposium conducted at the meeting of the Piaget Society, Philadelphia, PA.

Mead, G. H. (1934). *Mind, self, and society* (C. W. Morris, Ed.) Chicago: University of Chicago Press.

Mead, M. (1931). The primitive child. In C. Murchison (Ed.), *A handbook of child psychology* (pp. 669–87). Worcester, MA: Clark University Press.

Miller, P. (1982). *Amy, Wendy, and Beth: Learning language in south Baltimore.* Austin: University of Texas Press.

Moll, L. (1993). *Vygotsky and education: Instructional implications and applications of sociohistorical psychology.* New York: Cambridge University Press.

Ochs, E. (1988). *Culture and language development.* Cambridge, England: Cambridge University Press.

Ochs, E., & Schieffelin, B. (1984). Language acquisition and socialization. In R. LeVine and R. Shweder (Eds.), *Culture theory: Essays on mind, self, and emotion* (pp. 276–320). Cambridge, England: Cambridge University Press.

Piaget, J. (1965). *The moral judgment of the child.* New York: The Free Press.

Rogoff, B. (1982). Integrating context and cognitive development. In M. E. & A. L. Brown (Eds.), *Advances in developmental psychology* (Vol. 2, pp. 125–70). Hillsdale, NJ: Erlbaum.

Rogoff, B. (1998). Cognition as a collaborative process. In W. Damon (Series Ed.) & D. Kuhn & R. S. Siegler (Vol. Eds.), *Handbook of child psychology: Vol. 2. Cognition, perception, and language* (pp. 679–744). New York: Wiley.

Rogoff, B., & Lave, J. (1984). (Eds.). *Everyday cognition: Its development and context.* Cambridge, MA: Harvard University Press.

Rogoff, B., Mistry, J., Göncü, A., & Mosier, C. (1993). Guided participation in cultural activity by toddlers and caregivers. *Monographs of the Society for Research in Child Development,* 58 (Serial No. 236).

Shweder, R. (1990). Cultural psychology: What is it? In J. W. Stigler, R. A. Shweder, & G. Herdt (Eds.), *Cultural psychology: Essays on comparative human development* (pp. 1–43). Cambridge, England: Cambridge University Press.

Shweder, R., Goodnow J., Hatano, G., LeVine, R., Markus, H., & Miller, P. (1998). The cultural psychology of development: One mind, many mentalities. In W. Damon (Series Ed.) & R. M. Learner (Vol. Ed.), *Handbook of child psychology: Vol. 1. Theoretical models of human development* (pp. 865–937). New York: Wiley.

Shweder, R., & Sullivan, M. (1993). Cultural psychology: Who needs it? *Annual Review of Psychology, 44,* 497–523.

Vygotksy, L. S. (1978). *Mind in society.* Cambridge, MA: Harvard University Press.

Wertsch, J. V. (1985). *Vygotksy and the social formation of mind.* Cambridge, MA: Harvard University Press.

Wertsch, J. V., McNamee, G. D., McLane, J. G., & Budwig, N. A. (1980). The adult–child dyad as a problem-solving system. *Child Development, 51*, 1215–21.

Whiting, B. B. (1976). The problem of the packaged variable. In K. F. Riegel & J. A. Meachem (Eds.), *The developing individual in a changing world* (Vol. 1). Chicago: Aldine.

Whiting, B. B., & Edwards, C. P. (1988). *Children of different worlds.* Cambridge, MA: Harvard University Press.

Whiting, B. B., & Whiting, J. W. M. (1975). *Children of six cultures.* Cambridge, MA: Harvard University Press.

Whiting, J. M. H. (1954) The cross-cultural method. In G. Lindzey (Ed)., *Handbook of social psychology* (pp. 523–31). Reading, MA: Addison-Wesley.

Whiting, J. M. H. (1968). Methods and problems in cross-cultural psychology. In G. Lindzey & E. Aronson (Eds.), *The handbook of social psychology* (2nd ed.) (pp. 693–728). Reading, MA: Addison-Wesley.

Yowell, C. (1997). Risks of communication: Early adolescent girls' conversations with mothers and friends about sexuality. *Journal of Adolescence, 17*, 172–96.

PART TWO

Children's Engagement in the World

2 Children's Daily Lives in a Mayan Village: A Case Study of Culturally Constructed Roles and Activities

Suzanne Gaskins

Children must become competent members of their adult communities for both their own survival and that of the culture. Despite attempts to study this process from a number of disciplines such as psychology, anthropology, sociology, and education, it has proved difficult to characterize the process, including when the process begins and ends, the structure of the information transmitted (e.g., does it come in bundles or in discrete pieces for the child to piece together), what roles are filled by the various participants (e.g., how is responsibility for learning distributed), what the process actually looks like (e.g., what role does explicit instruction or internalization play), or even how much variability there is in such factors as these across cultures and across individual children. There is not even agreement on where one should look for evidence of the process. In the past, evidence has been sought in changes over time of the internalized constructions of individual children, in the shared understandings of the adult members of a culture, and in the structure and principles of those cultural institutions that have the explicit goal of transmitting information, such as Western schools. All of these attempts have provided unsatisfying answers, too general and abstract and too partial to capture the complexities and variations in the process that children and their caregivers and peers display in their everyday lives.

Recently, and in part in response to the limitations of previous work, there has been a growing interest among Western researchers in under-

This chapter represents insights from fieldwork over the last 18 years. During that time, the people of the village where I worked have repeatedly welcomed me into their homes to watch and participate in their daily lives, and they have patiently answered my questions and guided me toward understanding. There is no adequate way to thank them for their kindnesses to me and my family. In the process of writing this chapter, John A. Lucy and Artin Göncü provided me with many helpful comments on earlier drafts, and the end product is much better as a result.

25

standing development and socialization not as static phenomena to be found in individual children or in cultural belief systems or in institutional structures but as dynamic processes that can be observed and analyzed through the study of the behavior of children engaged in daily activities with other people. This approach was spawned in large part by Vygotsky's social/historical theory of development (1987 [1934]). Vygotsky argues that the behavior which leads to development occurs first on the interpersonal plane, through the co-construction of social interaction between the child and someone more knowledgeable. Only later can the child internalize, on the intrapersonal plane, what he or she has already been able to accomplish with others. Related work by his Russian colleagues and students (e.g., Leont'ev, 1979; Luria, 1976) emphasizes the importance of activities as the appropriate unit of analysis, increasing the centrality of both actions and context in the analysis (also see Farver, Gauvain, Göncü et al., and Guberman, this volume).

Contemporary psychological theorists who draw from this Soviet perspective and place activity at the center of their arguments, such as Rogoff (1990) and Lave and Wenger (1992), argue that one should not study individuals as independent units alone but always as individuals engaged in activity in context. Such approaches dissolve the artificial divisions constructed in the classic nature–nurture debate, recognizing instead the interdependence of both forces in development. This approach is harmonious with emerging theories in other social sciences, such as sociology, anthropology, and linguistics, in which human behavior and communication are situated in "practice" (Bourdieu, 1977) – and should be studied as situated behaviors, as activity in context – rather than as abstract structures in either society or the individual.

Although an activity theory approach to development corrects for the abstract nature of much of the previous research, and promises to ground the theory in the specifics of naturally occurring, observable behavior, it often assumes that the narrow context of the moment of action is enough to interpret behavior adequately. However, activity in context is going to have important effects on development primarily in the consistent patterns of daily activity that children experience. Therefore, it is the sources of those repeated patterns that will have the ultimate influence on development. In order to understand the developmental process as occurring through activity in context, one must study not only the individual instances of behavior observed but must also account for the sources of consistency in experience. This entails taking a broad view of context (Bronfenbrenner, 1979). To do this one must return to the traditional concerns about group beliefs and institutional practices now used in the service of understanding the sources of patterned activity that children engage in everyday. (For further elaboration of this view, see Tudge et al., this volume.)

This chapter takes the view that the process of development can be understood only by such a dual research agenda. First, one must study children engaged in their daily activities to observe the unit of child-in-activity-in-context that represents the locus of the developmental process. Second, one must also study the cultural belief systems and institutions that are responsible for consistency in the everyday contexts of behavior experienced by children (Gaskins, 1994). Given this perspective, it follows that generalizations about how culturally motivated patterns of activity influence the developmental process which are based on only one culture will be limited. Once development is conceived of as being situated in activity in context, and once that context is recognized as being culturally ordered, cultural comparison must be an inherent part of the developmental research agenda. A series of such dual-faceted case studies, which integrate both child activity and ethnographic context, would provide the foundation for a legitimate comparison of children's engagement across cultures and would allow us to begin to assess the relationship of culturally structured activity to development.

A good example of the potential of case studies is recent work on language socialization. Ochs and Shieffelin, in their work in Samoa and among the Kaluli of Papua New Guinea (Ochs, 1988; Ochs & Shieffelin, 1984), have demonstrated how patterns of language socialization observed in children's everyday lives are related to cultural systems. They describe significant cultural variation found in how caregivers speak to, with, and about children, and how these patterns change developmentally. From ethnographic work, they describe how the behaviors reflect culturally based theories about the social status of children and their capacity and appropriateness as communication partners.

Two related goals are addressed by studying diversity through case studies. The first goal is to understand the range of variation and the influence it has on development. To do this, one must have analyses of cultural systems that are both adequate and accurate, and they must facilitate comparison. Extensive ethnographic case studies of everyday behavior meet these criteria. The second goal is to ground generalizations about development in adequate data. The possibility of discovering generalities about development lies within the accumulation of detailed case studies of particular cultural systems and how children engage in culturally specific activities generated by such systems. Mead (1963) made a similar argument long ago that the universal process of becoming a member of a culture (socialization) cannot be understood except by studying the process of children becoming adults in specific cultures (enculturation).

This chapter is a report of one such case study. It describes young Yucatec Mayan children's engagement in their world. Four kinds of activity are described, and for each, there are patterns in children 1 to 5 years of age that are distinctively Mayan and that differ from patterns found in Western children. The chapter also presents three cultural principles of engagement that come from more general Mayan cultural beliefs and practices and are necessary for interpreting the observed behavior of young children. The act of simply describing the children's activity, without taking into account the cultural principles of engagement that define the context, could lead to significant interpretive misunderstandings about the meanings of the activity and the importance of the differences between Mayan and Western children. When each kind of children's behavior described is interpreted by the principles of engagement, it facilitates a culturally appropriate understanding of not only what the children and the other people around them do but also why they do it. The interpretation yields an overall picture of young Mayan children's behavior and the Mayan cultural context as a distinct and logically integrated system.

Ethnographic Context

In order to understand the interpretative arguments that follow, one must know a little about the Yucatec Mayan culture itself. A brief general description of the Maya is followed by more detail about the house compound and the kinds of daily activities that might occur there.

General Background

The Mayan Indians of Yucatan, Mexico, are historically related to the ancient Mayan peoples whose civilizations flourished during the pre-Columbian era. The Spanish conquest was particularly destructive of high culture but left most daily traditions intact. Many of these practices persist today in traditional remote villages now melded with both colonial Spanish and modern Mexican culture. The research discussed here has been conducted over a period of 17 years in a remote, traditional Mayan village in the county of Chemax, located in the eastern part of the state of

Yucatan, Mexico. It reflects an accumulated total of about 5 years of fieldwork in this village. All work has been done in Yucatec Maya, the language spoken in the village.

Both men's and women's work is organized around corn and associated agricultural and religious practices (for good descriptions of these traditional practices, see Redfield & Villa Rojas, 1934, and Steggerda, 1941). Most families, by working hard and relying on the grace of God, are able to produce enough to be fed, clothed, and sheltered, at least to some minimal standard, but only a few are able to accumulate significant wealth.

Almost all of the men are subsistence farmers, raising primarily corn, beans, and squash for their own family's consumption. They use a slash-and-burn system of farming that uses almost no modern technology. The fields surround the village and can be as far away as a 2-hour walk. During the periods of the year when cultivation is demanding, men are gone to their fields most days (except Sunday) from sunrise to sunset. During other times of the year, they stay home some days to do chores or take care of other business. Many men now also seek wage labor either by working in neighbors' fields, by selling produce and livestock, or by working at temporary jobs in the nearby Caribbean-coast tourist area. A man is aided in all his work by his sons as they become old enough. By the time a son is 8 or 10, he will be of significant help to his father. By the time he is 15, he will be able to claim a field of his own to cultivate, even though his father will still closely supervise his work.

Corn is also the center of daily life for women. If a woman does not have small children, she sometimes helps her husband in the fields, but her primary responsibility is to run the house and the yard. Two or three times a day, a woman must prepare corn for grinding, prepare beans or some other side dish, and make tortillas for her family, forming them by hand and cooking them on a griddle over the open wood fire. These tasks take many hours. She also washes her family's clothes by hand and takes care of the livestock and garden. Her work is constantly interrupted by the demands or needs of her children. Besides actually taking care of children herself, she also supervises the household work and caretaking responsibilities of the older children. A women is aided in her work by her daughters and by those sons not old enough to work the fields.

Typical Household

A typical family consists of a mother, a father, and several children in a house compound (50 × 50 meters). With a family this size, there are usually two houses in the compound. Traditional houses have stick walls, thatched roofs, and dirt floors. They are oval in shape. An average size is about 6 meters long and 4 meters wide. Each house has both a front door and a back door in the long sides of the ovals, but no windows. Extra light comes through the spaces between the sticks that form the walls. The houses are usually placed close together, most often one behind the other.

The yard of the typical compound is cleared of jungle and is planted with produce-bearing trees and plants as well as decorative flowers and bushes. The areas between the two houses and behind the back house are kept cleared and swept and are used as general work areas, weather permitting. Chickens and turkeys roam throughout the yard, and there are coops for them several meters from the houses. At the back of the compound, there is often a pigpen sectioned off on one side and an area of overgrown bush on the other side to provide some privacy for bath-rooming. Nowadays, there is usually electricity in both houses and a hose in the compound through which is water is pumped from a central well for 2 hours a day.

Both houses are used as general living space during the day and become sleeping space during the night, using colorful woven hammocks hung from the internal frames of the houses. The front house is closest to the compound entrance and is more public in nature. There are several hammocks in the front house, along with a few other possessions, perhaps a treadle sewing machine and chair, a large pile of unshucked dried corn, and a table with a picture of the family's saint, with some flowers and two candles on it. Clothes are usually stored in this house, perhaps in a couple of cardboard boxes set up on boards in the corner. Important papers and other items of value are often stored here as well. All of the family use this house during the day for various activities, and if there are many children, the older ones sleep in this house, usually two to a hammock.

The back house is a more private space. Only the family and close relatives and friends use the back house regularly. It also has a few hammocks, a fire pit at one end of the oval, a sloped bathing area at the other end of the oval (if there is no alternative bathing area constructed in the compound), a high table used for food preparation and storage of kitchen implements and food supplies, a small, low, round table used to make tortillas and to eat, and a number of low stools. A number of cooking utensils and food items can be found throughout this house, with perhaps a basket to hold shucked corn, an open bag of unshelled dry beans, various pots and buckets around the fire pit, a large ceramic pot and several large plastic buckets to hold water, and a stack of firewood. The parents sleep in this house, along with some of the younger children. A child who is still nursing would sleep in the parents' hammock.

Example of Typical Household Routine

The following "slice of life" scene, showing how a typical 18-month-old Yucatec Mayan girl might be engaged in her world, serves as a brief introduction to the daily life of a young Mayan child. (This typical account has been constructed from my field notes on the basis of observing several 18-month-old children. They have been merged into the following collage to allow a number of points to be illustrated efficiently.)

It is midmorning on a weekday, and Mari is walking around in the yard of the compound looking for something to do. She is dressed in a short, white, shiftlike dress with brightly colored embroidered flowers at the neck and hem, identical in style to her mother's and sisters' traditional dress but lacking the underskirt that girls begin to wear around the age of 10 or 12. Everyone in her family is busy working. As he does most mornings, her father left at dawn with his three oldest sons (ages 13 to 20) to go to their cornfields, which are about an hour's walk away. They will not be home until late afternoon. (Her mother, her sisters, and her younger brother and she stay at home within the compound except for errands, social visits, and any special public religious events when they occur.) Her two oldest sisters (ages 17 and 19) are washing clothes in cement washing tubs, which are placed in the yard under trees several meters from the house.

When Mari goes near her sisters to watch, they tell her to stay out of the mud and to go away. She ignores them and walks over to the shallow tub of water they are using and puts her hand in. Then she drops a rock into the tub, fishes it out, and drops it in again. One sister yells at her not to get wet, but Mari ignores her. Her sister calls to their mother that Mari won't listen to her. Mari's mother, who is near the back house washing the eating table and stools, looks up and harshly repeats the sister's order to leave the washing area, reminding her that the water is cold and may make her sick. Mari drops the rock into the tub a few more times, as her sister continues to scold her, before leaving.

Mari walks between the two houses. She looks in at the doorway of the front house and sees another sister (age 9) sweeping the dirt floor with a broom made of palm leaves. She knows she is not supposed to go into the house while her sister is sweeping, so she walks the few meters to the back house and finds another sister (age 11) tending the fire and stirring the corn that is cooking. Mari goes into the back house and walks over to her sister near the fire. The sister tells her to shoo the chickens out of the house and to give them some corn outside. Mari runs around the house, chasing the chickens out through the back door of the house into the yard, laughing as she does it. The sister calls to her to remind her to feed the chickens, and Mari comes back into the house. Her sister fills a gourd with dried corn from a basket, and Mari takes it outside and sprinkles it on the ground not far from the back door. The chickens quickly gather to eat the corn, and Mari watches them as they eat.

Near where she is standing, her mother is still washing the furniture. Mari turns to watch her mother and then goes over to her. She pulls a leaf from a nearby bush, dips it in the bucket of water her mother is using, and begins to scrub a stool with it. (Her mother is using a leaf as well to scrub with, but it is a special leaf with an abrasive surface.) Her mother laughs and calls to the two oldest daughters to take a look at Mari washing the furniture. Mari doesn't look up from her work but continues to scrub diligently, pouring water over the stool from time to time using a gourd. Eventually, she turns the ground to mud, and her mother takes the leaf and gourd away from her, picks Mari up and sets her down away from the mud. She then calls Mari's youngest sister (age 3) to come and take her to where she and her brother (age 5) are picking fruit and eating it in the back of the yard. The 3-year-old comes, invites Mari to come with her to eat the fruit, and takes her hand. Mari follows her sister to the back of the yard where the three small children pick and eat the fruit. From the beginning to the end of this scene, Mari has said nothing to anyone.

Three Cultural Principles of Engagement

Several things happened (or did not happen) in this short scene that suggest that this young child's engagement in her world is significantly different from that of a Western middle-class child of the same age. In order to give meaning to the events presented, however, one must have an accurate cultural framework. There are three cultural principles of engagement that motivate many of the interesting events of this observation as well as having general application to Mayan children's engagement in their world. These three principles – primacy of adult activities, importance of parental beliefs, and independence of child motivation –

are necessary to interpret Mayan children's behavior in a culturally meaningful way. In daily life, they work together hand in hand to produce a
particular character to children's behavior across a wide age range that is
typically Mayan and distinct from Western children's behavior.

1. Primacy of Adult Work. *As is true for all Mayans, life in the compound as experienced by children is structured around adult work activities. In particular, it is not structured around young children's interests
or desires, nor around adult goals for children.*

Unlike children in many industrialized cultures where economic production has been removed from the home, Yucatec Mayan children's
daily activities are primarily structured by adult work activities. These in
turn revolve around the immediate work needs of the household and the
family's participation in social and religious events within the household
and the larger community. Children are legitimate cultural participants
through this avenue, even as they are learning how to participate appropriately. They take part in both work and social activities from their
second year on, with their roles and level of participation changing as
they become more competent. There is a strong sense that adult work
must get done and that the child should not interrupt it. What children are
doing (as long as it is not dangerous or disruptive) is of secondary interest.
There is little if any attempt on the part of caregivers to create experiences
for children based on the children's desires (beyond taking care of their
immediate needs) or the adult's explicit goals as parents, and conversely,
there is little if any attempt on the part of children to initiate or control
social interaction. At the same time, in such situations, there is little
motivation for encouraging children to participate at the cutting edge of
their capabilities, because such participation increases errors and the need
to monitor children's behavior. Rather, children are allowed to participate
only in those parts of an activity where they already possess some competence. The rest of the activity is done by someone else.

In the foregoing example, everyone in the compound is working or
occupied in some activity, leaving Mari to find something to do on her
own. The child herself makes only one overture to be included in a work
event, and her real motivation is questionable, because it includes playing
with water, which she clearly enjoys doing. Her participation is tolerated,
even though her contribution is limited, until she begins to make a mess.
Then she is summarily dismissed. She is also told to do one simple chore,
which she is able to do with minimal help and which she does quickly
and cheerfully. She follows a number of simple rules already, such as

staying out of the way of the sister who is sweeping, being careful of the open fire pit, and doing a task when she is told to do it. (She has more trouble curbing her interest in water, even when reminded, but that is discussed later.)

This principle – that primary activities in the compound are related to adult priorities – means that young children can be engaged only with the primary activities to the extent that their abilities and understanding allow them to do so. In many cases, this means that children are decidedly peripherally engaged in such activities, although true participation in work activities is possible even at a very young age, as we see when Mari feeds the chickens. The two other options available to children when participation is not possible are to observe the primary activity or to engage in a secondary activity. Such secondary activity is likely to be tolerated at best and discouraged or punished at worst, but rarely actively supported through advice or participation by adults and older siblings. Mari is engaged primarily in the first option – much of what she does during this observation is to seek out things to watch. The other two young children in the compound are engaged in the second option; they have distanced themselves from being immediately observed and are having a snack of fruit that they pick from a tree. In either case, the child can be called on at any time to do some chore or errand. In this observation, Mari was asked to shoo the chickens out of the house, and her siblings were asked to take care of her. In both cases, they did what they were asked and then went back to doing what they were doing before the interruption. In the case of feeding the chickens, Mari's sister patiently reminded her a second time (recognizing that her young sister was not able to hold two commands in her head at a time) and facilitated her accomplishing the chore by providing Mari with the corn, but she did not bribe or praise her for doing the chore – her compliance was assumed and was forthcoming.

2. Importance of Parental Beliefs. *Cultural understandings about the nature of the world and about the nature of children significantly shape children's experiences.*

Many of a young child's experiences are shaped by the physical and social environment in which they take place. The child's physical environment, in turn, is shaped not only by the physical geography of the place but by the ways in which the culture chooses to engage that environment. Beliefs – about what is good and bad, important and irrelevant, safe and dangerous – are culturally specific and guide the construction of the child's daily environment (Harkness & Super, 1996; also see Farver, Göncü et al., Haight, and Tudge et al., this volume). All parents share the goals of maintaining a child's health and producing an adult child who is able to sustain himself or herself economically and function as a competent member of the group (LeVine, 1969). But what is perceived as necessary and relevant to achieve these goals is a matter of cultural understanding. Culturally specific beliefs guide a parent in deciding what a child should (and should not) experience, given their age, abilities, and circumstances, in order to stay healthy and become competent adults.

Many health concerns engage Mayan parents of young children. There are environmental hazards – such as the fire pit, rocky terrain that causes many falls, and dangerous insects and snakes – from which the child must be protected. Anyone with a small child in the same environment would share such concerns (although how to address them might differ). Other dangers perceived by Mayan parents stem from understandings of the nature of human bodies and the nature of the universe – dangers that Western parents would not share. There is a belief that one must maintain a balance between "cold" and "hot" elements in one's body and environment or else risk sickness. There are spirits and creatures that try to steal children or tempt people to come into their power. There is "evil eye," an illness that can be given to a child just by a person looking at him, if that person holds such powers. These abstract beliefs lead to very specific limitations on children's activities – where they can go, what they can eat, and what they can play with – all with the goal of ensuring the child's well-being.

Cultures also differ in how they understand the nature of young children and how children become adults. These influence the kinds of interactions parents have with their children and the kinds of environments and experiences they construct for them. The Maya believe that the source of development is internal and preprogrammed – it just "comes out by itself." Development and socialization are both thought to be ongoing, gradual, and continuous processes. Parents are not particularly concerned about monitoring children's developmental progress nor in structuring experiences to improve or hasten it. There is an expectation that children will learn to be safe and will learn to work, but such learning is seen as a natural outcome of participation in daily life. Again, there is no sense of intentional teaching or unusual encouragement needed (Gaskins, 1996).

Mari's sister and mother discouraged her from playing with the water and rocks. From a Western middle-class point of view, they deprived her of an opportunity to explore a rich and varied play medium and stifled her curiosity. But from Mari's mother's point of view, she was protecting her daughter from a significant and imminent danger, stemming from the Maya's belief in the importance of keeping symbolically cold and hot things in balance. Mari's playing in the water put her at risk of exposing herself to too much of a "cold" thing and increased her chance of getting a stomach ache. (Secondarily, if she were allowed to get all muddy for no reason, it would require someone to take time away from her work to clean her up, which would be a violation of the first principle, discussed previously.) Even if such a belief about hot and cold did not exist, Mari's mother would not share her Western middle-class counterpart's enthusiasm for the opportunity to explore in the water because she believes that much of the child's development, especially the way she comes to understand the nature of the world, is a result of maturation rather than experience.

Mari's mother also holds the belief that her youngest daughter is not yet old enough to be held responsible for her own actions; rather, her siblings are held responsible for her behavior (Gaskins & Lucy, 1987). Thus, when the older sister complains to her mother that Mari will not listen to her, she is not only enlisting her mother's help but is trying to ensure that she will not be seen as negligent. Mari receives no punishment for not listening nor for making mud when washing the stools. Her mother tries to motivate her through warning of the danger of the water, but she is not surprised when that doesn't work. Distraction with food (offered by her sister at her mother's order) and removal from the scene are used instead; such kinds of redirection are common ways of dealing with young children's undesirable or inappropriate behavior.

3. Independence of Child Motivation. *In line with the Mayan culture's general respect for individuals, many of a young child's activities are determined by the child's own interests and motivations, as well as by her own understandings of cultural expectations and restraints. Moreover, little self-directed behavior is socially manipulative (beyond direct requests), and the child has little expectation that she will have much influence on the activities of others.*

As mentioned previously, young children are not able to be full participants in adult activities, and when their help is not needed, they are usually expected to find something to do on their own or with their other young siblings. Thus, even while Mayan children are much more involved in ongoing, adult-directed work activities than are Western children, they are also given a much greater range of independence in general in deciding what they will do moment by moment. There are far fewer attempts by parents to organize or influence their children's behavior, and even young children are given the responsibility to make many decisions themselves (e.g., when to start school, whether to take medicine, how much to sleep and eat). A corollary to this is that children presume that they should act independently and seldom display attention-getting behavior or ask others to help them find something to do. Although they demonstrate an intense interest in what other people are doing, they do not rely on others to be entertained. Within the confines of safety concerns and adult priorities, children are left to their own devices and are content to be so.

No one creates something for Mari to do until it is expedient to distract her from the mud she has made washing the stool. She is free to roam in the yard and houses, and although there is general monitoring of her behavior to make sure she is safe, she is given a great deal of leeway in her movement. There are not many options of what to do in Mari's compound. She is kept from playing with water in this example, but she would also be kept from playing with dirt, household implements, food, and so on. She offers some passive resistance when told not to play with the water, but she understands enough that she gives it up in the face of significant scolding. She does not try to use things in the house that are not for playing, even though they are within reach. She is happy to do a chore when it is asked of her, and she accepts the offer to pick fruit when it is offered to her.

One of the more interesting things to do is to watch other people and events, and this Mari does a lot. She watches her sisters and mother work, she watches the chickens eat, and she is content and even happy to do so. She asserts her interest in her mother's work by imitating it – whether this should be called play or work is difficult to say, because it depends on Mari's own understanding of her actions. But it is clear that she does not engage in the imitative behavior to gain favor from her mother. When her mother comments on her behavior to the others, Mari appears to take no notice. Whatever her motivation, it is not social manipulation. Nor does she seek to gain her mother's attention in other ways. She doesn't speak the entire time, and the only speech directed to her are commands, telling to do something or not to do something. Mari's mother's comment about the danger of the water, given with the intention of making her stop out of fear, is the only speech directed to her that yields any information about the environment. In general, and within the constraints of the situation, much of Mari's behavior is self-directed and independent of others.

Mayan Children's Activities

These three cultural principles of engagement – primacy of adult activities, importance of parental beliefs, and independence of child motivation – can be used to help us interpret Mayan children's engagement in a wide range of activities. This section describes several different categories of children's behavior, and for each, the cultural principles are used to avoid interpretive pitfalls.

The decision of which activity categories to use to describe activities in and of itself is not a neutral research act (Gaskins, 1994). Although those who have looked at Western children's activities have often included play, work, and instruction, these activities appear to be generated from the researchers' interests rather than from an analysis of how children spend their time or what they value. Ethnographic observation of Mayan children suggests that one must develop a different nexus of categories if one wants to include the activities that take up a majority of their time and seem to characterize accurately how children are engaged in their world. The goal is to develop an exhaustive and mutually exclusive set of categories that are observable and culturally meaningful. Using these criteria, work and play both seem to be appropriate categories for including in a description of Mayan children's daily activities, even though they do not take up most of the children's time nor are they as well differentiated in time and space as they seem to be for Western children. Instruction does not seem to be as appropriate. For young children, it is rarely an action defined independently of other actions. Learning of specific skills usually takes place within work. In addition, it appears from ethnographic observation that a great deal of Mayan children's time is spent in maintenance activities (e.g., eating, sleeping, and being taken care of) and social orientation (e.g., making requests or observation of ongoing household activities). These four categories, then – maintenance activities, social orientation, play, and work – are used to organize the following description of Mayan children's activities.

To illustrate how these four activities are distributed in individual Mayan children's daily lives, I observed three children in one household for 9 hours over a period of 4 days. Using spot observations, I recorded for each child what specific activities he or she was engaged in at each 5 minute mark. Thus, in an hour, I sampled each child's behavior 12 times. In 9 hours, this yielded 106 observations for each child. The children were 20 months old, 3½ years old, and 5½ years old. The two younger children were girls; the older child was a boy. The baby was home for all the observations, the little girl was home for 85.8% of the observations, and the older boy was home for only 51.9% of the observations. I then classified my observations into the activity categories: maintenance activities, social orientation, play, and work (and a residual category of "other" to check on the exhaustiveness of the other categories). In Table 2.1, the numbers for each child reflect the percentage of time at home spent in each activity. Thus, each child's numbers add up to 100%, even though they varied in how much of the 9 hour time period was spent at home.

This quantification exercise on three children produces a distribution that is similar to those found in ethnographic descriptions I have made of many other children in the village. The order of frequency found was maintenance activities, social orientation, play, and work. In fact, somewhere between two-thirds and three-quarters of each of the children's time at home was taken up with maintenance activities and social orientation, neither of which is customarily considered in the Western literature as activities to be studied. The relatively low numbers in the "other" category serves to illustrate that the first four categories of activities adequately characterize almost all of the observations.

These four ethnographically derived categories are used in the following description of young children's activities. It must be remembered throughout, however, that children's ongoing behavior does not always slice up neatly into sustained periods of time engaged in one of these activities to the exclusion of the others. Perhaps even more so than with Western children, Mayan children's moment-to-moment experiences are a constant interweaving of all four kinds of activities. For instance, child-independent activities such as eating or pretend play are constantly interrupted by adults requesting that some chore or errand be done. And any activity may be suspended when some event occurs in the household that merits watching. Likewise, more than one activity can occur at the same time. For instance, Mayan children can be observing others while snacking on fruit for extended periods of time, and some work, such as childcaretaking, is often integrated into play activities. Thus, while the categories themselves are culturally derived, the expectation that behavior will fall neatly into one or the other of them is not. At the same time, even when two activities are concurrent, it is usually possible to

Table 2.1. *Observed Activities for Three Mayan Children*

	Maintenance	Social Orientation	Play	Work	Other
Reina (F) 20 months	46.2%	26.4%	23.6%	0%	3.8%
Chula (F) (3½ years)	42.9%	25.3%	18.7%	12.1%	1.1%
Chuco (M) (5½ years)	34.5%	29.1%	27.3%	5.5%	3.6%

distinguish which of the child's behaviors contributes to each. In this sense, the categories are formally exclusive, even though they may co-occur.

Maintenance Activities

Early Self-Maintenance. Young children in all cultures require some maintenance activities. The list of those activities defined for young Mayan children by their culture is not all that different from those defined for Western children. They must eat, sleep, bathe and groom, dress, urinate and defecate, and be in safe locations engaged in safe activities. One-year-old Mayan children are expected to do none of these on their own. Except for feeding at mealtimes and nursing, two activities that are usually supported by the children's mothers, much of the maintenance support is likely to be given by older children in the compound.

By the time children are 5, they are usually expected to take responsibility for doing almost all of their own maintenance activities, even though they may be prompted or checked on by adults. They decide what they wish to eat and how much of it; when, how long, and with whom to sleep; what to wear; and when to bathe (as long as they choose to bathe a minimum of once a day in the afternoon, which is the cultural norm). They take responsibility for all their own bathrooming, using the proper space provided in the yard. They may even be given responsibility for providing maintenance support to their younger siblings, under the direct guidance of the mother. Five-year-olds are also expected to be aware of most safety issues within the compound and to refrain from dangerous activity. They are no longer monitored from moment to moment, and, in fact, they may be out of the mother's sight, or even out of the compound, for long periods of time.

Three- and 4-year-old children are able to do many of these things as well, depending on their own motivations to take care of themselves and the household dynamics that determine how easy it is to provide a lot of childcare for them. But younger children are monitored much more closely than an older child, with their mother assuring that they are not doing something improperly or inappropriately. A 3-year old may already be able to bathe himself, for example, but with an older sibling assigned to provide the hot water from the fire and to watch him bathe, prepared to wash the child's hair more thoroughly or to make sure his feet are clean if necessary. For a fuller discussion of how young children come to do these activities independently, see the section, "Learning New Skills," later in the chapter.

From our Western understanding, it is a surprise that these children can achieve such high competence in self-maintenance so early with little or no pressure or encouragement from their parents. When one considers the amount of Western parental effort and concern that goes into getting a child to sleep through the night, to become toilet trained, or to eat properly, the Maya pattern is indeed distinctive. In addition, the amount of say that a child is given in making choices about eating and sleeping and the amount of responsibility the child is given to avoid danger verges on parental neglect from our perspective.

This early independence in personal maintenance is consistent with the three cultural principles of engagement. Both the importance placed on adult activities and the belief that the child's understanding is a result of maturation make the adults have little investment in being needed by the child or in feeling obligated to provide the child with overly supportive parenting attention. Likewise, because the child is self-motivated, there is little need to try to manipulate the adult's attention through emphasizing needs or feigning helplessness. Nor is there a struggle in these realms for establishing who is in charge, the parent or child, as often happens in these realms in middle-class Western families. Children accept help as long as it is needed and accept responsibility to do what they can on their own; parents provide only what help is actually needed according to children's abilities. Children are carefully monitored until they demonstrate adequate competence. The basic understanding of the caretaking roles of parents and children is fundamentally different from the West, and it yields early competence and low stress for both the parent and the child.

Nonmeal Eating. The other most salient fact about children's maintenance activities is the sheer amount of time spent in nonmeal eating. In the spot observations, one-third to almost one-half of children's time was spent on self-maintenance, and most of that time was spent in nonmeal eating. Children are given lots of snacks and spend a great deal of time consuming them. The most common snack for very young children is tea biscuits or other crackers. Once the danger of choking on pits and seeds is past (sometime between ages 2 and 3), children's most popular snack is the fruit available in most yards. A variety of native fruits usually are quite time-consuming to eat (skin to peel, large and attached pits, etc). It is not uncommon for young children to spend an hour or more at a time so occupied.

Such extended periods of time spent in snacking is not unheard of for Western children, especially toddlers. So the main interpretive danger here is assuming a similarity between such activities when there are some important differences. One reason parents support and encourage snacking is because of the advantage gained for adult's work by having their children happily and safely occupied for long periods of time. (This is a shared value with Western parents, but it is more important for the Maya given the primacy of adult work.) If a young child is interfering with work, one of the most effective enticements to get them out of one's way is offering the prospect of a snack. This technique was illustrated in the case reported previously – when Mari's mother has her slightly older sibling take her away from the mud and the mother's work to eat fruit off a tree in the yard. Even though Mari did not initiate the activity, it would not be surprising if she stayed at the fruit tree with her siblings for at least a half-hour or longer, requiring only minimal long-distance monitoring by her mother and allowing the morning chores to be finished without further interruption.

Snacks are culturally supported more generally by the belief that if children are hungry, then they must be given food, and preferably the food they desire – this in a culture where plentiful food and spare change are not always available. A great deal of disposable daily income goes toward buying children things to snack on, and it is almost always given as an example of why a person needs to earn more money. Even fruit eaten off a tree represents a real economic commitment to children by parents, because fruit that is not eaten by the family can be sold.

Finally, picking and eating fruit is an activity that children frequently choose to do on their own. Fruit trees are usually a short distance from the house, so children are removed a bit from the moment-to-moment household activity, and they can talk to each other alone. At the same time, it is close enough to watch most of what's going on in the compound and to be called upon when needed to do a chore or errand. Few other spaces within the compound serve the same purpose. Because it is culturally valued to be engaged in some activity at all times, snacking serves as an available and acceptable escape from the household activity and is also relaxing and enjoyable.

All three principles of engagement suggest that nonmeal eating is an important and valued activity for Mayan children and their caretakers. Rather than serving simply as a time filler and pacifier, it serves as a culturally supported activity that fulfills some important expectations about what children should do with their time and what parents should provide for their children.

Social Orientation

After maintenance activities, social orientation is the next most frequent activity for all three children observed in the spot observations. Although some of the observations were of simple conversations such as direct requests, most of the behavior in this category was silent observation of events occurring in the compound. These spot observations are consistent with more general ethnographic observation. Much of a young Mayan child's time is spent observing other actors in the compound. At 1 year of age, Mayan infants spend less than 20% of their time looking at other people and things. About two-thirds of that watching is directed toward people, and the rest is directed toward objects and animals of interest in their vicinity (Gaskins, 1990). This is actually less than American children are reported to look at things, with the difference between the two groups coming in the amount of time spent looking at Mother (presumably in the American sample, at least some of that is in face-to-face interaction or active attempts at social engagement rather than in the more common Mayan pattern of detached observation) (Clarke-Stewart, 1973). Between the ages of 2 and 5, as children become more engaged in the larger social world, they increase the amount of time spent in observation of activities, as shown in the foregoing spot observations. During this period, their ability to understand events and monitor actions at a distance improves, so that a 5-year-old will of course know more about what is going on in a compound than a 2-year-old, even though they may spend the same amount of time observing. But often by age 2, and certainly by 3, a child can report accurately where every member of her household is and what he or she is doing (as long as the activities are familiar to the child and evident from observable behavior or conversation). This is true even for those members who are not present. The child appears to be keeping sort of a running tab on compound activities through careful observation.

Thus, while young children are allowed a great deal of independence and self-direction, a lot of energy is put toward understanding the moment-to-moment pulse of the compound. This kind of behavior is similar to that of the adults, who are careful observers and monitor village activity in the same way. The cultural goal is to know everything that is going on, and young children mimic that goal, even at a very young age, at the level of the family and compound itself. In a compound with many people and animals in it, there is almost always some activity going on, so such observation is almost always an option for the child, and frequently it is done in parallel with whatever else the child is doing, because one can lose track of what is going on if one does not pay close attention at all times. Just like their parents, children frequently pause in their play or their work to watch something if it promises to be interesting.

It is worth noting that the child's primary motive for knowing where people are and what they are doing appears to be simple awareness of events, rather than trying to take part in them or influence them. Most of the time, when a child is observing social events, there is no related action that follows. Often, there is no observable reaction in the observer at all, even when events are dramatic or emotional. One little girl of 3, for instance, sat at a distance watching her older sister crying in the yard for over 30 minutes. For most of that time, the little girl did not take her eyes off her sister, but neither did she approach her nor comment on the behavior to anyone else. She just watched.

So even though there is a great deal of social orientation in young Mayan children, it does not imply a great deal of social interaction, especially with adults. Children at this age do not initiate conversations with adults unless they are making a specific request for something they need or want at the moment. They are expected not to do anything that will disturb the adults who are around, including running around or making a lot of noise. (On those rare occasions when only children under the age of 10 are home, the levels of rambunctiousness and noise rise significantly.) Adults rarely speak to young children unless it is to tell them to do something (or not to do something) or to offer information they think the child needs to do a task. Also, caregivers are more likely to comment to someone else about a young child's behavior than they are to talk to the child himself. (This was seen in the case of Mari.) Young children are more likely to talk to other children, especially those near their own age, but even when they do, there are often long periods of silence. It was not unusual that Mari did not speak once, even though she responded by actions when she was told to do things.

One corollary to the observance of behavior is that children from a very early age are able to sit quietly when necessary with little fussing or wriggling. Before the road into the village was improved, a trip by truck to the supply town was 3 hours long. Children of all ages were content to sit quietly on or near their parent or sibling for the entire duration of the trip. Children can also sit during a religious service or a dance for a long time, requiring only minimal attention or distraction. In fact, when given a choice, they often choose to attend such events and sit quietly than to stay home and have more freedom of movement.

To the Western eye, this degree of patience in a young child strikes one as remarkable. It would be easy to miss the behavior in the first place if one observed the children only superficially, because the behavior is only looking, not actions taken by the child. If Western observers did notice the amount of observation done by young children, they would likely interpret it as withdrawal or passivity, a lack of engagement.

Either would be a serious mistake. As was seen in the case of maintenance activities, the pervasive social observation found in young Mayan children is consistent with the three cultural principles of engagement and, when interpreted from their perspective, yields a picture of strong engagement with the world through focused observation. With the world of adult activities considered primary, children are left to negotiate their way through that world causing minimal disruption. The only way they can hope to do that is to pay attention to what is going on all the time, and to make the best sense of events and activities as their limited understanding will allow them. Before entering a social space occupied by others, it is prudent for Mayan children to take into account what is already happening and to judge whether or not it is appropriate to be there at all, whether they may speak or should be quiet, and so on. Mayan understandings of responsibility also promote careful social observation. If children are to be held responsible for a younger sibling's behavior (Gaskins Lucy, 1987), or if they are supposed to notice if the pig has escaped from the pen to the garden, they better be aware of what is going on. And because children operate as somewhat independent agents, again it is critically necessary to be aware of moment-to-moment events in the compound, to guide their choices of where to go and what to do. These three cultural principles of engagement yield a significantly different social space for young Mayan children than for their Western counterparts. From this perspective, social observation can be seen as an effective strategy for operating within that social space for young children who are still learning the system, rather than as evidence of passivity or disengagement, as we might be tempted to interpret it from our own (Western) cultural experiences.

Play

Play is assumed in Western theory and research to be a significant and unique activity for young children (Garvey, 1990). In particular, symbolic play has received a tremendous amount of attention from developmentalists who argue that it serves various functions such as tension reduction and wish fulfillment (Freud, 1950), assimilation of experiences (Piaget, 1962), and expansion and consolidation of understanding (Vygotsky, 1967). Whether play is as prevalent and serves the same functions in all cultures has never been adequately examined (Haight, this volume; Schwartzman, 1978), especially for symbolic play (Gaskins & Göncü, 1992).

In describing how Mayan children play at different ages, it is important to understand not only what the play itself looks like but how play fits into the distribution of activities. We have already seen for the spot observations done on the three children that play is not the predominant activity of any of the three children (being less frequent than both maintenance activities and social orientation) but that it is more frequently engaged in than work at these young ages. Play appears to occupy somewhere between 20% to 25% of a young child's time. In 1-year-olds, play occurs even more of the time (around 35%), which is similar to the amount of play found in American children at that age (Clarke-Stewart, 1973; Gaskins, 1990). Remember that Mayan children this young spend less time engaged in the social activity of observation. One can generalize that play is a significant activity for Mayan children from ages 1 to 5, even though it is not the dominant one.

One must then ask what Mayan children's play looks like. For children under the age of 2, most of their time is spent in manipulative play with objects (or substances). For 1-year-olds, about one-third of their total time is spent in object manipulation, the same as for American middle-class children (Clarke-Stewart, 1973; Gaskins, 1990). There is almost no time spent in other kinds of play by the Mayan 1-year-old. In extended observations of sixteen children (12- and 18-month-olds), examples of large-motor, social, or symbolic play were missing for most of the children observed and were very rare for the rest. In addition, there were no examples of verbal play with these children. Up to age 1½, then, Mayan children's primary form of play is small-motor manipulation of objects. For example, the 20-month-old who was observed in the spot observations previously reported spent 76% of her play time in simple manipulative play.

A child of 2, however, spends more and more time with siblings away from the mother and is included, to the extent possible, in whatever play the other children are doing. Children between the ages of 2 and 5 spend much of their play time in large-motor play, such as climbing trees, chasing each other, twirling around to get dizzy, and chasing bugs. The two older children (ages 3½ and 5½) observed in spot observations, for example, spent 60% to 65% of their play time so engaged.

The literature on Western children's play focuses primarily on symbolic play. Interestingly, not only do Mayan children spend only a small portion of their day in play, but they also spend very little of it in symbolic play. Again, the spot observations provide a helpful quantitative perspective. The 5½-year-old boy was never observed engaged in symbolic play during the 9 hours of observation. The two girls (ages 3½ and 20 months) were each observed playing symbolically three times during the 9 hours, one of those times together, representing in total about 3% of the total time observed.

On the basis of quantity alone, we can argue that symbolic play must serve very different functions for Mayan children than it does for Western children, who have been so heavily studied. But there are important qualitative differences in their symbolic play as well. For young Western children, age 2 and under, symbolic play often occurs with the support of an adult, who provides objects, models, and themes and who encourages symbolic or pretend behavior in the young child (Haight & Miller, 1992). But symbolic play is usually thought of in Western culture as being a dominant play form of preschool children, which disappears as the child reaches school age. When it is a social event, it most frequently includes children of about the same age, who jointly construct and maintain the play situation.

The contexts in which symbolic play occurs for Mayan children are very different from those for Western children. Symbolic play usually occurs in two kinds of contexts in the Mayan household. The first context is within the house or compound. Here, young children, up to the age of 5, can be seen in engaging in short instances of symbolic play that they spontaneously create, usually using as props household objects that are not intended for play. Examples from the two girls observed include the

20-month-old using a rope that is hung by one end from the rafters to produce a curve suggestive of a hammock and then pretending to sit and swing on the curve, or, with her sister (age 3½), putting small unripe fruit on the wheel of a wheelbarrow tipped on its side and turning the wheel around, pretending to grind corn. Instances like these tend to feature one specific and unelaborated act and last no more than a minute or two. They were the only kind of symbolic play observed during the 9 hours of spot observations. They are rarely acknowledged and almost never supported by adults or older children, who often cut short the children's pretense because of inappropriate use of household objects.

A second context yields a more extended kind of symbolic play (Gaskins, 1989). A large age-mixed group of children from a single compound do engage in symbolic play from time to time, usually at some distance from the house and without direct supervision or support of adults. Older children, sometimes as old as 12 or 13, organize the play event and assign specific roles to the younger children. The themes of these play sessions are taken directly from adult life, most of them daily events, and they are repeated over and over again with little variation. The primary role that young children take in this extended play is to do the specific actions that they are told to do by the older children who orchestrate the pretend scenarios. The frequency of such events varies greatly from family to family, depending on whether the adults discourage or tolerate them. They were not observed at all during the spot observations.

For Mayan children between the ages of 2 to 5, then, symbolic play is either momentary cases of symbolic relationships being expressed spontaneously by a child or the enactment of specific behaviors that are generated by older children and are realistic representations of adult daily activities that are repeated from one play session to the next. There is little opportunity in either case for the kind of emotional and cognitive work to be done that is assumed inherent in symbolic play by Western researchers (Gaskins & Göncü, 1992). And whichever of these two forms the symbolic play takes, it is a very small part of the child's overall activities.

There has been a tendency in Western research to interpret a lower rate or a lower level of complexity in symbolic play as evidence of a deficit in non–middle-class or non-Western children (cf., Farver; Göncü et al.; this volume), presuming that a lot of complex and creative symbolic play is inherently important, or even necessary, for children's "optimal development." The evidence from the Maya suggests that symbolic play *is* perhaps inherent, because with little or no support from their parents, very young Mayan children show evidence of spontaneous symbolic expressions, and older children engage in extended symbolic play of realistic adult activities. But the importance that has been placed on symbolic play by Western researchers is not found in the three Mayan principles of engagement.

Play is not culturally supported as an activity – at best, it is tolerated, and often it is discouraged. By definition, play is in contrast to the primary activity of adult work. It is sometimes tolerated when it gets children out of the way of adults' work. This is an attitude often expressed by mothers, who are home all day with the children. But it is discouraged if it conflicts with work (e.g., if the children make a lot of noise while playing) or if it prevents children from being able to take part, even to a marginal extent, in the work at hand. Most fathers do not tolerate children's play; they argue, even for young children, that they should be working instead. Indeed, the amount of play is much less in most households when the father is home.

Mayan parents' goals and beliefs about development are also relevant. The importance of play for development that is assumed by many Western parents is not recognized by Mayan parents. Because they believe that development is primarily internally generated, such experiences as play are not seen as relevant. The only major justification given by Mayan parents for the value in children's play, beyond keeping them busy so adults can work, is that it is good to see young children play because then one knows they are not sick (Gaskins, 1996). This illustrates the Mayan preoccupation with children's illness, which is a reasonable concern in a culture where a generation ago about half of the children did not live to adulthood, and where medical services still are often unavailable, unaffordable, or unreliable.

Yet, in line with the third principle of independence of motivation, when children are allowed to play, they are allowed to play according to their own agenda with almost no adult interference other than removing household items from the play and insisting on physical safety. For young Mayan children, the play that is demonstrated is truly self-motivated. It is not based on adult structuring or praise nor is it geared to gaining adult attention – the "Mommy, watch me!" phenomenon so often seen in Western children's play. From age 1 on, children's play is primarily independent of adult supervision and participation, and conversely, social overtures to adults during play are almost nonexistent (Gaskins, 1990).

When one evaluates Mayan play from this culturally informed perspective, one concludes that play, and especially symbolic play, is a less frequent and less socially dominant form of activity for young Mayan children than it is for young middle-class American children. But one should conclude not that there is therefore a deficit in Mayan children but rather only that they spend their time on other, more culturally significant activities. The larger perspective allows us to see not only what the Mayan children do not do but how their culturally constructed environment leads them to do things other than play. In turn, it allows us to consider play in American children as a culturally supported activity. As such, it should lead us to explore not only how play becomes more frequent and complex when it is culturally supported but also what cultural principles of engagement of our own might lead both parents and researchers to value it so highly.

Work

Although work is the least frequent of the four categories of Mayan children's activities described here, it nonetheless is very important for several reasons. First, although it reflects only a small percentage of young Mayan children's time, it is much more time than American children of the same age spend at work. Second, it is the one category of the four that will continue to increase in frequency as children get older. Thus, by age 5, it provides just a hint of the kinds of activities that will come to dominate the children's activity by the time they are 10 or 12, a good example of continuity in socialization (Benedict, 1938). Third, even at this age, work takes precedence over all other activities in the sense that if there *is* a job that a young child can do, then that work becomes more important than any other activity. The relatively low amounts of work done by children up to age 5 is a reflection more of their abilities than of any principle that values work differently for children than for adults.

What work is actually done by young Mayan children? The list is remarkably long. Children of this age do simple household chores such as putting things away or fetching things from the other house or the yard, or tending to the livestock or garden (as we saw earlier when Mari was asked to chase the chickens and feed them). Children are often asked to go beyond the compound to go shopping, run errands, or to deliver messages throughout the village. This was in fact part of the reason that the 5½-year-old was out of the compound almost half of the time. They are sometimes sent with older siblings to cut firewood in the nearby jungle and to carry it home, to take a horse into the bush to feed, or to deliver food midday to the men and older boys working in the distant cornfields. Children are asked to take care of any younger sibling or cousin in the household, for long periods of time, carrying the infant around on the hip, entertaining the infant, or putting the infant to sleep. If the mother is working, children usually bring the infant to her only to nurse. Younger caregivers are consistently monitored and instructed by the mother in what needs to be done, but 5-year-old children are expected to be able solely to take care of a younger child for perhaps 1 to 2 hours at a time while the mother works out of the compound or goes on errands.

Of the four categories of activities, work is the only one for which there are significant differences between the sexes at this young age. Although both boys and girls are expected to work, much of the work that is to be done around the house is "women's work" and as such is more readily assigned to girls, although boys are asked to do it if there are no girls available (just as girls are asked to do more traditionally male work if there is no boy available). Girls are more likely to be asked to do work involving food preparation, caregiving, and housecleaning. The running of errands, delivering of messages, and tending of the garden is equally shared. Boys are more likely to be sent into the jungle with an older sibling for the chores that are to be done there, and to be given responsibility for livestock. Such sex differences are more pronounced by age 5 than they are earlier, and that trend continues as the children get older.

In the spot observations made on the three children, we see a significant increase in the amount of time the children spend working as they grow older. At 20 months, the youngest child was never observed in any activity one could call work. (This is not to say that children of this age never work. I have seen many examples of children this age engaged in simple, momentary chores and have even seen an 18-month-old sent shopping to the store down the street.) But by 3½, the older girl is observed in 12% of the observations in the compound to be engaged in some work activity. And she was out of the compound 15% of the total time of observing, quite likely engaged during some of that time in doing errands. By age 5½, only 5% of the boy's time observed in the compound involved work, but he was gone for half of the observations, again likely to be engaged in errands for at least some of that time because this is a common task given to children of this age. If half of their time out of the compound is presumed to be related to work (and general observation suggests it would be more likely to be more than half, not less), then the estimate of the 3½-year-old's total time spent in working rises to about 17% and the 5½-year-old's to about 27%.

It is important to note when one is talking about work at such young ages that the tasks the children are being given are not difficult for them nor very lengthy. Many of the things they do take no more than a minute or two. Some, especially those that involve leaving the compound, take longer but still are not hard to do. The simplicity of the chores, and the small proportion of the day that they take up, might lead someone from outside the culture to minimize their importance. This would be a serious mistake because the chores, while differing little in outward appearance from those given to Western children, are an integral part of Mayan adult work activities and represent a critical component in how Mayan parents think their children need to grow up in order to be competent workers.

For all children over the age of 1½ or 2, they are expected to do whatever chores they are asked to do, quickly and effectively. Adult work relies on an ever-ready supply of children to fetch things from the yard or a neighbor, to run to the store to buy something, or to do any number of other small jobs. It is very difficult to run a household without young children to do these chores. In a sense, young Mayan children are always on call for their parents and older siblings. It is assumed that nothing that the child is doing is more important than what the older person wants them to do. So, although work does not take up much of the young children's time, the potential for work is there all the time, and the child is indeed a legitimate and valuable participant in household work activities.

The assumption of children's availability and regular demands to do small chores and errands flows directly from the first cultural principle that work comes first. Anything that the child can do to make the adult's job easier is expected, because the adults' work is primary. Children are presumed to be part of the work process in the compound as soon as they can understand commands and walk competently, and they contribute to the work to be done from the beginning. Of course, as their competency grows, their participation becomes more central and extensive, until, as a teenager, they can do the equivalent of an adult's job.

The early inclusion of children in work, which some Western observers have been inclined to interpret as exploitation, actually stems not only from need but also from a desire on the parents' part to ensure that their children grow up to be good at the work they must do. Mayans believe that development stems from an internal source but that children must participate regularly in work in order to become motivated and competent. Thus, from their point of view, when they give their children chores to do, they are engaged in responsible parenting.

Most of the time, Mayan children do not perceive constant demands on their time as negative. From an early age, they demonstrate a desire to be included in the dominant work activities of the household, to an extent that is difficult for an American parent to imagine. Mayan children take pride in newly developed skills and the confidence that adults come to place in them to do new tasks independently as their competence grows. It is far more common to see a child respond cheerfully and often eagerly to a command than it is to see him avoid or resent it, even when it interrupts some other activity. By the time children are 5 years old, it is not unusual to see them do some chores spontaneously and take responsibility for tasks beyond those assigned to them. Thus, there is a harmony among the three cultural principles in the area of children's work.

Learning New Skills

In each of these categories of activities – maintenance, social orientation, play, and work – children become more competent as they grow older. It is perceived by the Mayans that children learn to do something when they are ready. But the rate at which they achieve competence in a particular activity depends not only on the children's own talents and motivation but also on the opportunities they have to participate in the relevant activities. The opportunities to work and engage in self-maintenance occur more often when adults need children to participate in increasingly integrated ways in those activities. Conversely, the opportunity to play and observe occurs more often when the children are *not* engaged in much work and self-maintenance. The timing of all of these opportunities is determined by a number of factors beyond the children's interests and abilities, including the family structure (e.g., oldest sons and daughters tend to learn maintenance and work skills early, whereas children with many older siblings are exposed to more extended and complex play situations), sources of family income (especially whether or not they are located in the compound, e.g., a lot of livestock or a small store in the home to tend), family resources (e.g., whether there is money to pay an outsider to do some work), parents' education and modernity (parents who have been to school or are more modern tend to support earlier school and play than do uneducated or more conservative parents), and particular family events (e.g., a birth, a serious illness, or an extended absence of someone).

Despite the variations in timing that occur across individuals and compounds, all children come to possess all the skills that they need for self-maintenance and for basic economic sustenance by the time they are in their teens. They do so by mutual participation in adult work activities, where they are called upon to do those parts of a task that they are able to do and are present to observe those parts they are not yet able to do. Mayans recognize the importance of children's participation for the learning of skills and therefore place a very high value on it. (Jordan [1989] provides a complementary analysis of the training of traditional Yucatecan Mayan midwives very similar to the general socialization of children discussed here.)

Such systems of instruction have been described by researchers in ethnographic studies of children in a variety of other cultures (e.g., Childs & Greenfield, 1980; Fortes, 1970 [1938]; Gay & Cole, 1967; Hogbin, 1970 [1946]; LeVine & LeVine, 1963; Maretzki & Maretzki, 1963; Minturn & Hitchcock, 1963; Raum, 1940; Read, 1960; Romney & Romney, 1963; Williams, 1970). From this evidence, one might conclude that learning through activity in context has been documented as a frequently preferred mode across cultures, and that it needs therefore to be included in any theory of learning, socialization, or development. Despite this evidence, most theorists do not address it. Exceptions include Bruner (1972) (knowing how vs. knowing that), Scribner and Cole (1973) (informal education), Rogoff (1990) (apprenticeship), and Lave and Wenger (1992) (situated learning and legitimate peripheral participation). (For other examples, see Gauvain, Guberman, and Pappas, this volume.)

If children from a wide range of cultures are learning primarily through activity in context, it may have significant implications for the kinds of knowledge and cognitive structures and processes they develop. The qualitative differences between learning through activity in context and learning as a decontextualized, abstract, verbal activity were emphasized by Vygotsky (1987 [1934]). For him, the integration of everyday and scientific concepts that comes through schooling is necessary for the final stages of cognitive development. Contemporary psychological research on implicit vs. explicit cognitive processes (which are related to contextualized vs. decontextualized learning) also suggests important differences; for example, implicit processes are less affected by differences in age and intelligence, and they have less transfer to other contexts. (See

Borofsky [1994] and Cole [1990] for more complete discussions of this point.)

Although there is little systematic instruction, there are two important ways in which Mayan parents influence their children's learning. First, they ask their children to do only those things that the child can already do reasonably well, thereby ensuring the child's ability to participate legitimately. Second, they give a lot of directions and microlevel corrections while the child is engaged in the task. Such a style of instruction is similar to Vygotsky's notion that learning for the child occurs first on the *interpersonal* level through mutual activity before it can be internalized and realized on the *intrapersonal* level. Although this may very well be the mechanism that allows learning to occur for Mayan children, it is also important to realize that Mayan parents' understanding of their behavior is somewhat different; Mayans are engaged first and foremost in getting their work done, not in teaching or apprenticing their children. Thus, asking children to do only what they can already do, and correcting them when necessary, are expedient strategies for getting the maximal amount of work done with the fewest errors. The task is never bent to structure the children's' activities in a way to allow them to learn a maximal amount. For this reason, it is not scaffolding in its most precise sense (Wood, Bruner, & Ross, 1976). Although specific directions are given, there are few explanations, rhetorical reflections, probing questions, or reformulations of the problem. Likewise, children are unlikely to ask questions, try to exceed their ability, or exhibit frustration when they are relieved of a task. If a child cannot do a part of the task or requires too many directions, the adult takes over the part of the task that is proving difficult. The child then can observe the activity and re-engage when he or she is able to contribute in a useful way. The smoothness with which this occurs, over and over again in a single day, suggests that both parent and child share a common goal of getting the task done.

The interaction between work and play is interesting in this context. Before children are truly able to participate in a task, they are allowed to imitate the task alongside those who are really working. We saw an example of this when Mari began to wash furniture next to her mother. It is difficult to know what Mari thought she was doing, but her mother clearly did not think she was contributing to getting the stools clean. Yet she tolerated her presence, and even her mud, up to a certain point. Mari's mother explained her patience in the following way. She interpreted Mari's behavior as indicating an interest in participating in the work to be done, even though she did not yet possess the skills that would allow her to participate. Thus, she allowed the behavior to go on, even when it was a slight inconvenience; in fact, she took pleasure in it and commented about it to her other daughters. Seeing such behavior exhibited by Mari would lead her to begin to ask Mari to do more chores that are within her ability. Thus, the parent takes the child's imitative behavior as a sign of readiness, tolerates it to encourage the child's motivation, and then provides a structure for that motivation to be realized in tasks within the child's ability.

Thus, the fact that Mayan children make so few mistakes is a sign not only of their competence but also of their parents' ability to judge which tasks lie just within their child's abilities. The Vygotskian model of a zone of proximal development has the child achieving things through social interaction that are just beyond his grasp to do alone. The Mayan model has the child achieving things as a legitimate participant in a shared activity where the child never goes beyond what he or she can actually do. Both require the adult to structure the environment according to the child's abilities, but the motivation of the adult and the experience for the child in the two systems are very different.

Conclusions

This chapter has formulated three cultural principles of engagement for young Mayan children that were developed from general ethnographic knowledge of the Mayan culture and extensive observations of Mayan children engaged in everyday activities. The three principles are (1) primacy of adult work activities, (2) importance of parental cultural beliefs in structuring the children's activities, and (3) independence of Mayan children's motivation. These three principles were used to interpret four different categories of activities in which Mayan children engage: maintenance activities, social orientation, play, and work. For each category of activity, we can see from the description alone that Mayan children's engagement with the world looks significantly different from Western children's engagement. But the description alone did not provide an adequate basis for an interpretation of the children's behavior that was culturally accurate or meaningful. With the three cultural principles of engagement, it was possible to understand what engagement in that activity might actually mean to the child or how it might be valued by the culture. In fact, for each category of activity, because Mayan children do not do what Western children do, a culturally naive researcher might miss important behavior or interpret it as evidence for deficits in development.

Only by considering the full range of children's activities and the cultural principles that underlie and motivate them is one able to approximate a culturally adequate understanding.

For example, symbolic play, supposed in Western research to be important if not critical for development, is neither a frequent nor a well-elaborated activity for Mayan children. How should such a fact be interpreted? It may be that children receive a similar sort of stimulation from some other activity, but it is also possible that children who do not engage in sustained and complex symbolic play are less advanced in some ability, such as creativity, for example, than those who do (although evidence demonstrating direct influences of symbolic play in any domain of development is quite limited). Rather than stopping at the conclusion that Mayan children are not developing optimally, one must ask what activities the children are engaged in instead of symbolic play (or its substitute) and how those activities in turn influence their development, perhaps in areas very different from those influenced by symbolic play.

By making such a move, one acknowledges the cultural marginality of play for the Maya. It is true that the opportunity to engage in complex, extended, and creative symbolic play is not provided to Mayan children by their culture. But it is important to recognize as well that symbolic play for Mayan children does just what the parents want it to do. It meets their expectations of keeping children out of the way and demonstrating that their children are healthy. But because it conflicts with a more important cultural value of adult work, and children's participation in it, it *should not* have an important role to play in Mayan childhood *if* the children are going to grow up to share the values of their culture and participate productively in its activities. All three of the other categories of activity – maintenance, social orientation, and work – are more relevant for children to engage in if they are going to grow up to be competent Mayans. And young Mayan children do more of these activities and are more competent at each of them than are young Western children. All three promote their peripheral but legitimate engagement in the adult world, which is the primary world that the culture provides for children. In contrast, Western-style play promotes central but artificial engagement in a child-dominant world, which is the primary world that Western culture provides for children.

It is true that there may be some costs to the Mayan child for engaging in such activities. Some of these may be in areas that Westerners value highly. At the same time, there will also be some benefits from these same activities, and by and large, they will be in those areas valued and supported by the Mayan culture. The description of Mayan children given here suggests that they certainly are more competent at the skills involved in basic maintenance activities and doing chores and errands. One could hypothesize that they would develop more quickly than Western children in such areas as attention, social cognition, independence, and following instructions. Beyond differences in rates of development, there may be different developmental endpoints as well, especially in such domains as understanding of self (and its relation to the group), self-esteem, and motivational structure. Such hypotheses can be developed, however, only as a result of studying Mayan children's development in the context of the entire range of their behavior and in the context of the cultural system as a whole, so that their development can be understood on its own terms rather than on ours.

To advance a cultural theory of development, it is first important to recognize that there can be multiple developmental outcomes. But it is perhaps even more important to recognize that there can also be multiple stances for judgment about the value of those outcomes. These two recognitions move us beyond comparative research that is motivated by an idea of a single optimal outcome in one specific area of behavior, where variation can only be interpreted as delay or deficit. It encourages us to consider the child's engagement with the world as part of a complex cultural system of interrelated activities. It provides an understanding of "optimal development" as a culturally relative concept.

This chapter has demonstrated that such an approach leads to a more complete and accurate picture of Mayan children's engagement in their world. But it also forces us as researchers to recognize that because development is integrally tied to children's activities in particular contexts, and because those activities and contexts are *necessarily* culturally structured and variable, we need to adopt a similar perspective for research on Western children. This perspective would be difficult to generate by studying children in only our own culture. It suggests that in addition to certain benefits, there might also be some costs incurred by our own children engaging in the sort of child-oriented world of play and nonresponsibility that we construct for them and reward them for, including such things as identity crises, social isolation or selfishness, erosion of intrinsic motivation for real-world tasks, and low self-esteem. In this sense, a culturally motivated approach can do more than provide more adequate answers. It can give us the insight to ask new questions and entertain insights about ourselves. This increased awareness of ourselves is increasingly important in the modern world, where we must interact and negotiate with members of other cultures every day (Geertz, 1994).

References

Benedict, R. (1938). Continuities and discontinuities in cultural conditioning. *Psychiatry, 1* (2), 161–7.

Bourdieu, P. (1977). *Outline of a theory of practice.* Cambridge, England: Cambridge University Press.

Borofsky, R. (1994). On the knowledge and knowing of cultural activities. In R. Borofsky (Ed.), *Assessing cultural anthropology* (pp. 331–48). New York: McGraw-Hill.

Bronfenbrenner, U. (1979). *The ecology of human development.* Cambridge, MA: Harvard University Press.

Bruner, J. (1972). Nature and uses of immaturity. *American Psychologist, 27*(8), 687–708.

Childs, C. P., & Greenfield, P. M. (1980). Informal modes of learning and teaching: The case of Zinacanteco weaving. In N. Warren (Ed.), *Studies in cross-cultural psychology* (Vol. 2, pp. 269–316). London: Academic Press.

Clarke-Stewart, K. A. (1973). Interactions between mothers and their young children: Characteristics and consequences. *Monographs of the Society for Research in Child Development, 38*(6–7, Serial No. 153).

Cole, M. (1990). Cognitive development and formal schooling: The evidence from cross-cultural research. In L. Moll (Ed.), *Vygotsky and education* (pp. 89–110). New York: Cambridge University Press.

Fortes, M. (1970 [1938]). Social and psychological aspects of education in Taleland. In J. Middleton (Ed.), *From child to adult: Studies in the anthropology of education* (pp. 14–74). Garden City, NY: Natural History Press for the American Museum of Natural History.

Freud, S. (1950). *Beyond the pleasure principle.* New York: Liveright.

Garvey, C. (1990). *Play.* Cambridge, MA: Harvard University Press.

Gaskins, S., (1989, February). *Symbolic play in a Mayan village.* Paper presented at the annual meeting of the Association for the Study of Play, Philadelphia, PA.

Gaskins, S. (1990). *Exploratory play and development in Mayan infants.* Unpublished doctoral dissertation, University of Chicago.

Gaskins, S. (1994). Integrating interpretive and quantitative methods in socialization research. *Merrill-Palmer Quarterly, 40*(3), 313–33.

Gaskins, S. (1996). How Mayan parental theories come into play. In S. Harkness & C. Super (Eds.), *Parents' cultural belief systems* (pp. 345–63). New York: Guilford.

Gaskins, S., & Göncü, A. (1992). Cultural variation in play: A challenge to Piaget and Vygotsky. *The Quarterly Newsletter of the Laboratory of Comparative Human Cognition, 14*(2), 31–35.

Gaskins S., & Lucy, J. A. (1987, December). *Passing the buck: Responsibility and blame in the Yucatec Maya household.* Paper presented at the annual meeting of the American Anthropological Association, Philadelphia.

Gay, J., & Cole, M. (1967). *The new mathematics in an old culture.* New York: Holt, Rinehart, and Winston.

Geertz, C. (1994). The uses of diversity. In R. Borofsky (Ed.), *Assessing cultural anthropology* (pp. 454–67). New York: McGraw-Hill.

Haight, W., & Miller, P. J. (1992). *Pretending at home: Early development in a sociocultural context.* Albany: State University of New York Press.

Harkness, S., & Super, C. (1996). Introduction. In S. Harkness & C. Super (Eds.), *Parents' cultural belief systems* (pp. 1–23). New York: Guilford.

Hogbin, H. I. (1970 [1946]). A New Guinea childhood: From weaning till the eighth year. In J. Middleton (Ed.), *From child to adult: Studies in the anthropology of education* (pp. 134–62). Garden City, NY: Natural History Press for the American Museum of Natural History.

Jordan, B. (1989). Cosmopolitical obstetrics: Some insights from the training of traditional midwives. *Social Science and Medicine, 28*(9), 925–44.

Lave, G., & Wenger, E. (1992). *Situated learning: Legitimate peripheral participation.* New York: Cambridge University Press.

Leont'ev, A. N. (1979). The problem of activity in psychology. In J. Wertsch (Trans. and Ed.), *The concept of activity in Soviet psychology* (pp. 37–71). Armonk, NY: M. E. Sharpe, Inc.

LeVine, R. A. (1969). Culture, personality, and socialization: An evolutionary view. In D. Goslin (Ed.), *Handbook of socialization theory and research* (pp. 503–41). Chicago: Rand-McNally.

LeVine, R. A., & LeVine, B. B. (1963). *Nyansongo: A Guisii Community in Kenya.* Six Cultures Series. New York: John Wiley & Sons.

Luria, A. R. (1976). *Cognitive development: Its cultural and social foundations.* Cambridge, MA: Harvard University Press.

Maretzki, T., & Maretzki, H. (1963). *Taira: An Okinawan Village.* Six Cultures Series. New York: John Wiley & Sons.

Mead, M. (1963). Socialization and enculturation. *Current Anthropology, 4*(2), 184–8.

Minturn, L., & Hitchcock, J. T. (1963). *The Rajputs of Khalapur, India.* Six Cultures Series. New York: John Wiley & Sons.

Ochs, E. (1988). *Culture and language development.* Cambridge, England: Cambridge University Press.

Ochs, E., & Schieffelin, B. (1984). Language acquisition and socialization. In R. LeVine & R. Shweder (Eds.), *Culture theory: Essays on mind, self, and emotion* (pp. 276–320). Cambridge, England: Cambridge University Press.

Piaget, J. (1962). *Play, dreams and imitation in childhood.* New York: Norton.

61   *Children's Daily Lives in a Mayan Village*

Raum, O. F. (1940). *Chaga childhood: A description of indigenous education in an East African tribe.* London: Published by the Oxford University Press for the International Institute of African Languages and Cultures.

Read, M. (1960). *Children of their fathers: Growing up among the Ngoni of Nyasaland.* New Haven: Yale University Press.

Redfield, R., & Villa Rojas, A. (1934). *Chan Kom: A Mayan village.* Chicago: University of Chicago Press.

Rogoff, B. (1990). *Apprenticeship in thinking: Cognitive development in social context.* New York: Oxford University Press.

Romney, K., & Romney, R. (1963). *The Mixtecans of Juxtlahuaca, Mexico.* Six Cultures Series. New York: John Wiley & Sons.

Schwartzman, H. B. (1978). *Transformations: The anthropology of children's play.* New York: Plenum.

Scribner, S., & Cole, M. (1973). Cognitive consequences of formal and informal education. *Science, 182,* 553–9.

Steggerda, M. (1941). *Mayan Indians of Yucatan.* Washington, DC: Carnegie Institution.

Vygotsky, L. S. (1967). Play and its role in the mental development of the child. *Soviet Psychology, 5,* 6–18.

Vygotsky, L. S. (1987 [1934]). *Thinking and speech.* In R. W. Rieber & A. S. Carton (Eds)., *The collected works of L. S. Vygotsky. Vol. 1: Problems in general psychology* (trans. by N. Minick) (pp. 39–285). New York: Plenum.

Williams, T. R. (1970). The structure of socialization process in Papago Indian society. In J. Middleton (Ed.), *From child to adult: Studies in the anthropology of education* (pp. 163–72). Garden City, NY: Natural History Press for the American Museum of Natural History.

Wood, D., Bruner, J., & Ross, G. (1976). The role of tutoring in problem solving. *Journal of Child Psychology and Psychiatry, 17,* 89–100.

3   Cultural Heterogeneity: Parental Values and Beliefs and Their Preschoolers' Activities in the United States, South Korea, Russia, and Estonia

Jonathan Tudge,[1] Diane Hogan,[2] Soeun Lee,[3]
Peeter Tammeveski,[4] Marika Meltsas,[5]
Natalya Kulakova,[6] Irina Snezhkova,[6] and
Sarah Putnam[1]

In this chapter we report on an ongoing program of research that has been underway since 1989. The aim of the research is to try to understand ways in which children become competent members of the cultural group into which they are born. Our assumption is that what counts as "competence" is culturally relative and can be understood only in terms of the prevailing values and practices of the members of any cultural group. Becoming competent is the result of ongoing interpretations, actions, and interaction in which children (and others) engage with social partners. We have therefore observed everyday activities of young children and their partners in those activities and gathered data from their parents about their values and beliefs relating to bringing up children. Although the project has since broadened in scope, our initial focus was on industrialized societies from the northern hemisphere. In a series of interconnected studies, data were collected in cities of equivalent size and cultural amenities in societies that differed, at least until recently, in ideology (capitalist

The authors are affiliated with: [1]The University of North Carolina at Greensboro, USA; [2]The Children's Research Centre, Trinity College Dublin, Ireland; [3]Chungbuk National University, Korea; [4]The Pennsylvania State University; [5]The University of Tartu, Estonia; [6]The Institute of Ethnology and Anthropology, Moscow, Russia. We wish to express our deep appreciation to the parents and children who gave so generously of their time. We also wish to thank the International Research and Exchanges Board (IREX, with funds provided by the U.S. Department of State [Title VIII]), and the Spencer Foundation for grants awarded to the first author, and to the University of North Carolina at Greensboro for the granting of a Kohler Fund Award, Research Assignment, and Excellence Foundation Summer Research Award to the first author. The data presented, the statements made, and the views expressed are solely the responsibility of the authors.

or socialist) and in values about social organization (relatively individualistic or collectivist).

Much cross-cultural research has been conducted with cultural groups that are as different as possible from each other. As Bornstein, Tal, and Tamis-LeMonda (1991) pointed out:

> Cross-cultural research is often geared to evaluate the distinctiveness of some phenomenon in a setting that is exotic or unique; frequently, it is undertaken to compare samples from contrastive settings in order to maximize the potential of uncovering differences. However, such a strategy potentially confounds childrearing aspects of culture with other factors. (p. 73)

For example, cross-cultural psychologists interested in issues of children's development have compared child rearing in an industrialized society (typically the United States) with equivalent practices in societies in which the parent generation has had little or no schooling (as in many parts of rural Africa or South America). It is clear as a result that behaviors, beliefs, practices, and so on that are considered competent in one cultural group are not seen as competent in another. Cultural groups differ widely in terms of such things as the appropriate age to wean the child from the breast, the age at which children should not be sleeping with parents, when it is worth trying to communicate with babies, and so on (Morelli, Rogoff, Oppenheim, & Goldsmith, 1992; New & Richman, 1996; Ochs & Schieffelin, 1984; Valsiner, 1989; Wolf, Lozoff, Latz, & Paludetto, 1996).

Although this work has been useful in alerting psychologists to the range of values, beliefs, and practices that are viewed as appropriate and competent, there has been a problem with this focus on cultural groups that are maximally different from each other. The problem is that within-society cultural differences have largely been ignored, and one group of families, most commonly white, middle-class, and from the United States, is typically compared with rural, minimally schooled, families in one or more nonindustrialized societies. For example, middle-class families in Boston have been compared with Kokwet families in Kenya and Efe hunter-gatherers in Zaire, middle-class families in Salt Lake City with rural Mayan families in Guatemala, and middle-class families in Wisconsin compared with rural families in Senegal (Bloch, 1989; Dixon, LeVine, Richman, & Brazelton, 1984; Morelli, Rogoff, & Angelillo, 1992; Morelli et al., 1992; Rogoff, Mistry, Göncü, & Mosier, 1991; Super & Harkness, 1982).

We do not wish to imply that the scholars engaging in this research believe that their findings can be generalized beyond the particular group being studied or that there is an assumption of within-society homogeneity. In fact, the richly contextualized descriptions of daily lives in these groups are meant to indicate their specific ecocultural niche. In this sense, their work is a conceptual world away from traditional research in developmental psychology as practiced in North America, where generalizability is the explicit goal and thus the impact of context is, supposedly, reduced to a minimum. Nonetheless, without any explicit discussion of within-society heterogeneity, problems in interpretation may occur. For example, by virtue of the fact that the families of "Orchard Town" were the only ones drawn from the industrialized world in the Six Cultures Study (Whiting & Whiting, 1975), they have come to serve as representative of families far beyond the confines of the small New England village where the data were collected. This is partly because we have an extremely limited amount of high-quality observational data of everyday lives in such families, unlike the comparative wealth of such data gained from the participants in more "traditional" anthropological studies, conducted in predominantly rural and non-or semi-industrialized societies (Bloch, 1989; Richards, 1977). But it is also the result of the lack of any explicit attention to the heterogeneous nature of industrialized societies or to the changes in social relationships over historical time. Readers of reports of the Six Cultures Study may thus be left with the understanding that, compared to mothers in Kenya, India, the Philippines, Mexico, and so on, mothers in the United States are more likely to be the social partners of their children. Even in the most recent report (Whiting & Edwards, 1988), no mention is made of possible variations across historical time (the 1950s, when the data were gathered, and the 1980s), across social class (all the families were of middle class or self-employed working class), across race (all the families were white), or across area (all the families lived in a small New England village).

The issue of heterogeneity has long been recognized, of course, but principally by those with a sociological background who explore racial, ethnic, or social class variability within societies or by psychologists who include these terms as independent variables of interest, but who go little beyond using what Bronfenbrenner and Crouter (1983) have termed "social address" models. In our view, it is important to go beyond such models and analytic strategies to explore the ways in which cultural groups who live at different social addresses engage in their everyday activities, the meanings that these activities have for them, and their consequences.

One of the approaches taken to heterogeneity has been to focus on immigrants, who have brought the values, beliefs, and practices of their original society (or rather, of their cultural group within that society) to their new society (Field & Widmayer, 1981; Goodnow & Collins, 1990; Ninio, 1979, 1988; Okagaki & Sternberg, 1993; Pomerleau, Malcuit, & Sabatier, 1991). Comparisons of immigrants and nonimmigrants (or different groups of immigrants to the same area, or even the relative length of time immigrants have been in a place) are relatively easily accomplished. There is a price to be paid, of course, because it is not possible to understand any differences between those who chose to remain and those who chose to come to a new society (chosen, perhaps, because of preexisting views of the nature of that society, including such things as the perceived goodness of fit or opportunities for success).

A second approach to heterogeneity has been to explore the impact of differential extent of engagement in schooling. This research has been conducted for the most part in societies that are currently industrializing and making it more possible, and desirable, for children to attend school. In the research of LeVine, Miller, Richman, and LeVine (1996), for example, it is clear that the longer time mothers spent in school the more likely they were to believe that their children could be communicative partners and the more likely they were to respond contingently to their children. This relationship held true even when other important factors, such as access to resources, neighborhood, and husband's education were taken into account. Moreover, when the babies were retested when they were almost 3 years old, those whose mothers had behaved more contingently scored higher on tests related to subsequent school performance. Amount of schooling has other benefits, of course, including both more general and school-specific cognitive competence, likely to help schooled children get better jobs and pass on the benefits to their children in turn (Rogoff, 1981; Stevenson, 1982). The way in which schooled members of a culture engage with children also is different from those without schooling (Wertsch, Minick, & Arns, 1984).

In industrialized societies, also, level of education has been found to play a role in beliefs and practices, although it is difficult to disentangle the confounding factors of education and socioeconomic status, given that level of education is often a determining factor in the type of occupations that are attainable (see, for example, Hoff-Ginsburg & Tardif, 1995).

However, a number of studies have focused specifically on education, indicating that parents have differing ideas about development and engage in different practices, as a function of level of education. For example, Palacios and Moreno (1996) studied ethnically homogeneous Spanish parents and adolescents, varying in terms of education and urbanicity, and found quite different "cultural models" of parenting coexisting within the same society. Other studies have examined changes in maternal beliefs about child rearing as a function of parent education programs (Holden, 1995).

A third approach to heterogeneity has been to examine, explicitly, two or more groups from within the same society, whether differentiated by race, ethnicity, or social class in the United States (for example, Wolf et al., 1996), or implicitly, by choosing for comparative purposes matched groups from two or more societies. As McGillicuddy-DeLisi and Subramanian (1996) pointed out with regard to their study of the beliefs of Tanzanian and U.S. mothers, matching groups on such characteristics as parental education, degree of affluence, occupation, and so on does not mean that the two groups have been equated. However, a matching strategy does acknowledge the heterogeneity that exists in both societies. Bornstein et al. (1991) were more explicit about the issue of heterogeneity in their study of parenting in the United States, Japan, and France, choosing equivalent-sized cities and mothers and babies that were carefully balanced on a whole range of characteristics, including demographic. It is this third approach that we adopted in our program of research by examining, in each society from which we have collected data, two groups that are differentiated by education and occupation.

Theoretical Foundation

The theoretical foundation for this project has been drawn from two related theories, Vygotsky's cultural-historical theory on the one hand, and Bronfenbrenner's ecological systems theory on the other. We have written more extensively about these theories and their relevance for research on young children elsewhere (Hogan & Tudge, in press; Tudge, 1996, 1997; Tudge, Gray, & Hogan, 1997; Tudge, Odero, Hogan, & Etz, 1998; Tudge & Putnam, 1997; Tudge, Putnam, & Sidden, 1993, 1994; Tudge, Putnam, & Valsiner, 1996; Tudge & Winterhoff, 1993). Here we would simply like to stress the following points. Both Vygotsky's and Bronfenbrenner's theories require that our understanding of development encompasses three interrelated factors – namely, aspects of the individual, of the sociocultural and physical context (at both the immediate, interpersonal level as well as at the broader, cultural-historical level), and the passage of time (also see Gaskins, this volume). In Bronfenbrenner's (1989) ecological systems theory, context is differentiated into the microsystem (where children are engaged in activities with partners), mesosystem (relations among two or more microsystems), exosystem (a context, such as the parent's workplace, in which the child is not present but which nonetheless influences the child's microsystem), and macrosystem (the values, beliefs, and practices of a cultural group). Time can be thought of in two distinct senses, in one sense as the microgenetic processes of interaction that occur between the developing individual and those around him or her, and in the other sense as the passage of historical time that has helped to shape the culture.

The links between these different aspects or levels are multidirectional; culture or context does not cause or "explain" individual development any more than individuals create culture. Instead, the causal link between the different levels of these theories is one that has been termed transactional, co-constructive, or dialectical. This is what Bronfenbrenner had in mind when he argued, borrowing from Lewin, that development is a function of person and environment (Bronfenbrenner, 1988, 1989, 1993, 1995). Similarly, Vygotsky's "general genetic law" that all higher psychological functions are social prior to being individual takes for granted that "social" in this context necessarily includes the individual (Tudge, 1997; Vygotsky, 1978, 1994). Individual and social factors are thus mutually constitutive. The appropriate unit of analysis is one that involves neither individual nor social factors alone but rather one that encapsulates both. Human activity constitutes such a unit, for any such activity, including that of a child playing alone, as simultaneously individual and social.

The link between the cultural-historical level and the individual level is to be found in everyday activities. Vygotsky defined one such link as activity that creates a "zone of proximal development" or the ways in which a child manages to understand or achieve something at a more competent level (culturally defined) after having been helped to do it with the assistance of someone already more competent (Vygotsky, 1978, 1987; also see Guberman, this volume). Similarly, Bronfenbrenner (1993) defined "proximal processes" as the "engines of development" for children, by which he meant engagement with others in "progressively more complex activities and tasks" (p. 11).

These views of the links between culture and individual development are similar to those of cultural anthropologists and cultural psychologists who define culture in terms of the values, beliefs, activities, and practices that continue from generation to generation (see Farver, Gaskins, Göncü et al., and Haight, this volume). These values, practices, and so on are not simply adopted wholesale by the parents from the culture in which they live and then transmitted by the parent generation to the child generation in any unidirectional fashion (McGillicuddy-DeLisi & Subramanian, 1996). Although cultural messages are available through books, television, and other forms of mass media, and thus may appear to be the source of such messages, members of the culture are of course responsible for producing that material. Moreover, some parents pay more attention to some messages than others, ignore some while enthusiastically endorsing others. Some families encourage certain types of activities in their children and discourage others, while other families encourage quite different activities. Simultaneously, the children themselves are engaged in a constant process of figuring out what the appropriate practices are, what to believe, how to act, and so on. As they interpret the messages (both explicit and implicit) that are made available by members of the parent generation, the messages are transformed in subtle ways, in such a fashion that there is never a straightforward copy from one generation to the other, but the practices, activities, and beliefs are reproduced in novel ways (Valsiner & Litvinovic, 1996). Cultures, in other words, continually develop just as the members of those cultures develop.

If we accept this definition of culture, as one involving delineated values, beliefs, practices, and activities, it is clear that culture and society are not synonymous, and that within societies many cultures are to be found. (Although these cultural groups are sometimes known as ''subcultures,'' we will not use that term because it carries with it the pejorative meaning of being subordinate, as opposed to the dominant cultural group within society.) Within-society cultural groups, like cross-societal cultural groups, can be identified to the extent to which they encompass different lifestyles, resources, and opportunity structures; espouse different values and beliefs; engage in different types of activities; encourage different practices in their young; and try to pass on to them their values and beliefs. This position is similar to Bronfenbrenner's (1993) definition of the macrosystem. Examples of within-societal cultural groups in the United States include racial or ethnic groups, regional groups, and socioeconomic groups.

In our research we have, until now, concentrated on socioeconomic groups as our example of within-society cultures. The primary reason for this stems from the work of the sociologist Melvin Kohn (1977, 1979, 1995; Kohn & Schooler, 1983; Kohn & Slomczynski, 1990), whose interest has long been in the role of parental position in the social stratification system as an influence on parental values and beliefs about child rearing. This work is particularly relevant to Bronfenbrenner's theory, because it proposes a link between the macrosystem (values of a cultural group) and the microsystem (parental child-rearing practices) via the exosystem of parental workplace experiences.

In both the sociological and psychological literature, there has been a great deal written about values, beliefs, attitudes, and ideas, without any great definitional or conceptual clarity being achieved (see, for example, discussions by Goodnow & Collins, 1990; Harkness & Super, 1996; Sigel, McGillicuddy-DeLisi, & Goodnow, 1992). Kohn (1977) defined values as "conceptions of the desirable" (p. 10). He argued that all parents want certain things for their children – to do well at school, to be happy, become successful in later life, and so on. However, they differ in the emphasis they place on some characteristics, and especially on the extent to which they value self-directed independent behavior in their children. Why should these different emphases be related to position in the social stratification system? For Kohn, the most important determining factor was parental occupation, and specifically experiences at work. People with higher education, and who work in the professional sphere, typically have occupations that are complex and nonroutine, and that require working with people. In order to do well in jobs such as these, parents have to exhibit a lot of self-direction; not surprisingly, Kohn argued, these parents value these qualities for their children. By contrast, parents who do not have higher education and whose jobs are nonprofessional are more likely to be relatively routinized and to work with things rather than people. Their success at work has required them to follow directions carefully, directions that others have often established for them. These parents are relatively more likely, therefore, to want their children to learn to obey rules and to conform to external standards.

Kohn did not observe what actually occurred in families, but Luster and his colleagues (Luster, Rhoades, & Haas, 1989) went one step beyond. Although they accepted Kohn's definition of values, they argued that beliefs represented a mediating factor, defining them as "parents' ideas on how they can help their children achieve valued outcomes" (1989, p. 40). Luster et al. collected observational data from 60 mother–

child dyads from New York State, heterogeneous in terms of social class. In addition to collecting data about mothers' values and beliefs about child rearing, Luster and his colleagues, using observations, examined the extent of similarity between mothers' expressed values and beliefs and the ways in which they treated their children. Luster's data supported his hypothesis that beliefs serve as a mediating link between values and behavior, as well as for the most part supporting Kohn's general thesis of a relationship between class and values. Our intention was to use the work of both Kohn and Luster, but to collect far more observational data than Luster and his colleagues had done, so that we would be able to focus on children's everyday activities.

In this research, we decided to focus on families in several industrialized societies, all of which are at an approximately similar level of technological complexity (United States, Korea, Russia, and Estonia). In each society, we have collected data from families from a medium-sized city (approximately 100,000 to 700,000 inhabitants) from two separate groups, divided by education and occupation. That is, in each city some of the participants have higher education (the equivalent of a college degree in the United States) and occupations that are professional, while other participants do not have higher education and have jobs in the nonprofessional sphere. For simplicity's sake, we refer to these groups as "middle class" and "working class," respectively, although we recognize that these are simply labels that in this case refer to differences that are a function of education and occupation.

We have thus three related interests. First, whether it is possible to find differences in values, beliefs, and activities at the "society" level (to the extent to which these cities can in any sense represent their society as a whole). This was particularly interesting, given that the cities are from societies that differ in terms of both ideology and family orientation toward collectivism and individualism (Bronfenbrenner, 1970; Choi, Kim, & Choi, 1993; Kim & Choi, 1994; Kirveennummi, Räsänen, & Virtanen, 1994; Lee, 1992; Schwartz, 1994; Triandis, 1993, 1995; Tudge, 1991), but which nonetheless are not so drastically different from each other in degree of industrialization as those most often compared. Our second interest, derived from Kohn, Luster, and others, was whether social class (as we have defined it) distinguishes parents in terms of their values and beliefs. Our third interest, assuming that differences in values and beliefs were found, was whether children actually behaved in ways that reflected their parents' differing values and beliefs.

Methodology

Observations

Families were asked to keep their daily routines unchanged as much as possible during the observation period. Each child was observed, wherever he or she was, for 20 hours over the course of a week to capture the equivalent of an entire waking day. Observations were continuous in 2- and 4-hour blocks, but activities were coded only during 30-second "windows" every 5½ minutes, using modified spot observations (Tudge, Sidden, & Putnam, 1990). Activities were coded as being "available to" the child if they occurred within his or her hearing or sight. Children were coded as being "involved in" the activities if they were physically participating or were observing. As well as observing which activities were available to the child and which he or she became involved in, we coded how activities were initiated and by whom, the manner in which the child became involved in any activity, any partners in activity, their respective roles, and so on.

The activities in which we were interested were lessons (4 categories); work (5 categories); play, exploration, and entertainment (10 categories); conversation (3 categories); and "other" (6 categories, including sleeping, eating, etc.). (For full details of the coding scheme, refer to Tudge et al., 1990). In brief, lessons were defined as involving the deliberate attempt to impart or receive information in four areas: academic (spelling, counting, learning shapes and colors, etc.); interpersonal (teaching etiquette or "proper" behavior); skill/nature (how things work, why things happen); and religious lessons. Work was defined as "activities that either have economic importance or contribute to the maintenance of life" (Tudge et al., 1990) and was broken down into work involving no technology, clear technology (such as sweeping with a broom), or more complex technology (such as using a vacuum cleaner). Play (including exploration and entertainment) was defined as activities that were being engaged in for fun or for their own sake, with no apparent curriculum (which would constitute a lesson) or sense that the activity had economic importance (work). Types of play included pretend/role play, play with an academic object (such as looking at a book), playing with objects typically designed for children, play with adult objects, other types of play (such as chase or rough and tumble), and watching television. Thus a child looking at a book or being read to would be coded as engaging in "play with an academic object," whereas a child asking what a particular word was, or being asked to name colors, would be coded as being involved in an academic lesson. Conversation was defined as talk that was not related to an ongoing activity and had a sustained or focused topic. Talking that accompanied play, work, or a lesson was not coded as conversation. During any 30-second window, more than one activity could occur and could be coded.

One of our interests in conducting this research was not simply to document similarities and differences in children's everyday activities but to focus on variability in those activities that might be expected to relate to later academic competence. As yet, we have follow-up data only on the U.S. children (Odero, Hogan, & Tudge, 1996; Tudge et al., 1998), but the research is designed to be longitudinal, with teachers and parents providing information on their perception of the children's social and academic competence in their first years of formal schooling. Accordingly, we have examined with particular interest those activities we felt might be most relevant to academic competence – namely, the academic and skill/nature lessons in which children were involved, their play with academic objects, and their conversation with adults. We focus for much of the chapter on these activities.

Questionnaire and interview

Following the observation period, the parents were interviewed and completed questionnaires to assess, among other things, their values and beliefs about child rearing.[1] In order to assess values, we used the same Q-sort methodology that Kohn (1977) had used. Parents are asked to choose, from a list of 13 values, the three that they rank highest and the three they rank lowest. From these 6, the parents then choose the one they value most and the one they value least. Of these 13 values, 5 relate to self-direction (e.g., "have self-control," "have good sense and sound judgment"), four to conformity (e.g., "have good manners," "obey their parents well"), and four are related to neither (e.g., "gets along well with other children"). A high score on this scale represents a higher value for self-direction compared to conformity, with scores that can range from a minimum of 10 to a high of 26.[2]

---

[1] In Greensboro, the interview and questionnaire data gathering occurred only during a second phase of the study, approximately 3 years after the first.

[2] A self-direction score was computed by summing the scores for the six values chosen, in the following fashion. All "filler" items were scored 3. Of the

In order to assess their beliefs about child rearing, we asked parents to complete the Parents' Opinion Survey (Hogan & Tudge, 1994), which had been adapted for use with parents of school-age children from the Parental Beliefs Survey (Luster, 1985, cited in Luster et al., 1989), and which deals with parental beliefs about appropriate child rearing. Parents were asked to circle the response that best represented their opinion for each of the 59 items, on a 6-point Likert scale. Responses ranged from "strongly agree" to "strongly disagree." In this chapter, we refer to three subscales: beliefs about spoiling the child by attending closely to him or her (for example, "I worry about spoiling my child by being an overattentive parent"); beliefs regarding freedom in and around the home (for example, "As long as the child is safe and the object will not be damaged, he/she should be allowed to play with almost any object in the house that interests him/her"); and beliefs regarding discipline and control (for example, "The most important task of parenting is disciplining the child"). These were the three subscales that were most related to self-direction and conformity.

Participants

Greensboro, NC, USA. This town consists of approximately 200,000 inhabitants, located approximately 250 miles (400 km) south of Washington, DC. The city was founded early in the nineteenth century and by the end of the century was an important textile manufacturing center (Putnam, 1995). The city's economy is still based in manufacturing, primarily of textiles, furniture, and tobacco products, but much employment is also to be found in the banking and insurance industries as well as in the five colleges and universities within the city borders. Participants were recruited from birth records if they lived in one of two areas (each 2 to 3 sq km) judged to be relatively homogeneous in terms of housing and racial background. A total of 20 families with young children were recruited from these two communities (one of which was middle class, in which most parents have higher education and tend to work in professional occupations, and one of which was working class, in which parents typically do not have higher education and tend to work in the nonprofessional sphere). Acceptance rates from those initially contacted were quite

nonfiller items, the most-liked value was scored 5, liked values scored 4, not liked values scored 2, and least-liked values scored 1. Conformity items were reverse scored.

high (64% and 78% in the middle-class and working-class communities), and the two groups of families that participated consisted of 11 middle-class families and 9 working-class families with children aged from 30 to 48 months. The families were clearly differentiated by education (no working-class parent had a college degree, whereas virtually all middle-class parents had at least a degree) and by occupation criteria, using Hollingshead (1975) rankings.

Suwon, South Korea. This town of approximately 700,000 inhabitants is located approximately 70 kilometers from Seoul and is one of the satellite cities around the capital. It houses a branch of Seoul National University. As was the case with each of the non-U.S. cities, our intention was to locate families that were the closest equivalent to "middle-class" and "working-class" families in U.S. terms. This translated into choosing two groups of families that were distinguishable in terms of education and occupation in the same manner as in the U.S. groups. This proved to be relatively straightforward in Suwon, where two communities were located. In one of them lived families who were mostly well educated (most of whom had at least a college degree) and in which the fathers had professional occupations, whereas the other consisted primarily of working-class parents, none of whom had completed a college education.

Inspection of birth records was not possible in Suwon, so we contacted community representatives who had detailed information about people residing in the community. They helped us to locate potential participants, and screening calls were then made to gain information about parental education and occupation. Families had to meet the same educational and occupational criteria as was the case in Greensboro. Twelve families participated in Suwon, divided equally by community and gender. However, recruitment was far more difficult in Suwon than in the other cities. Of 36 families who were contacted in the middle-class community, 13 (36%) were willing to participate, but seven of the children were enrolled in preschools that did not permit observations. In the working-class community, 16 families were contacted, of whom 7 (44%) were willing to participate, but one child was enrolled in a preschool that did not permit observations.

Obninsk, Russia. This town is situated about 100 kilometers south of Moscow and has approximately 120,000 inhabitants. It is a new town, built in the 1950s, around a nuclear power plant, which is no longer in use. Because of the need for scientists and skilled technical workers, two institutions of higher education (*VUZ*) were established, as well as a number of polytechnical institutes of lesser standing. The town was built on what had been an old estate, owned by the Obninsk family, but few traces of its past remain. Perhaps because of its recent birth, and perhaps because of the demand for skilled workers, Obninsk appears more prosperous than equivalently sized cities in Russia. Compared to the large and stolid apartment complexes that are typical of many Russian cities, those in Obninsk are relatively stylish, using color and architectural features to enhance the buildings' appearance.

As with other cities in the former Soviet Union, it is not possible to find areas of the city that are differentiated by social class, type of occupation, and so on. Well-educated professional families are likely to live next door to less-educated workers. Although there are some small single-family dwellings around the outskirts, the vast majority of the city's population lives in apartment complexes. Half of the Russian families consisted of parents who had the equivalent of a U.S. college education or higher and whose primary occupation was judged to be professional (many parents held more than one job, as a way of supplementing their income). The other half had no more than the equivalent of high school in the United States and worked in the nonprofessional sphere. It was not possible to recruit families in the same manner in the Russian town because there was no possibility of identifying families from birth records. We therefore used our initial contacts to recruit via a "snowball" technique. In the middle-class group, all the fathers and all but two of the mothers had completed a higher education degree (typically a 5-year program involving completion of a thesis), whereas in the working-class group, no one had more than the equivalent of a high-school education or "incomplete secondary education" followed by courses in a technical college.

In other respects, these two groups of families were quite similar. For example, they lived in very similar apartment complexes in the same areas of town. In terms of total family income, the group of parents with higher education earned, on average, only slightly more than their counterparts without higher education. It is thus clear that although in terms of education and occupation the two groups in Russia differed from each other in a way very similar to those in the USA, in terms of income and housing the two groups of Russian families did not differ at all. This was in marked contrast to the two groups of U.S. and Korean families.

Tartu, Estonia. This city, of approximately 100,000 inhabitants, is located 180 kilometers south of Tallinn, the capital of Estonia. It is an old city (the first recorded reference stemming from 1030), founded on the banks of the Emajogi river. The University of Tartu was founded in 1632 and is the preeminent institution of higher education in Estonia. The city also has an agricultural university and a teacher education college, as well as local industries, primarily light industry including a brewery, sawmill, the production of furniture, plastics, footwear, and leather goods, as well as enterprises that produce concrete building materials and car parts.

The city may be thought of as being divided into three main areas: the heart of the city, close to the river, where the town hall and university are situated, and where older single-and joint-family dwellings (many of which are wooden) are to be found; the area north of the river, which consists almost entirely of large apartment complexes, predominantly either five or nine stories high, built in the Soviet era; and areas south of the center, which have many old single-family dwellings, as well as new houses that are currently being built. As is the case in Obninsk, and quite unlike the situation in Greensboro, there is no clear division between areas of the city in terms of the inhabitants' occupations; factory workers and doctors are likely to live next to one another and are as likely to be found in the rather unattractive apartment complexes as in the architecturally more interesting new houses.

As was the case in Greensboro, two areas of the city were selected, one of which consisted solely of apartment complexes and the other from an area of single-family houses, both new and old. Each area was smaller than its Greensboro equivalents, approximately 1 square kilometer, but with a similar or higher density of families. Each area was bounded by large roads or by the river. Families were located from birth records, as was the case in Greensboro. Workers at the local ministry supplied names and addresses and occasionally some basic demographic details (such as educational level) of families living in the relevant streets and with children of the approximate age. Of the 34 families who were contacted, 67% agreed to participate, from which 20 families were selected, equally divided by social class. As was the case in Obninsk, the families were clearly differentiated by educational level and by occupational status, but they were not differentiated by income.

Analytic Strategy

Our intention is not to argue that we have drawn samples from known populations, much less to say that these participants were randomly drawn. Our participants consist of families who were recruited from specific cultural groups from specific cities. Although it is possible that similar results might have been found if we had drawn from different groups or different cities, this is a question for further research. We thus do not wish to generalize our findings to people living in smaller villages or towns or larger cities, or from a different part of the respective countries, or from different ethnic or racial groups. As we are thus not interested in using our data to infer what might be true of other sets of families, inferential statistics are not required to test whether differences between these groups are significant; a difference is simply that, a difference. On the other hand, the selection process was designed to include as many as possible of the families with children of the appropriate age from within the communities we chose, and the acceptance rates were good enough to make us reasonably confident that these groups are not unrepresentative of similar types of families living in similar circumstances elsewhere. Therefore, we analyzed the data using a nonparametric statistic (Kruskal Wallis) and have reported significant differences ($p < .05$) where appropriate. Moreover, because we collected values and beliefs data on both parents (where possible) in each family, we have analyzed the data separately for mothers and fathers to ensure independence of the units of analysis.

Results

Values and Beliefs

Although we collected the data on the parents' values and beliefs about child rearing after having collected the observational data, we shall first discuss their values and beliefs. With regard to parental values for self-direction, we had predicted that parents in Greensboro would score higher (indicating a greater value placed on self-direction) than their counterparts in the other cities, and that the groups of parents with a college education and a professional occupation ("middle class") would score higher than their counterparts who did not have a college degree and who worked in the nonprofessional sphere ("working class"). The first hypothesis was not supported; mothers and fathers (on average) scored surprisingly similarly in each of the cities. This was true despite the fact that Greensboro is part of a society that places more emphasis on individualism, whereas the parents in each of the other cities were raised in societies that are supposedly more collectivist (Korea and the former Soviet Union). However, middle-class parents scored significantly higher than their working-

Table 3.1. *Parents' Positive Evaluation of Self-Direction in Their Children, by City and Social Class*

	Mothers			Fathers		
	M	*SD*	*N*	*M*	*SD*	*N*
Greensboro (USA) – all	20.3	2.5	19	20.0	2.7	19
Middle class	21.5	1.71	11	20.7	2.8	11
Working class	18.6	2.4	8	19.1	2.8	8
Obninsk (Russia) – all	20.1	3.2	20	20.8	2.8	15
Middle class	21.4	2.5	10	21.9	1.8	7
Working class	18.7	3.4	10	19.9	3.4	8
Tartu (Estonia) – all	20.8	2.7	20	21.2	1.8	19
Middle class	20.9	2.9	10	22.1	1.2	10
Working class	20.7	2.5	10	20.2	1.9	9
Suwon (Korea) – all	19.2	2.4	9	19.3	3.5	9
Middle class	21.3	1.5	4	21.5	3.1	4
Working class	17.6	1.5	5	17.6	3.0	5

class counterparts in the case of both mothers ($p < .005$) and fathers ($p < .001$). See Table 3.1.

The situation was not quite so clear with regard to parental beliefs. The three beliefs in which we were interested were those relating to spoiling the child by giving him or her attention (where we expected working-class parents to score higher), beliefs about the importance of discipline and control when bringing up children (again, where working-class parents were expected to score higher), and the belief that children should have freedom to explore things in and around the home (where we expected middle-class parents to score higher). As can be see in Table 3.2 (for mothers) and Table 3.3 (for fathers), in each case the results were mostly as expected. Working-class parents across the four cities were more likely than their middle-class counterparts to believe that children would be spoiled if they received a lot of attention (mothers: $p < .005$; fathers: $p < .001$) and to believe in the importance of control and discipline (mothers: $p < .05$; fathers: $p < .001$). By contrast, the middle-class mothers, across the cities, were more likely to endorse freedom in and

Table 3.2. *Mothers' Beliefs about Freedom around the Home, Control and Discipline, and Spoiling, by City and Social Class*

	Freedom		Control		Spoiling		
	M	SD	M	SD	M	SD	N
Greensboro (USA) – all	3.7	0.9	3.7	1.1	2.4	0.9	19[a]
Middle	3.8	1.0	3.4	1.3	1.8	0.7	11
Working	3.6	0.8	4.2	0.6	3.1	0.8	8
Obninsk (Russia) – all	3.6	0.7	3.4	1.0	2.9	0.8	20
Middle	3.9	0.7	3.1	1.1	2.9	0.7	10
Working	3.3	0.6	3.7	0.9	3.0	0.9	10
Tartu (Estonia) – all	3.4	0.6	3.0	0.8	3.1	0.9	20
Middle	3.6	0.6	2.7	0.7	2.7	0.7	10
Working	3.2	0.6	3.2	1.0	3.0	0.9	10
Suwon (Korea) – all	3.4	0.5	4.0	0.7	3.8	0.6	10
Middle	3.5	0.7	3.9	0.8	3.8	0.3	4
Working	3.4	0.6	4.2	0.8	3.9	0.7	6

[a] Only 7 U.S. working-class mothers responded to all the questions about freedom, and only 10 U.S. middle-class mothers responded to all the questions about control.

around their homes for their children ($p < .05$), although middle-class fathers only tended to score higher ($p < .08$).

At the city level, significant differences were found for the concern about spoiling in the case of both mothers ($p < .005$) and fathers ($p < .001$), with Suwon mothers and fathers being the most concerned and Greensboro parents the least concerned. The data were less clear-cut in the case of the other beliefs, although fathers were significantly differentiated in terms of allowing freedom ($p < .001$). Fathers in the two cities that were part of the former Soviet Union (Obninsk and Tartu) were less interested in freedom for their children than were fathers in Greensboro and Suwon. Mothers, however, did not differ significantly. By contrast, fathers were not different in terms of beliefs about control and discipline, whereas mothers differed significantly ($p < .02$), with those in Greensboro and Suwon more interested in control than their counterparts in Obninsk and Tartu.

Table 3.3. *Fathers' Beliefs about Freedom around the Home, Control and Discipline, and Spoiling, by City and Social Class*

	Freedom		Control		Spoiling		
	M	SD	M	SD	M	SD	N
Greensboro (USA) – all	3.7	0.4	3.4	1.0	2.7	0.7	19[a]
Middle	3.8	0.4	3.0	0.9	2.4	0.8	11
Working	3.5	0.4	4.0	0.7	3.1	0.2	8
Obninsk (Russia) – all	3.3	0.9	3.7	1.1	3.6	0.8	15
Middle	3.8	0.9	3.2	1.1	3.1	0.8	7
Working	2.9	0.6	4.2	1.0	3.9	0.6	8
Tartu (Estonia) – all	3.0	0.6	3.4	1.2	3.7	0.9	19
Middle	3.1	0.6	2.9	1.0	3.4	0.7	10
Working	2.9	0.5	4.1	1.1	4.1	1.0	9
Suwon (Korea) – all	3.8	0.5	4.0	0.8	4.3	0.5	11
Middle	3.8	0.6	3.6	1.1	4.1	0.3	5
Working	3.8	0.4	4.5	0.2	4.4	0.5	6

[a] Only seven U.S. working-class fathers responded to all the questions about freedom.

Because of the issue of independence of the units of analysis, we discussed mothers' and fathers' values and beliefs separately. However, a comparison of Tables 3.2 and 3.3 reveals that in all cases fathers were more concerned about spoiling their children than were mothers ($p <$ .005). The data are not so clear with regard to values for self-direction or beliefs about freedom and control, although mothers in Obninsk and Tartu were consistently more likely than fathers to believe that children should be free around the home, and correspondingly less likely to believe that control and discipline were important.

Children's Activities

Initially, we were interested simply in the amount of different types of activities in which these children were involved. We made approximately 180 observations of each child in the study. In any one observation period (lasting 30 seconds), the children could be involved in (and coded in) more than one activity. Excluding activities in the "other" category

Table 3.4. *Children's Involvement in All Activities, by City and Social Class*

	Play		Lessons		Work		Conver-sation		
	M	*SD*	*M*	*SD*	*M*	*SD*	*M*	*SD*	*N*
Greensboro (USA) – all	94.6	25.2	11.5	5.7	13.9	7.2	19.7	11.0	20
Middle	81.1	20.5	13.1	5.7	13.3	9.3	24.7	11.5	11
Working	111.0	20.8	9.6	3.5	14.7	3.5	13.6	6.5	9
Obninsk (Russia) – all	86.5	11.5	21.4	6.2	20.1	6.9	17.1	7.5	10
Middle	83.5	7.9	23.7	6.6	20.0	7.1	19.0	8.9	6
Working	91.0	15.9	18.0	3.9	20.2	7.8	14.2	4.3	4
Tartu (Estonia) – all	105.5	15.1	16.9	5.9	23.7	10.3	19.3	11.1	20
Middle	109.5	16.6	18.8	6.4	27.5	10.5	23.2	12.9	10
Working	101.5	13.1	15.1	5.0	20.0	9.1	15.4	7.8	10
Suwon (Korea) – all	126.7	13.8	8.1	4.2	14.9	6.3	10.2	6.8	12
Middle	122.5	10.2	10.5	4.8	12.7	5.1	15.2	5.8	6
Working	130.8	16.6	5.7	1.0	17.2	7.1	5.3	3.0	6

(which included eating, bathing, sleep, uncodable), children in Greensboro were involved on average in 153 activities, those in Obninsk were involved in an average of 145 activities, those in Tartu in 165, and those in Suwon in an average of 160.

It is shown in Table 3.4 that in each of the four cities play was the activity in which the children were most often involved (not surprisingly, given their ages), with lessons, work, and conversation much less common. The children in the four cities significantly differed in their observations of each type of activity ($ps < .005$ in the case of play, lessons, and work; $p < .05$ in the case of conversation). Children in Suwon were most involved in play, in an average of 122 of the 180 observations, and those in Obninsk the least, in an average of 86 observations. The four groups also differed in terms of each of the other types of activities. In terms of lessons, for example, children in Obninsk and Tartu were more involved (averages of 21 and 17 observations) than their counterparts in Greensboro and Suwon (averages of 11 and 8 observations, respectively). The children in Obninsk and Tartu were also more likely to be involved in work, on average 20 and 24 of their observations, than children from

Greensboro and Suwon (averages of 14 and 15, respectively). The four groups of children also differed in terms of conversation, with children in Suwon less likely to be involved in conversation than children from the other three countries (an average of 10 observations for children in Suwon, compared to averages of approximately 20, 17, and 19 in the case of children from Greensboro, Obninsk, and Tartu).

However, it was also clear that there were within-city differences as a function of social class in terms of all activities with the exception of the amount of work in which the children were involved. For example, in terms of lessons ($p < .05$) and conversation ($p < .002$), children from middle-class families (that is, those in which the parents had a college education and professional occupations) were significantly more likely to be involved than those from working-class families. By contrast, working-class children tended to be ($p < .07$) more likely than their middle-class counterparts to be involved in play.

As mentioned previously, our main interest was to focus on subclasses of activities that we expected to relate to later academic competence. These were academic lessons, skill/nature lessons, play with academic objects, and conversation with one or more adults. Academic lessons were defined as those in which there was a deliberate attempt to impart information (or receive information; for example, by asking a question) about something of relevance to school or preschool. Asking a question about how many sides a square has, or information about a word when looking at a book, are examples of this type of lesson. Our goal was not to distinguish between occasions when children were learning or not learning, because our assumption was that children may learn no matter what activity they are engaged in. Looking at a book or playing with blocks or drawing or helping a parent cook are all opportunities in which learning may occur, but lessons were explicit (often didactic) attempts to teach the child something or explicit attempts to get information from someone viewed as more competent (usually, but not exclusively, an adult). Across the cities, there was a tendency ($p < .10$) for the children to be differentiated in terms of involvement in academic lessons. As is seen in Table 3.5, children in Obninsk and Suwon were somewhat more likely than those in Greensboro and Suwon to engage in these types of lessons. In terms of social class differences, middle-class children were, in each city except Obninsk, more likely than their working-class counterparts to engage in these types of lessons, and the overall effect of social class was close to significant ($p < .06$).

A similar pattern was found in terms of skill and nature lessons. These

Table 3.5. *Children's Involvement in Activities Most Related to Academic Competence, by City and Social Class*

	Academic Lessons		Skill/ nature Lessons		Academic Play		Conversation with Adults		
	M	SD	M	SD	M	SD	M	SD	N
Greensboro (USA) – all	2.6	3.6	3.8	2.6	8.1	6.8	18.3	10.0	20
Middle	3.7	4.4	4.6	3.1	9.5	7.4	23.0	10.7	11
Working	1.2	1.6	2.8	1.5	6.6	6.2	12.7	5.2	9
Obninsk (Russia) – all	4.1	2.2	11.8	5.0	9.0	4.7	14.2	5.9	10
Middle	4.0	2.2	14.2	4.4	7.8	3.7	14.8	7.0	6
Working	4.2	2.1	8.2	3.9	10.7	6.0	13.5	4.7	4
Tartu (Estonia) – all	2.6	3.1	9.2	4.6	5.4	4.8	16.8	11.1	20
Middle	3.3	3.9	11.1	4.3	7.3	5.7	19.9	13.4	10
Working	1.9	2.2	7.3	4.2	3.5	2.7	13.7	7.8	10
Suwon (Korea) – all	3.4	2.7	2.0	2.1	17.3	11.0	8.4	6.1	12
Middle	4.7	3.0	2.2	2.8	25.5	8.5	12.3	6.0	6
Working	2.2	1.7	1.8	1.5	9.2	5.4	4.5	2.9	6

lessons were defined as ones in which there were deliberate attempts to impart or receive information about the workings of the natural world (such as why the sun rises, or why it gets cold in winter) or about how to do things, such as tying shoelaces, mending a broken toy, and so on. Lessons about health and safety also were included in this category. Children in Obninsk and Tartu were far more likely to engage in these types of lessons than their counterparts in Greensboro and Suwon, with differences at the city level being significant ($p < .001$). In each of these cities, however, social class differences were such that middle-class children engaged in more skill/nature lessons than those from working-class backgrounds ($p < .05$).

Play with academic objects was defined as play with any object that was relevant to preschool or school but when there was no specific attempt to receive or impart information. Thus, for example, if a child was looking at a book, or being read to, or playing with magnetic numbers on the refrigerator, he or she was playing with an academic object but not engaging in an academic lesson. At the city level, differences in level of play were significant ($p < .005$); children in Suwon were almost twice as likely to play with academic objects as children in the other three cities, and more than three times as much as those in Tartu. However, it is apparent (see Table 3.5) that there were large differences between middle-class and working-class Suwon children, with the former playing with academic objects far more than any other group. In all groups except Obninsk, the same was true, though to a lesser extent: Middle-class children were more likely than their working-class counterparts to play with academic objects. These social class differences were also significant ($p < .05$).

The final activity of interest was conversation involving an adult. A conversation was defined in such a way that it was distinguished from talking that was simply an accompaniment to play, or work, or the talk that necessarily went along with lessons. Talking was defined as a conversation if it involved turn taking between interlocutors, with the topic of conversation being something separate from any other activity that was occurring. Thus, if two children were playing, but talking about something that they had seen on television the night before, that would count as a conversation. Similarly, talk between child and mother featuring what had happened at school earlier in the day or about where they would go on vacation would count as conversation.

Looking first at the city level, these groups of children significantly differed in the extent to which they were involved in conversation with adults ($p < .02$), with children in Greensboro most likely and children in Suwon the least likely. However, as has been consistently the case, there were significant differences between the social classes ($p < .005$), with middle-class children more likely to be involved in conversation with adults than their working-class counterparts. As can be seen from Table 3.5, these class differences were particularly noticeable in Greensboro and Suwon, less so in Obninsk and Tartu.

This pattern of results by and large is nicely supportive of Kohn's general thesis. At the level of parental values and beliefs about child rearing, the citywide differences are not great, and the most interesting findings are those regarding social class differences. Across these cities, from very different types of societies, middle-class parents were more likely than working-class parents to value self-direction in their children and to espouse beliefs about child rearing that were supportive of those values. Moreover, and here we have been able to extend Kohn's work in much the same way as Luster and his colleagues did with their sample of mothers from the northeast USA, the activities of their children seem for the most part consistent with the parental values and beliefs. Specifically, middle-class children in each of the cities were more likely than their working-class counterparts to engage in activities that were likely to help them become more independent and self-reliant once they entered school.

It is possible to make the connection between values, beliefs, and activities more tight, however. If middle-class parents are more likely to value self-direction, it should be possible to find direct evidence of self-directing behavior on the part of the children themselves. For this reason, we were also interested in knowing just how activities were started. We coded whether they began because someone *other* than the child began them or whether the child, either alone or in conjunction with someone else, began them. The latter would be a direct indication of self-direction on the part of the child. We therefore examined each of the activities of interest in terms of whether the child was involved in starting them.

As predicted, middle-class children across the four cities were significantly more likely than their working-class peers to initiate academic lessons, play with academic objects, and conversation with adults ($ps <$ .05), although they were not significantly more likely to initiate skill/nature lessons. (Full details are provided in Table 3.6.) It was also the case that there were differences at the city level in the case of the initiation of skill/nature lessons ($p < .001$), play with academic objects ($p < .02$), and conversation ($p < .05$); these were not significant in terms of initiation of academic lessons.

Discussion and Conclusion

We had three goals in mind when designing this program of research. The primary goal was to try to understand the ways in which children become competent members of the culture into which they are born. The research was set within an ecological systemic framework derived from Bronfenbrenner and Vygotsky; for this reason, it was important to examine macrosystemic variation – examining groups that were likely to differ in terms of values, beliefs, and practices. We were dissatisfied by comparisons of societies at different levels of technology, typical of much cross-cultural research, and we were interested in examining societies that were industrialized. This allowed us to focus on cultural groups without the confounding influence of such factors as schooling and urbanicity. Part of this goal was thus to discover whether parents, from societies that

Table 3.6. *Children's Initiation of Activities Most Related to Academic Competence, by City and Social Class*

	Academic Lessons		Skill/ Nature Lessons		Academic Play		Conversation with Adults		
	M	SD	M	SD	M	SD	M	SD	N
Greensboro (USA) – all	0.9	1.6	0.9	1.4	5.1	4.1	8.7	6.6	20
Middle	1.4	2.0	1.4	1.7	5.9	3.7	11.5	7.7	11
Working	0.3	0.7	0.3	1.5	4.1	4.6	5.3	2.4	9
Obninsk (Russia) – all	1.0	1.6	2.6	1.9	3.8	2.5	6.5	3.2	10
Middle	1.0	1.5	3.2	1.9	3.7	2.5	6.5	3.5	6
Working	1.0	2.0	1.7	1.7	4.0	2.9	6.5	3.1	4
Tartu (Estonia) – all	1.2	1.6	2.5	2.7	3.2	3.1	7.0	5.6	20
Middle	1.7	1.9	3.3	3.3	4.5	3.6	8.3	6.5	10
Working	0.8	1.1	1.8	1.7	1.9	1.7	5.8	4.5	10
Suwon (Korea) – all	0.5	1.0	0.0	0.0	11.6	9.5	3.6	2.7	12
Middle	1.0	1.3	0.0	0.0	16.5	10.6	5.0	2.7	6
Working	0.0	0.0	0.0	0.0	6.7	5.1	2.2	1.9	6

were industrialized but which differed in terms of ideology and in societywide views regarding independence and interdependence, would differ in terms of their values and beliefs.

It was thus surprising to us that we found no differences in parents' (either mothers' or fathers') valuation of self-direction in their children in any of the cities – we had expected that the parents from Greensboro would have evaluated this higher than parents from the other cities, given prevailing beliefs that parents in the United States are interested in fostering children's independence. By the same token, we had expected that Greensboro parents would have believed to a greater extent than other parents that it was important to provide their children freedom in and around the home, to be less interested in control and discipline, and to be less worried about spoiling their children by paying them a lot of attention – all things that might be more expected in groups that emphasize interdependence rather than independence. As was true of values for self-direction, the pattern of results was not as expected; it was not the case that the Greensboro parents were clearly distinguishable from parents in the other cities.

One possible explanation, at least with regard to Russia and Estonia, relates to the changes that have occurred over the past decade, with the breakup of the Soviet Union. As Russian and Estonian parents have observed such changes, away from collectivism and toward an economy based on individualism and competition, they may have revised their views about the characteristics needed to succeed. Where once the ability to compromise and conform may have been the characteristics most conducive to a successful work life, now initiative and independence in thought and action may be perceived to be more important. On the other hand, it is also possible that clear differences in ideology between the two societies were only minimally reflected in families' values, beliefs, and practices even prior to the collapse of the Soviet Union. Without equivalent data from the 1980s, we cannot be sure.

However, according to Bronfenbrenner, macrosystem and society are not synonymous, and there are within-society groups that qualify as macrosystems. Bronfenbrenner's theory thus forces researchers to at least consider the within-society heterogeneity that is the feature of all societies. In our case, we decided to focus on social class, instantiated as differences as a function of education and occupation. Our data made clear that even if the cross-city differences in values and beliefs did not fall into a consistent pattern, the same cannot be said of social class. In terms of both values and beliefs, the results were precisely as predicted. Middle-class parents in each city were more likely than their working-class counterparts to evaluate positively self-direction in their children and were more likely to believe in the importance of allowing their children freedom in and around the home. By contrast, working-class parents were consistently more likely than those from the middle class to believe in the importance of controlling and disciplining their children and more likely to believe that one could spoil one's children by being overly attentive. In terms of Bronfenbrenner's theoretical perspective, social class is truly a cultural factor by virtue of these differences in values and beliefs. There is something about social class, or rather the conditions of life associated with class, that makes a difference in parents' values and beliefs. These results clearly support Kohn's work linking social class and values, as well as that of Luster and his colleagues connecting class, values, and specific child-rearing beliefs.

From the perspectives of both Vygotsky and Bronfenbrenner, it is crucial to focus not simply on the broadest aspect of culture as a means of "explaining" development. Instead, it is necessary to examine what Bronfenbrenner termed the "proximal processes" of development – children's everyday activities within their microsystems. The final goal of the research was therefore to evaluate the extent to which there is a relationship between parents' socioeconomic status and their children's activities. Although some revealing differences were found in activities considered at the most general of levels (specifically, that middle-class children in each city were more likely than their working-class counterparts to engage in lessons and conversation), more interesting were the patterns found when we focused on those activities most linked to future competence. With two exceptions, middle-class children were more likely than those from a working-class background to be involved in academic lessons, skill/nature lessons, play with academic objects, and conversation with adults. The exceptions were from Obninsk, where children were not distinguished in terms of academic lessons and where working-class children played appreciably more than their middle-class counterparts with academic objects. The working-class children in Obninsk, in addition, were only slightly less likely than those from the middle class to engage in conversation with adults (the magnitude of the difference was less than in any other city). Some of the data from Obninsk and Tartu may perhaps be explained by the fact that, in the face of greater uncertainty that the State will look after its citizens, parents are more interested in providing their children with the skills they view as essential. On the other hand, parents in both Obninsk and Tartu have long needed to use certain types of skills (for example, sewing, gardening, building, and repairing) in their everyday lives, given limited availability and/or high prices of valued goods and the desire to supplement diets by growing their own vegetables. These are activities in which their children were likely to be involved, and skills that parents would expect their children to learn. In Obninsk, moreover, any connection between occupation and values is likely to be weakened by the fact that many of the parents (but particularly those with higher education), like those in Russian society as a whole, have to work at two occupations in order to make sufficient income and are much less likely than in the past to find occupations that fit their particular specialities (Kashenov, 1995; Khabibovskaya, 1995).

We were also able to look more directly at self-direction in the children, by examining the extent to which the children themselves were involved in initiating these activities. Again, the results were revealing – in virtually every case, middle-class children were more likely than those from working-class families to initiate activities. Of course, if middle-class parents believe that these activities are more important for their children to engage in, they may provide more of them than do working-class parents. But at least some of these activities were started by the children themselves, an indication that they had already internalized their parents' value for self-direction. It also indicates the extent to which children are co-constructing their own environments, rather than simply being the objects of a simple unidirectional transmission of values and practices, as would be expected from the perspectives of both Vygotsky and Bronfenbrenner.

The link between macrosystemic factors (such as social class) and what occurs in the microsystem may be explained by reference to the exosystem, a setting in which children are not directly involved but which nevertheless exerts a powerful indirect effect. For Kohn, parents' workplace experiences are key to understanding why parents' position in the system of social stratification is the key factor in determining the types of values that parents have – more important, he has argued, than education or income. Our data, however, are not able to show that. Our index of social class included both education (parents either with or without higher education) and type of job (professional or nonprofessional). However, in cases in which the mother did not work outside the home, we used the father's job as the occupational index. Most of the Obninsk and Tartu mothers had full-time occupations (reflecting the typical situation in both Russia and Estonia), but in Greensboro and Suwon, at least in the middle-class homes, many mothers did not work outside the home. It is therefore interesting to note that the difference between Greensboro middle-class and working-class mothers in terms of values for self-direction was actually greater than the corresponding difference for fathers. Similarly, in terms of beliefs, Suwon and Greensboro mothers were not differentiated by class any less than were fathers. This finding casts some doubt on Kohn's general thesis that the workplace experiences of extent of routinization, complexity of work, and extent of supervision are the key variables relating to parental values and beliefs about child rearing. Education may be at least as significant a factor, as others have argued in a variety of different contexts (LeVine et al., 1996; Palacios & Moreno, 1996; Wright & Wright, 1976).

Kohn has changed his mind over the years regarding the role played by education in the development of values. Early in his career (Kohn, 1977), he had argued that education played a central role, and drew on the work of Bowles and Gintis (1976) to suggest that value for self-direction might be fostered by length of time in school, given that the longer children stay in school, the greater are their chances to exercise (and be valued for) self-direction. Subsequently, Kohn appeared to believe that education's effect on values was primarily indirect, arguing that "a large part of the reason why education affects psychological functioning is because education is determinative of job conditions, which in turn have a strong effect on psychological functioning" (Kohn & Slomczynski, 1990, p. 98). In his latest work, however, Kohn has not attempted to determine whether education or job conditions are related, arguing instead that it "is not that education and job conditions are competing for importance; they are part of the same process" (Kohn, 1995, p. 149). Both educational and occupational self-direction are important in the development of values.

The potentially important role of educational self-direction is not relevant only to the United States; the school systems in many countries, including the four that are the focus of this chapter, are highly didactic, with little or no opportunity for students to exercise independence of thought prior to entering higher education, and then only in carefully circumscribed domains (Kerr, 1990; Long, 1990; Tudge, 1991). The situation is often different at university level, where students are more likely to be encouraged to exercise independent thought. Moreover, it is not the case in any industrialized society that there is any clear one-to-one relationship between occupation related to a particular social class position and the opportunity to exercise self-direction, and some positions require more education on the job itself. In other words, the relations between education and occupation are complex and cannot be separated in this study.

What is clear, however, is that we need to pay more attention to the heterogeneity involved in all societies, particularly those that are industrialized or currently industrializing, or developing in other ways, such as the social/political changes currently taking place in the former Soviet Union. In this study, we focused on variations as a function of education and/or occupation, two of the critical attributes of social class. In each of the countries in which we collected data, we studied families from only one city (so holding regional differences and urban–rural differences constant), in which the participants did not differ by race or ethnicity. Nonetheless, the within-city differences, solely a function of social class, were at least as large as the cross-city (cross-societal) differences. When contrasting groups at different levels of industrialization, is it not altogether surprising to find differences in patterns of child rearing or beliefs about child rearing. Interest in cross-cultural differences must not blind us, however, to the heterogeneous nature of all cultures.

References

Bloch, M. N. (1989). Young boys and girls play at home and in the community: A cultural-ecological framework. In M. N. Bloch & A. D. Pellegrini (Eds.), *The ecological context of children's play* (pp. 120–54). Norwood, NJ: Ablex.

Bowles, S., & Gintis, H. (1976). *Schooling in capitalist America*. New York: Basic Books.

Bornstein, M. H., Tal, J., & Tamis-LeMonda, C. S. (1991). Parenting in cross-cultural perspective: The United States, France, and Japan. In M. H. Bornstein (Ed.), *Cultural approaches to parenting* (pp. 69–90). Hillsdale, NJ: Erlbaum.

Bronfenbrenner, U. (1970). *Two worlds of childhood: USA and USSR*. New York: Russell Sage.

Bronfenbrenner, U. (1988). Interacting systems in human development. Research paradigms: Present and future. In N. Bolger, A. Caspi, G. Downey, & M. Moorehouse (Eds.), *Persons in context: Developmental processes* (pp. 25–49). Cambridge: Cambridge University Press.

Bronfenbrenner, U. (1989). Ecological systems theory. In R. Vasta (Ed.), *Annals of child development* (Vol. 6, pp. 187–249). Greenwich, CT: JAI Press.

Bronfenbrenner, U. (1993). The ecology of cognitive development: Research models and fugitive findings. In R. Wozniak & K. Fischer (Eds.), *Development in context: Acting and thinking in specific environments* (pp. 3–44). Hillsdale, NJ: Erlbaum.

Bronfenbrenner, U. (1995). Developmental ecology through space and time: A future perspective. In P. Moen, G. H. Elder, Jr., & K. Lüscher (Eds.), *Examining lives in context: Perspectives on the ecology of human development* (pp. 619–47). Washington, D.C.: American Psychological Association.

Bronfenbrenner, U., & Crouter, A. C. (1983). The evolution of environmental models in developmental research. In P. H. Mussen (Ed.), *Handbook of child psychology: Vol. 1. History, theory, methods* (pp. 357–414). New York: Wiley.

Choi, S., Kim, U., & Choi, S. (1993). Indigenous analysis of collective representations: A Korean perspective. In U. Kim & J. W. Berry (Eds.), *Indigenous psychologies: Research and experience in cultural context* (pp. 193–210). Newbury Park, CA: Sage.

Dixon, S. D., LeVine, R. A., Richman, A., & Brazelton, T. B. (1984). Mother–child interaction around a teaching task: An African–American comparison. *Child Development, 55*, 1252–64.

Field, T., & Widmayer, S. M. (1981). Mother–infant interactions among lower SES black, Cuban, Puerto-Rican and South American immigrants. In T. Field, A. Sostek, P. Vietze, & P. H. Leiderman (Eds.), *Culture and early interactions* (pp. 41–62). Hillsdale, NJ: Erlbaum.

Goodnow, J., & Collins, W. A. (1990). *Development according to parents: The nature, sources, and consequences of parents' ideas.* Hillsdale, NJ: Erlbaum.

Harkness, S., & Super, C. (1977). Why African children are so hard to test. In L. L. Adler (Ed.), *Issues in cross-cultural research. Annals of the New York Academy of Sciences, 285*, 326–31.

Harkness, S., & Super, C. M. (1996). Introduction. In S. Harkness & C. M. Super (Eds.), *Parents' cultural belief systems: Their origins, expressions, and consequences* (pp. 1–23). New York: Guilford.

Hoff-Ginsburg, E., & Tardif, T. (1995). Socioeconomic status and parenting. In M. H. Bornstein (Ed.), *Handbook of parenting: Vol. 2. Biology and ecology of parenting* (pp. 161–88). Mahwah, NJ: Erlbaum.

Hogan, D. M., & Tudge, J. R. H. (1994). *Parents' Opinion Survey.* Unpublished scale, University of North Carolina at Greensboro.

Hogan, D. M., & Tudge, J. R. H. (in press). Implications of Vygotskian theory for peer learning. In A. M. O'Donnell & A. King (Eds.), *Cognitive perspectives on peer learning.* Mahwah, NJ: Erlbaum.

Holden, G. W. (1995). Parental attitudes toward childrearing. In M. H. Bornstein (Ed.), *Handbook of parenting: Vol. 3. Status and social conditions of parenting* (pp. 359–92). Mahwah, NJ: Erlbaum.

Hollingshead, A. B. (1975). *Four Factor Index of Social Status.* Unpublished manuscript, Yale University.

Kashenov, A. (1995). The problem of prevention of mass unemployment. *Questions of Economics, (5),* 53–57. [In Russian].

Kerr, S. T. (1990). Will glasnost lead to perestroika? Directions of educational reform in the USSR. *Educational Researcher,* October, 26–31.

Khabibovskaya, E. (1995). Secondary employment as a way of adapting to economic reforms. *Questions of Economics (5).* [In Russian].

Kim, U., & Choi, S.-H. (1994). Individualism, collectivism, and child development: A Korean perspective. In P. M. Greenfield & R. R. Cocking (Eds.), *Cross-cultural roots of minority child development* (pp. 227–57). Hillsdale, NJ: Erlbaum.

Kirveennummi, A., Räsänen, M., & Virtanen, T. J. (Eds.). (1994). *Everyday life and ethnicity: Urban families in Loviisa and Võru 1988–1991.* Helsinki: Suomalaisen Kirjallisuuden Seura.

Kohn, M. L. (1977). *Class and conformity: A study in values* (2nd ed.). Chicago: University of Chicago Press.

Kohn, M. L. (1979). The effects of social class on parental values and practices. In D. Reiss & H. Hoffman (Eds.), *The American family: Dying or developing?* (pp. 45–68). New York: Plenum.

Kohn, M. L. (1995). Social structure and personality through time and space. In P. Moen, G. H. Elder, Jr., & K. Luscher (Eds.), *Examining lives in context: Perspectives on the ecology of human development* (pp. 141–68). Washington, DC: American Psychological Association.

Kohn, M. L., & Schooler, C. (1983). *Work and personality.* Norwood, NJ: Ablex.

Kohn, M. L., & Slomczynski, K. M. (1990). *Social structure and self-direction: A comparative analysis of the United States and Poland.* Oxford: Basil Blackwell.

Lee, S. (1992). *Culture and preschoolers' activities: The United States and Korea.* Unpublished doctoral dissertation, University of North Carolina at Greensboro.

LeVine, R. A., Miller, P. M., Richman, A. L., & LeVine, S. (1996). Education and mother–infant interaction: A Mexican case study. In S. Harkness & C. M. Super (Eds.), *Parents' cultural belief systems: Their origins, expressions, and consequences* (pp. 254–69). New York: Guilford.

Long, D. H. (1990). Continuity and change in Soviet education under Gorbachev. *American Educational Research Journal, 27*(3), 403–23.

Luster, T. (1985). *Influences on maternal behavior: Child-rearing beliefs, social support, and infant temperament.* Unpublished doctoral dissertation, Cornell University, Ithaca, NY.

Luster, T., Rhoades, K., & Haas, B. (1989). The relation between parental values and parenting behavior: A test of the Kohn hypothesis. *Journal of Marriage and the Family, 51,* 139–47.

McGillicuddy-DeLisi, A. V., & Subramanian, S. (1996). How do children develop knowledge: Beliefs of Tanzanian and American mothers. In S. Harkness & C. M. Super (Eds.), *Parents' cultural belief systems: Their origins, expressions, and consequences* (pp. 143–68). New York: Guilford.

Morelli, G. A., Rogoff, B., & Angelillo, C. (1992). *Cultural variation in young children's opportunities for involvement in adult activities.* Paper presented at the American Anthropology Association meetings, San Francisco.

Morelli, G. A., Rogoff, B., Oppenheim, D., & Goldsmith, D. (1992). Cultural variation in infants' sleeping arrangements: Questions of independence. *Developmental Psychology, 28,* 604–13.

New, R. S., & Richman, A. L. (1996). Maternal beliefs and infant care practices in Italy and the United States. In S. Harkness & C. M. Super (Eds.), *Parents' cultural belief systems: Their origins, expressions, and consequences* (pp. 385–404). New York: Guilford.

Ninio, A. Z. (1979). The naive theory of the infant and other maternal attitudes in two subgroups in Israel. *Child Development, 50,* 976–80.

Ninio, A. Z. (1988). The effects of cultural background, sex and parenthood on beliefs about the timetable of cognitive development in infancy. *Merrill-Palmer Quarterly, 34,* 369–88.

Ochs, E., & Schieffelin, B. B. (1984). Language acquisition and socialization: Three developmental stories and their implications. In R. A. Shweder & R. A. LeVine (Eds.), *Culture theory: Essays on mind, self, and emotion* (pp. 276–320). New York: Cambridge University Press.

Odero, D., Hogan, D. M., & Tudge, J. R. H. (1996, April). *Preschoolers' everyday activities and their long-term implications for perceptions of competence: A longitudinal study of the transition from home to school.* Paper presented at the annual meeting of the American Educational Research Association, New York City.

Okagaki, L., & Sternberg, R. J. (1993). Parental beliefs and children's school performance. *Child Development, 64,* 36–56.

Palacios, J., & Moreno, M. C. (1996). Parents' and adolescents' ideas on children: Origins and transmission of intracultural diversity. In S. Harkness & C. M. Super (Eds.), *Parents' cultural belief systems: Their origins, expressions, and consequences* (pp. 215–53). New York: Guilford.

Pomerleau, A., Malcuit, G., & Sabatier, C. (1991). Child-rearing practices and parental beliefs in three cultural groups of Montreal: Quebecois, Vietnamese, Haitian. In M. H. Bornstein (Ed.), *Cultural approaches to parenting* (pp. 45–68). Hillsdale, NJ: Erlbaum.

Putnam, S. E. (1995). *Everyday lessons of North American preschoolers: Social class as cultural community.* Unpublished doctoral dissertation, University of North Carolina at Greensboro.

Richards, M. P. M. (1977). An ecological study of infant development in an urban setting in Britain. In P. H. Leiderman, S. R. Tulkin, & A. Rosenfeld (Eds.), *Culture and infancy: Variations in the human experience* (pp. 469–93). New York: Academic Press.

Rogoff, B. (1981). Schooling and the development of cognitive skills. In H. C. Triandis & A. Heron (Eds.), *Handbook of cross-cultural psychology* (Vol. 4, pp. 233–94). Rockleigh, NJ: Allyn and Bacon.

Rogoff, B., Mistry, J., Göncü, A., & Mosier, C. (1991). Cultural variation in the role relations of toddlers and their families. In M. H. Bornstein (Ed.), *Cultural approaches to parenting* (pp. 173–83). Hillsdale, NJ: Erlbaum.

Schwartz, S. H. (1994). Beyond individualism/collectivism: New cultural dimensions of values. In U. Kim, H. C. Triandis, C. Klagitcibasi, S.-C. Choi, & G. Yoon (Eds.), *Individualism and collectivism: Theory, methods, and applications* (pp. 85–119). Newbury Park, CA: Sage.

Sigel, I. E., McGillicuddy-DeLisi, A. V., & Goodnow, J. (Eds.). (1992). *Parental belief systems: The psychological consequences for children* (2nd ed.). Hillsdale, NJ: Erlbaum.

Stevenson, H. W. (1982). Influences of schooling on cognitive development. In D. A. Wagner & H. W. Stevenson (Eds.), *Cultural perspectives on child development* (pp. 208–24). San Francisco: Freeman.

Super, S., & Harkness, C. M. (1982). The infant's niche in rural Kenya and metropolitan America. In L. L. Adler (Ed.), *Cross-cultural research at issue* (pp. 47–56). New York: Academic Press.

Triandis, H. C. (1993). Collectivism and individualism as cultural syndromes. *Cross-Cultural Research, 27,* 155–80.

Triandis, H. C. (1995). *Individualism and collectivism.* Boulder, CO: Westview Press.

Tudge, J. R. H. (1991). Education of young children in the Soviet Union: Current practice in historical perspective. *The Elementary School Journal, 92* (1), 121–33.

Tudge, J. R. H. (1996). Studying peer collaborative problem-solving from a Vygotskian perspective. *Cognitive Studies: The Bulletin of the Japanese Cognitive Science Society, 3* (4), 14–16.

Tudge, J. R. H. (1997). Internalization, externalization, and joint-carving: Comments from an ecological perspective. In B. Cox & C. Lightfoot (Eds.), *Sociogenetic perspectives on internalization* (pp. 119–31). Mahwah, NJ: Erlbaum.

Tudge, J. R. H., Gray, J., & Hogan, D. A. (1997). Ecological perspectives in human development: A comparison of Gibson and Bronfenbrenner. In J. Tudge, M. Shanahan, & J. Valsiner (Eds.), *Comparisons in human development: Understanding time and context* (pp. 72–105). New York: Cambridge University Press.

Tudge, J. R., Odero, D. A., Hogan, D. M., & Etz, K. E. (1998). *Relations between the everyday activities of preschoolers and their teachers' perceptions of their competence in the first years of school.* Unpublished manuscript. University of North Carolina at Greensboro.

Tudge, J. R. H., & Putnam, S. A. (1997). The everyday experiences of North American preschoolers in two cultural communities: A cross-disciplinary and cross-level analysis. In J. Tudge, M. Shanahan, & J. Valsiner (Eds.), *Comparisons in human development: Understanding time and context* (pp. 252–81). Cambridge: Cambridge University Press.

Tudge, J. R. H., Putnam, S. A., & Sidden, J. (1993). Preschoolers' activities in socio-cultural context. *Quarterly Newsletter of the Laboratory of Comparative Human Cognition, 15,* 71–84.

Tudge, J. R. H., Putnam, S. A., & Sidden, J. (1994). The everyday activities of American preschoolers: Lessons and work in two socio-cultural contexts. In A. Alvarez & P. Del Rio (Eds.), *Perspectives in socio-cultural research: Vol. 4. Education as cultural construction* (pp. 110–21). Madrid: Fundacion Infancia i Aprendizaje.

Tudge, J. R. H., Putnam, S. A., & Valsiner, J. (1996). Culture and cognition in developmental perspective. In B. Cairns, G. H. Elder, Jr., & E. J. Costello (Eds.), *Developmental science* (pp. 190–222). New York: Cambridge University Press.

Tudge, J. R. H., Sidden, J., & Putnam, S. A. (1990). *The cultural ecology of young children: Coding manual.* Unpublished manuscript, University of North Carolina at Greensboro.

Tudge, J. R. H., & Winterhoff, P. A. (1993). Vygotsky, Piaget, and Bandura: Perspectives on the relations between the social world and cognitive development. *Human Development, 36,* 61–81.

Valsiner, J. (1989). *Human development and culture: The social nature of personality and its study.* Lexington, MA: Lexington Books.

Valsiner, J., & Litvinovic, G. (1996). Processes of generalization in parental reasoning. In S. Harkness & C. M. Super (Eds.), *Parents' cultural belief systems: Their origins, expressions, and consequences* (pp. 56–82). New York: Guilford.

Vygotsky, L. S. (1978). *Mind in society.* Cambridge, MA: Harvard University Press.

Vygotsky, L. S. (1987). *The collected works of L. S. Vygotsky: Vol. 1. Problems of general psychology.* New York: Plenum.

Vygotsky, L. S. (1994). The problem of the environment. In R. Van der Veer & J. Valsiner (Eds.), *The Vygotsky reader* (pp. 338–54). Oxford: Blackwell.

Wertsch, J. V., Minick, N., & Arns, F. (1984). The creation of context in joint problem solving: A cross-cultural study. In B. Rogoff & J. Lave (Eds.), *Everyday cognition: The social context of the development of everyday cognitive skills* (pp. 151–71). Cambridge, MA: Harvard University Press.

Whiting, B. B., & Edwards C. P. (1988). *Children of different worlds: The formation of social behavior.* Cambridge: Harvard University Press.

Whiting, B. B., & Whiting, J. W. M. (1975). *Children of six cultures: A psychocultural analysis.* Cambridge: Harvard University Press.

Wolf, A. W., Lozoff, B., Latz, S., & Paludetto, R. (1996). Parental theories in the management of young children's sleep in Japan, Italy, and the United States. In S. Harkness & C. M. Super (Eds.), *Parents' cultural belief systems: Their origins, expressions, and consequencies* (pp. 364–84). New York: Guilford.

Wright, J. D., & Wright, S. R. (1976). Social class and parental values for children: A partial replication and extension of the Kohn thesis. *American Sociological Review, 41,* 527–37.

PART THREE

Children's Engagement in Play

4 Activity Setting Analysis: A Model for Examining the Role of Culture in Development

Jo Ann M. Farver

Cultural diversity in early childhood has been documented with increasingly detailed evidence over the past decade, but the implications of these efforts for our understanding of child development remain unclear. This problem stems in part from a common methodological error of treating culture as an "unexamined independent variable" (Rogoff, Gauvain, & Ellis, 1984). Therefore, we often learn that culture is related to a particular psychological construct, but we learn little about the specific elements of culture that contribute to the proposed relationship (Betancourt & Lopez, 1993). Moreover, as Gauvain (1995) has pointed out, there is nothing psychologically meaningful about being a member of a particular culture. However, what is important is *how* growing up in a particular community contributes to an individual's development and leads to different psychological outcomes.

B. Whiting (1976) refers to culture and other status characteristics such as ethnicity, social class, age, and gender, as "packaged variables" that need to be "unwrapped" to be scientifically meaningful. She argues that the study of cultural effects on individuals requires a closer examination of contexts in which human activities take place, an understanding of the specific processes and experiences that may be associated with different types of behavior, and more detailed analyses of children's early learning environments.

In this chapter, I first discuss how activity setting analysis can be effective in "unpackaging" culture to identify how broad cultural factors are translated into specific contexts that influence children's daily activities and the development of relevant skills and behaviors. Second, I illustrate my view of this model by providing empirical examples from my research that examined cultural influences on children's early social interaction and play behavior in European-American, Indonesian, Mexican, and Korean-American communities.

99

The Activity Setting Model

The activity setting approach is conceptually grounded in three different yet historically connected schools of thought. It is derived from (1) Vygotsky's (1978) model of socially mediated cognition and Soviet activity theory (Leont'ev, 1981; Wertsch, 1985, 1991), (2) the Whitings' behavior setting concept (Whiting, 1980; Whiting & Edwards, 1988) and ecological cultural models (Super & Harkness, 1986), and is elaborated in (3) the work of Weisner, Gallimore, and Tharp (Tharp & Gallimore, 1988; Weisner, 1984; Weisner, Gallimore, & Jordan, 1988). Common to these theoretical perspectives is the emphasis on the importance of social and cultural experiences in shaping children's thinking and interpreting the world, and the shifting of analysis from a focus on the *individual child* to the *child-in-context*. The model presented here extrapolates from several viewpoints. However, it is most consistent with Weisner and Gallimore's interpretation of activity settings, and it represents an extension and application of their ideas.

Central to the activity setting approach is Vygotsky's (1978) notion that children's development unfolds from experience in socially structured activities through the internalization of the processes and practices provided by society and its members. Vygotsky proposed that all uniquely human and higher forms of mental activity are jointly constructed and transferred to children through interaction and shared activities with other people. This process, which occurs within the zone of proximal development, enables the child to use partially mastered skills with the assistance and supervision of more skilled and experienced members of the culture. In this sense, collaborative activities with people who are more expert in the use of a culture's material and conceptual tools, serve as "cultural amplifiers" (Rogoff & Gardner, 1984) that scaffold children's learning and thereby drive and shape development.

In his extension of Vygotsky's work, Wertsch (1985) emphasizes the notion of activity as the basic unit of human psychological functioning. Wertsch (1991) states that "human beings are viewed as coming in contact with, and creating their surroundings as well as themselves, through the actions in which they engage. Thus action, rather than human beings or the environment considered in isolation, provides the entry point into the analysis" (p. 8). (For an elaboration of activity theory, see Göncü et al., this volume). From this standpoint, human activity is grounded in an implicit set of assumptions about appropriate social roles, cultural goals and values, individual motives for action, and the behaviors of the participants in a particular setting. Accordingly, activities have objective as well as subjective features. They are *determined* by the physical context and are *created* in the setting by the participants themselves.

As Wertsch claims, activity settings can be thought of as abstract theoretical constructs. However, drawing from a second school of thought (Whiting, 1980; Whiting & Edwards, 1988), activity settings can also be conceptualized as a unit of analysis. Harkness and Super provide an ecological model in which activity settings are used to describe how aspects of physical and psychological environments may lead to different developmental outcomes for children.

Super and Harkness (1986) pose the concept of the developmental niche to express the idea that children's particular developmental contexts have not only evolved through time but also have been adapted to the constraints imposed by the subsistence base, the climate, and the political economy of a region (Weisner, 1984, p. 335–6). As a unit of analysis, the developmental niche broadly includes the physical and social setting in which the child lives, culturally regulated customs of childcare and child rearing, and the psychology of the caregivers. These three components function in an interrelated fashion to mediate children's development within a larger cultural context.

Super and Harkness propose that the characteristics of children's physical and social environments (i.e., the age and sex of the "company they keep") set the course for particular developmental outcomes. Parents and other caregivers adapt their daily routines or customs of childcare to the ecological and cultural settings in which they live. Predominant beliefs or "parental ethnotheories" (Harkness & Super, 1996) about what is desired and appropriate child behavior guide a caregiver's particular approach to child socialization. Therefore, the regularities within the settings, customs, and caregiver cultural belief systems organize children's developmental experiences and provide the information from which children construct the rules of their culture (Super & Harkness, 1986).

In a third school of thought, Weisner and Gallimore integrate Vygotsky's insights about the role of social interaction in psychological development, Soviet activity theory, the behavior setting concept, and Harkness and Super's ecological model in a way that allows researchers to quantify specific features of children's physical and social settings, which are instrumental in determining their early learning environments. Weisner and Gallimore's approach is grounded in ecocultural (*eco*logical-*cultural*) theory, which emphasizes that a family's major adaptive task is to construct and maintain a daily routine through which they can organize and structure their children's activities and development (Weisner, Matheson, & Bernheimer, 1995). The circumstances of everyday routines create opportunities for the culturally meaningful activities and sensitive interactions on which a child's development depends. Ecocultural theory also proposes that ecological/cultural effects are mediated through the activity settings of the daily routine. Activity settings provide opportunities for children to learn and develop through forms of mediated social learning embedded in goal-directed interactions (Weisner, 1989a). In this sense, culture "is instantiated in local activity settings that shape interaction and thought" (Weisner, 1989b, p. 14).

As conceptualized by Tharp and Gallimore (1988), activity settings are "contexts in which collaborative interaction, intersubjectivity, assisted performance, and learning occur" (p. 72). Activity settings are made up of everyday experiences rather than a deliberate curriculum, and they contain ordinary settings in which children's social interaction and behavior occur. They are the who, what, where, when, and why of daily life. The examples include:

> the father and daughter collaborating to find lost shoes, the preschooler recounting a folk tale with sensitive questioning by an adult, the child who plays a board game through the help of a patient brother, the Navajo girl who assists her mother weaving and who eventually becomes a master weaver herself. (p. 72)

In the ecocultural model, the activity setting is the basic unit of analysis. There are five specific components that are essential to know in understanding an activity and its consequences: the personnel, tasks, cultural scripts for conduct, motives, and goals (Weisner, 1989b). First, analysis of the *personnel present* and their availability in activities throughout a child's daily routine are determined by broad eco-cultural factors such as the economic and social organization of a community, individual families' daily routines, their economic livelihood, and household demography. Variations in family experiences may produce different combinations of people with different kinds of roles to play in placing a child's life on a particular developmental path. For example, young children who grow up in homes where both parents work spend much of their early years in the company of same-age peers in settings where they are cared for by unrelated adults. In contrast, children living in rural settings whose parents also both work may be cared for at home by older siblings and/or other family members.

Second, data are gathered on the *nature of the activities or tasks being performed* and the child's involvement in them. For example, what is going on in a setting might include caregiving, schooling, household chores, playing, or a combination of these.

Third, activity setting analysis involves determining the *purpose of the activities or tasks*. This includes understanding the meaning of the activity in the minds of the individuals and their reasons for doing it. For example, an activity or task may be physically similar across settings, but the motivation behind the activity and its underlying meaning may be different. Similarly, activities that may appear superficially different may have common underlying meanings for the actors. In either case, the motivations surrounding an activity directly influence how individuals behave, how they interact, and how they proceed to carry out the task.

Fourth, information is also obtained on the *scripts that guide children's participation* in these activities, everyday tasks, and routines; the patterns of their social interaction; and the cultural norms for self-expression. For example, in individualistic societies, children are conversational partners with adults, they are encouraged to join adult activities, and they learn through formal teaching by adults. On the other hand, children who are reared in collectivistic communities are often expected "to be seen and not heard," their activities are separate from those of adults, and they learn primarily by observing and imitating adult behavior.

Fifth, activity setting analysis involves collecting data on *salient cultural values, goals, and beliefs*. Adults organize children's environments based on their inherent developmental goals and the experiences they believe will help children become productive members of their community. Within activity settings, children have opportunities to learn and develop through modeling, apprenticeship, and other forms of socially mediated learning. However, the particular structuring and organization of children's mundane everyday activities will have a profound impact on the kinds of skills and behaviors they develop. Therefore, variations within activity settings may provide multiple paths that can lead to similar or different developmental outcomes.

In summary, activity setting analysis facilitates the comparison of a developmental phenomenon across similar contextual dimensions by combining the material aspects of the activity with participants' socially constructed meanings. Also, this model provides a means to consider simultaneously cultural features at several levels, and to examine how ecological factors determine children's development by influencing families' daily routines, the individuals with whom they interact, the activities in which they engage, and the scripts that guide their behavior. Finally, the model provides a way to overcome some methodological challenges common to cross-cultural research. Historically, the data on which current developmental theory rests were collected with European and American children who were raised in predominantly white middle-class families. Because the discipline itself and our methods for conducting research are products of Western European intellectual traditions, the obvious risk is that we have constructed a theory of development that is applicable to a small segment of the world's population. Activity setting analysis addresses ethnocentric biases by allowing researchers to examine development in *context* to consider if our current theories are culturally specific or are generalizable to children being raised in different environments. By examining diversity in human experience, we can isolate aspects of development that are similar across societies and can begin to understand the respective roles of nature and nurture in determining behavior.

Illustrative Studies

To illustrate the use of the activity setting model, I draw on examples from my research on young children's social interaction and play behavior. First, I discuss two studies that compare toddlers' play behavior with their mothers and older siblings in the United States, Mexico, and Indonesia. (See Farver, 1992a, b, 1993; Farver & Howes, 1993; Farver & Wimbarti, 1995, for further information on procedures, coding schemes, and data analysis.) Second, I present data from a series of studies that examined European- and Korean-American children's play in their preschool settings. (See Farver, Kim, & Lee, 1995; Farver & Lee, 1997, for further information.) Although these studies focused primarily on children's pretend play, I also refer to other activities available to children to identify the nature and significance of play in each cultural setting, and I discuss how children's work, school activities, and assigned household chores may compete with opportunities for play. Due to limitations of the data, certain activity setting features are discussed together.

Toddlers' Social Pretend Play with Their Mothers and Older Siblings

Pretend play is of research interest because its appearance and development during the toddler period marks the beginning of social interaction based on commonly understood symbols rather than on objects. Social pretend play is the outward manifestation or expression of young children's growing ability to think about that which is not immediately present and to begin to communicate these ideas to a partner (Howes, 1988). The complexity of children's social pretend play is also a developmental indicator of their emerging cognitive abilities, language skills, and social competence. Children who are skilled at pretense often have a flexible repertoire of social behaviors, socially relevant cognitive skills, and a willingness to cooperate, to share, and to compromise. These skills are acquired and developed through play interaction with peers and lay a foundation for positive social adjustment in later life.

Research with Western populations has shown that children's early pretend play develops in social contexts during interaction with more experienced partners (Dunn & Dale, 1984; Fiese, 1989; Garvey, 1990). Many investigations have focused on the mother as the more experienced and skilled play partner (Beizer & Howes, 1992; Haight & Miller, 1993; O'Connell & Bretherton, 1984). Such studies report that mothers "scaffold" or support young children's play efforts by arranging play situations, providing props and suggestions, and coordinating the interaction, which in turn allows children to perform beyond their existing level of competence.

Unfortunately, there is little research to support the generalizability of this pattern of mother–child play to other cultures. Children's play and social behavior can be expected to vary in settings where mothers are not available and willing play partners, where playing with children is culturally inappropriate adult behavior, and where play is not considered a valuable and productive activity. (See Gaskins, Göncü et al., and Haight, this volume, for further discussion.) Therefore, the purposes of the toddler studies were to investigate Western theoretical assumptions about children's play behavior in two non-Western societies, to examine the distinctive roles of mothers and older siblings as play partners, and to understand how different sociocultural contexts shape children's early social interaction and play behavior with different partners.

These studies were carried out in three communities in the United States, Mexico, and Indonesia (Farver, 1992a, b; Farver & Howes, 1993; Farver & Wimbarti, 1995). Participants were 90 children and their mothers and older siblings: 30 American, 30 Mexican, and 30 Indonesian; 10 from each community, at ages 18, 24, and 36 months. Half of each age group were girls.

The American sample included white working-class families residing in a city of about 40,000 residents in an economically depressed county in northern California. Participants lived in nuclear family households with two to five children ($M = 2.45$ children). In most families, the older siblings who participated in the study were first born (ages 4.5 to 7 years; $M = 5.5$ years), and the target children were second born. About half the families owned their homes. The remainder lived in rented houses, mobile homes, or apartments. Parents had at least a high-school education. Fathers worked in the building trades as truck drivers, retail store clerks, and similar occupations. Mothers were not employed outside the home.

The Mexican families were recruited from a small town of about 5,000 residents located on the Pacific Coast 1,700 miles south of the U.S. border. Participants resided in extended family households that included both parents, their two to six children ($M = 3.3$ children), grandparents, and/or paternal siblings and their children. The older siblings who participated in the study were first born or second born (ages 3.5 to 7.4 years; $M = 5.1$ years), and the target child was second or third born. Mexican families held title to their land and lived in modestly furnished concrete block homes. Most parents had the equivalent of a primary-school education (about seventh grade) and could read and write some Spanish. Fathers were employed in *syndicados* (unionized) construction-related jobs (tile setters, masons, concrete finishers) or as automobile mechanics, craftsmen, or truck drivers. Several mothers worked in the home by selling their garden produce, eggs, or soft drinks.

The Indonesian families came from a Javanese neighborhood in the city of Yogjakarta. Participants resided in a working-class *kampung*, which is a densely populated urbanized version of a rural village with concrete block houses set close together in rows along narrow walkways. Typical extended family households included both parents, their two to five children ($M = 3.2$ children), grandparents, paternal siblings, and domestic help (who are generally treated as "fictive kin"). Older siblings who participated in the study were first or second born (ages 4.5 to 6.3 years; $M = 5.2$), and the target child was second or third born. Families owned their household compounds communally for generations. Both parents had the equivalent of a high-school education. Fathers were employed as shop clerks, staff of public services, taxi drivers, and craftsmen. Mothers did not work outside the home.

Data were collected using qualitative and quantitative research methods. The qualitative data collection began first. A graduate student and I collected the American data, in Mexico I was helped by two Mexican field assistants, and the entire Indonesian study was carried out by a graduate student who was familiar with the community. During the qualitative data collection, we observed children and their families in and around their homes for approximately 6 to 8 hours. Observations were unstructured so that family behavior might be as self-motivated and spontaneous as possible. The purpose of the observations was to ensure ecological validity of the subsequent experimental procedure, and to provide contextual information to interpret and inform the quantitative results with ethnographic descriptions of family life, child-rearing practices, and the settings children typically inhabited.

We recorded and analyzed the qualitative data using the grounded theory method (Glaser & Strauss, 1967), an inductive approach that consists of collecting, categorizing, coding, and analyzing the data to allow theories to emerge. These emerging theories can then be systematically tested, provisionally verified, discarded, or reformulated simultaneously as data collection proceeds. This method allows researchers to uncover patterns in participant behavior as it occurs in context and is dynamic in the sense that they can revise their understanding of the data as they work with the community. Thus, understanding becomes part of the data collection itself.

In the quantitative procedure, mother – and sibling – child pairs in the three communities were videotaped in their homes on two separate occasions as they played with wooden toys suggestive of imaginative play for about 20 minutes. Mothers and siblings were asked to "play with your child/younger sister or brother in any way you want." The order of the play sessions was counterbalanced. After the videotaped play sessions, mothers were interviewed and were asked to rate the importance of play for children, to indicate who plays most with the child, and to state their beliefs about the purpose of play for children.

The videotapes were transcribed verbatim and were coded by episode for partners' type of mutual involvement and complexity of play (e.g., solitary, parallel, simple social, and reciprocal/complementary play, and social pretend play), maternal and sibling play behaviors (e.g., join play, comment, suggest pretend, teach, praise, and reject/ignore), and partners' predominant affect (e.g., neutral, positive, negative, and shared positive).

Mothers' responses to the open-ended interview questions revealed that most American and Indonesian mothers believed that play was very important, contributed to children's social and cognitive skills, and provided educational benefits for children. In contrast, Mexican mothers considered play to be relatively unimportant and believed that its primary purpose was to amuse children. American toddlers' common play partners were their mothers and older siblings, whereas the Mexican and Indonesian toddlers' partners were their older siblings and mixed-age peers.

The analyses of the quantitative data showed that children in all communities engaged in increasingly more complex social pretend play from 18 to 36 months. However, there were cultural differences in partners' involvement and participation in play. Among the American families, children's play was more frequent and complex with their mothers than with their older siblings, whereas in the Mexican and Indonesian settings, the reverse was true. For the most part, Mexican and Indonesian mothers were reluctant to play with their children, and among the American families, the older siblings were ambivalent about playing with the younger children. Indonesian and Mexican sibling–child play behaviors were similar to American mother–child play behaviors. For example, American mothers and Indonesian and Mexican older siblings joined their younger partners' play episodes, provided comments, praised their partners, and made suggestions for pretend play. In contrast, Mexican and Indonesian mothers engaged in more teaching and less play behaviors, and American older siblings ignored or rejected their play partners' suggestions and often behaved aggressively in play.

To explore how the environmental contexts in which children develop were associated with the differences we found in the mothers' and older siblings' play behavior, we used the activity setting model to situate play within daily life in the three communities. We began by isolating the specific features of American, Mexican, and Indonesian children's activity settings.

First, during our observations we noted differences in the *personnel available* in the three communities. The American children inhabited relatively quiet and solitary activity settings. In the single-family homes, mothers and siblings were often the only personnel present. Typically, mothers were involved with their household chores while children busied themselves alone or with their siblings in their rooms, outdoors within fenced back yards, or watching television. Thus, young children's social contact was limited primarily to their older siblings and to occasional encounters with similar-aged peers in neighborhood parks.

The Mexican children inhabited busy, very social activity settings. Televisions and radios played loudly in most homes; unmuffled diesel trucks and buses roared by on the coast highway; street peddlers sold roasted corn, ice cream, and sweets; and household pets, chickens, and pigs wandered over fences and through the streets. In the extended family households, children were in the company of related kin, neighborhood children of varying ages, and older siblings who served as their caregivers. Mothers were in close proximity to their children while engaged in their daily chores, but we observed little interaction between them.

Although the Indonesian neighborhoods were not as "noisy" as the Mexican settings, Indonesian toddlers had many opportunities for social interaction and play with a variety of mixed-age companions. Similar to the Mexican setting, the Indonesian children and families were often in the company of extended family members, neighbors, and household help. Mothers busied themselves with adult-centered activities (i.e., light household chores, visiting, or cooking), while children were relatively free to play outdoors in mixed-age play groups in the care of their older siblings. Unlike most urban American settings, where being outdoors alone can be dangerous, in the Indonesian community even young children are quite safe to wander the boundaries of their immediate neighborhood. The Javanese view community members as *paguyban* (family), and neighbors keep a vigilant eye on stray children as well as on each other.

Differences in *the nature and the purpose of the activities being performed* were also apparent across the three samples. In the American setting, mother–child social interaction typically took place during meals, caregiving, and child-centered play activities. When mothers finished their work, they spent time with their children playing with toys or educational games, running errands by car, and visiting nearby parks. Their play included elaborate baby-care routines with dolls, tackle football in the back yard, "driving" toy cars and trucks to fictitious destinations, reading stories, coloring, and building elaborate structures with manipulatives. Young children rarely engaged in work activity with their mothers.

In the Mexican setting, mother–child social interaction and play occurred in work contexts such as doing the laundry, washing dishes, cooking food, or caring for real babies instead of dolls. Often children were given simple tasks, and while "working" alongside their mothers, they followed her model and directions and playfully imitated her behavior. Mothers did not "socialize" with their children. Instead, after the daily chores were done, mothers sat with other women in the afternoons sewing, watching television *novelas* (soap operas), reading comic book romance and adventure stories, or talking, while their children played together outdoors.

In the Indonesian community, mother–child social interaction and play occurred most frequently during caregiving activities, such as feeding, dressing, or bathing. Although there were instances when Indonesian mothers played simple games and engaged in short bouts of pretend play, mothers generally went about their daily chores, and children amused themselves with quiet play alone, with their siblings, caretakers, or other children. Similar to the American households, Indonesian children were not involved in their mothers' work.

We also observed differences in the *cultural scripts that influence children's participation* in activities, everyday tasks, and routines, in the patterns of their social interaction, and in the cultural norms for self-expression. For the most part, in the American setting mothers and children were considered conversational equals and sometimes play partners. Although children were expected to be able to entertain themselves, we observed that mothers sometimes organized play sessions by providing props and ideas and then joined in the children's play. The American mothers' inclination to play with their children may be attributable to the notion that an important parent job is to help children learn and that "playing is learning." During observations, we noted that American mother–child interaction often involved some kind of teaching/learning activity. Sometimes the teaching was formal and involved reading a story book with a simple question–answer format, coloring pictures, or playing simple games. At other times, teaching was embedded in other activities, such as asking the child to name colors or farm animals while playing with toys, naming objects while driving in the car, or discussing the correct sequence of events in a pretend tea party. In these teaching/learning contexts, mothers provided verbal support and followed their children's lead in play.

There were different scripts for interaction in the Mexican community. We observed that parents expect obedience from their children and they maintain their authority by using distant and formal communication styles in which children are not considered adult conversational partners. In teaching and learning contexts, adults typically provided models of behavior for young children to observe and imitate rather than providing formal instruction. We rarely found mothers or any adults asking children to name colors or to identify or count objects as a "game" or in a formal play context – this was considered "the school's job." We also noticed that children joined adult activities rather than vice-versa. As children were able to follow directions and to take on more household responsibilities, they were gradually incorporated into the work routines of daily life.

In the Indonesian setting, young children were expected to be seen and not heard. When outdoors, children were free to play loudly. However, when indoors and in the company of adults, they were expected to be quiet and reserved. Mothers were often in the proximity of children, but their activities were relatively separate. Children were not conversational partners with adults, and they did not enter adult activities. Similar to the Mexican mothers, the Indonesian mothers did not spend time formally teaching their children skills; instead, they relied on older siblings to keep the younger children entertained with learning activities, games, and play. We often observed children hovering on the edges of adults' conversations, socializing, and work. Indonesian children learn to be quiet observers of adult behavior until they are ready to take part in their community.

Lastly, there were differences in *salient cultural goals, values, and beliefs* in the three communities. In the American setting, child rearing tended to mirror the wider society's "individualistic" (Triandis, 1989) orientation. American parents value family harmony. At the same time, they also emphasize the development of self-confidence and encourage their children to be assertive and to respect the rights of the individual (Hoffman, 1988; LeVine, 1980; Richman, Miller, & Solomon, 1988; Whiting & Edwards, 1988). While these values are compatible, balancing them can sometimes be difficult. For example, we observed in the American homes that parents encouraged their children to play together, but they were also highly tolerant of their children's frequent conflicts, apparent rivalry, and aggressive behavior. We noticed that siblings had difficulty sharing objects, territory, play ideas, and parental attention. Among several families, we noted that as long as the younger children were content to play with the broken pieces to a game, the doll that was missing an arm, or a toy car missing the wheels, and on *their side* of the room, relatively harmonious sibling play could occur.

Similar to communities in other parts of Mexico, the lives of the families studied here were interwoven in their wider community (Tapia-Uribe, LeVine, & LeVine, 1994). Although traditional Mexican mestizo values have changed, and villagers have adopted "urban" ideas such as smaller family size and more egalitarian family attitudes (Alba, 1982; Suárez, 1978), most rural Mexicans remain "collectivistic" (Triandis, 1989) in their orientation. Families stress community interdependence and the maintenance of cooperative and harmonious social relationships (Tapia-Uribe et al., 1994). Mexican children are encouraged to develop positive social relationships with community members whom they are likely to know and depend on for most of their lives (Uribe et al., 1994). Sibling rivalry and conflicts of any kind among children are rarely tolerated and are usually punished.

These cultural values and child-rearing goals were reflected in the

Mexican siblings' relationships and in their social interaction and play behavior. We observed that older siblings were tolerant of their younger siblings' behavior and highly responsive to their needs. Young children who were distressed or crying were immediately picked up and comforted. Older siblings were quite willing to share with the younger children any activities, toys, and snacks bought from passing street peddlers. We noted that although much of this "motherly" behavior took place in the context of sibling caretaking, it was not limited to girls or to the caregiving context. We observed that older brothers also included young children in their play activities and that they were as helpful and friendly with younger children as were the older sisters.

Javanese society can also be considered "collectivistic" (Triandis, 1989) in its orientation (Koentjaraningrat, 1985). Indonesian children are not trained for eventual independence from their family or community. Instead, the personal attributes that promote group harmony, deference to authority, emotional restraint, and cooperativeness are emphasized in the socialization of the typical Javanese child (Geertz, 1961; Koentjaraningrat, 1985; Williams, 1991). Javanese child-rearing practice emphasizes emotional development, the importance of being *rukun* (maintaining harmonious relationships with siblings and other children), being *manut* (obedient), and *tepa-selira* (helping, sharing, and empathizing with others) as ideal human virtues, and children are taught early to approximate these ideals (Koentjaraningrat, 1985).

These values were reflected in the Indonesian children's everyday social interaction and play behavior. For example, we found that sibling interaction was relatively harmonious. Although there were disagreements over activities, play ideas, and taking turns, very few of these conflicts escalated into aggressive behavior. The older children were patient with their younger siblings' behavior and indulged them by "letting the young ones have their way because they are small and do not know any better." Few children were observed to cry, and those who did were quickly consoled by adults or other children. Within the neighborhood play groups, children shared activities, available toys, and food. We noted that play groups tended to be gender segregated, with much of the caretaking being done by girls.

By integrating our quantitative findings with our activity setting analysis, we found that Mexican and Indonesian older siblings developed skills in playing with young children to a greater extent than did the American siblings, and that in using these skills they played a role similar to the American mothers in constructing play episodes. The use of siblings as caregivers for young children, and the nature of the sibling relationships in the Mexican and Indonesian communities, fostered the development of these skills. Furthermore, sibling caretaking provided opportunities for older children to learn to scaffold play with younger siblings, and for the younger children to acquire skills and knowledge by participating in play activities with more competent partners. In the American sample, children experienced play with both their mothers and older siblings. However, because the American sibling relationships were often antagonistic, the children were unable to sustain or enjoy cooperative pretend play.

These findings challenge the prevailing notion that mothers are the "better" facilitators of children's early pretend play and that siblings provide "less than optimal educational environments" for young children's social and cognitive development (Macdonald, 1993). In settings where mothers are not considered playmates for children, and where siblings are cooperative, caring, and nurturant and there is an absence of sibling rivalry, siblings may provide stimulation that is cognitively challenging to supplement their mothers' more restrictive and less playful style of interaction (Edwards & Whiting, 1993). Furthermore, from a "Westerner's" perspective, play with siblings appeared to be more fun than play with mothers. Thus, the scaffolding or the social support provided by a more skilled partner (i.e., the *what*) may be essential to the development of children's pretend play, but *who* does the scaffolding, *how, when,* and *why* it gets done, may be culture-specific and highly dependent on the environmental context.

The activity setting model allowed us to analyze how variations in children's early educational environments influenced their play with different partners across the three communities. This mode of analysis also provided the basis to evaluate our theoretical assumptions about child development and to draw some overall conclusions about the effects of culture on children's development.

The Preschool Pretend Play Studies

Recent work has been influential in fostering positive attitudes toward children's play and in developing preschool curricula that provide children with opportunities for daily play activity. However, not all adults emphasize play in child rearing or education, leading to considerable variation in children's play in other cultures and among American minority populations. In the past, these cultural and ethnic differences were misinterpreted as signs of deficiency rather than variation. More recently, researchers who have begun to ''unpackage'' cultural effects on individuals have found that differences in children's play behavior can be more accurately attributed to the role of specific cultural practices that organize children's early learning environments (Roopnarine, Johnson, & Hooper, 1994). Factors that have been shown to influence preschoolers' play are time and space to play (Curry & Arnaud, 1984), access to objects (Gottfried & Brown, 1986), adult behavior and attitudes toward play (Curry et al., 1984), and availability of play partners (Garvey, 1990). (Also see Gaskins, Göncü et al., and Haight, this volume.)

These contextual factors are interrelated and are influenced by culture. For example, as shown in the toddler studies, children's activity settings are structured by adults' developmental goals for children and the socialization practices used to meet those goals. In building on this research, the overall purpose of the preschool studies was to examine how culture shapes and organizes the environments in which children's social interaction and play activity take place, and to understand how variations in these environments are associated with different developmental outcomes for children.

The studies were carried out with the help of two Korean graduate-student research assistants. The participating children were from middle-class, relatively recent Korean immigrant families, who attended all-Korean preschools in the Korean town community of Los Angeles, CA, and from white middle-class European-American families, who attended preschools in a small city in the southwest USA and in the Los Angeles suburbs. All of the preschools were year-round, full-day programs with adult–child ratios of 1:7 and with average group sizes of 16 children.

In the Korean preschools, the teachers and directors were middle-class Korean immigrants with varying degrees of educational background. The curricula were similar in philosophy and were designed by the directors and teachers of the individual preschools. Overall, the stated goals of the Korean programs were to teach academic skills (numbers, letters, and writing), to provide English and Korean language instruction, and to prepare children for public school.

In the European-American settings, the teachers were predominantly white and middle class and had completed at least the state-required course work for early childhood education. The directors, teachers, and community board members in the respective preschools designed the programs using Developmentally Appropriate Practice guidelines (DAP) (published by the National Association for the Education of Young Children in 1994).

Study One: European- and Korean-American Preschoolers' Pretend Play. The first study (Farver et al., 1995) was conducted with 96 preschoolers (48 Korean- and 48 European-American; half girls; $M = 50$ months), who were observed individually during free-play activity in their preschools. On four separate occasions, observers recorded children's play initiations and peers' responses, teacher–child social behaviors, complexity of social interaction and pretend play, and predominant affect every 60 seconds for 5 minutes.

Mothers completed a questionnaire concerning their beliefs about play, common play activities, and availability of play partners in the home. Teachers completed a Likert rating scale consisting of 16 items to measure each child's social competence with peers (i.e., "difficult," "hesitant," or "sociable"). Children's friendship status was determined using individual sociometric interviews, teacher ratings, and behavioral identification of common play partners during the social behavior observations. Children were given the Peabody Picture Vocabulary Test (PPVT-R) to provide an estimate of their cognitive functioning by measuring their receptive vocabulary. The Korean-American parents completed an acculturation questionnaire containing items about family demography, language preference, and cultural identification.

Quantitative analyses were used to compare children's observed social behaviors, play complexity, PPVT-R scores, teacher-rated social competence, and frequencies of teacher–child interaction for culture. The results showed that Korean-American children were more cooperative in their responses to peer-initiated play, displayed more neutral affect, were observed to be more unoccupied, and engaged in more parallel play than the European-American children. In contrast, the European-American children had more negative and aggressive responses to peers' play initiations, displayed more shared positive affect, and engaged in more social pretend play than the Korean-American children. The Korean-American children scored higher on PPVT-R, were rated by their teachers as being more "hesitant" with peers, and had, at most, one reciprocated friendship. The European-American children were rated by their teachers as being more "sociable" with peers, and they had two or more reciprocated friendships. The European-American children engaged in more social interaction with their teachers than the Korean-American children. Most

European-American mothers believed that play was a learning experience and was related to positive developmental outcomes for children, whereas most Korean-American mothers said that play was primarily for children's amusement.

Study Two: European- and Korean-American Preschoolers' Communication of Social Pretend Play. Study Two (Farver & Lee, 1997) extended our prior work by examining whether the cultural differences we found in the first study reflected limitations in children's ability to engage in social pretend play, or were instead related to facets of the culturally mediated contexts provided in the preschool settings. A second purpose was to understand how culture influences the expression of pretend play by exploring the communicative strategies children use to organize and maintain play with a partner, and the thematic content of their play episodes.

Ninety-two preschoolers (46 Korean- and 46 European-American; half girls; $M = 48.2$ months) were studied in two situations: during free play in their preschools, and in a quasi-experimental condition where children were paired with a self-chosen play partner and were provided with toys conducive with imaginative play.

Children in both groups were observed for a total of 20 minutes during free-play activities using the procedures described for Study One. In the experimental-play condition, dyads were videotaped for 20 minutes while they played with a *Fisher Price Castle* and its accompanying accessories (a king, queen, prince, princess, knight, horses and carriage, a dragon, beds, tables, and chairs).

The videotapes were transcribed verbatim. All statements made by the children, as well as any vocalizations, such as paralinguistic cues or behaviors that served a communicative function, were recorded. The transcriptions were keyed to the videotaped footage and were divided into twenty, 60-second intervals. Each 60-second interval was coded for the target child's highest level of play complexity. All 60-second intervals containing social pretend play were isolated and were coded for 10 communicative strategies: describe own action, describe partners' action, semantic ties, tag questions, directives, paralinguistic cues, call for attention, reject play, statements of agreement, and polite requests. Each 60-second interval that contained social pretend play was also coded for four play themes: family relations, everyday activities, danger in the environment (aggressive behaviors such as killing, shooting, crashing), and fantastic themes (extraordinary actions performed by fantasy characters).

Similar to our results from Study One, we found that during free play the European-American children engaged in more social pretend play than did the Korean-American children. However, in the toy-play condition, where children were provided with toys, time, and space to play, there were no significant cultural differences in the frequency of their social pretend play.

The results comparing children's communicative strategies showed that Korean-American children frequently described their partner's actions and used semantic ties, tag questions, statements of agreement, and polite requests, whereas European-American children described their own actions, used directives, and rejected their partners' play ideas and suggestions. Finally, for the Korean-American children, family roles and everyday activities were the common play themes, whereas among the European-American children, danger in the environment and fantastic themes were the most frequent.

Study Three: Individual Differences in European- and Korean-American Preschoolers' Play Behavior. Taken together, the results of our first two studies revealed distinct *between*-culture differences. However, it remained unclear how variability in children's skills and behaviors *within* each culture might contribute to differences in their social pretend play. Therefore, we designed a third study (Farver & Kim, under review) to examine individual and intracultural differences in European- and Korean-American children's play behavior. Specifically, we wanted to understand how intracultural variation in children's skills and behavioral characteristics might be associated with social pretend play in early childhood. Five sources of individual difference noted in the play literature on Western children were considered: behavioral style, social functioning, cognitive functioning, creativity, and child-rearing attitudes. We expected to find relationships among these variables that would be predictive of pretend play in the two cultures.

The participants were 60 preschool children, (30 European- and 30 Korean-American; half girls; $M = 55.33$ months). Children's social behavior and level of play complexity were observed during free-play periods in their preschools on six separate occasions using the procedure described for Study One and Study Two. To provide an estimate of children's creative potential or ideational fluency, three subsets of the Multidimensional Stimulus Fluency Measure – patterns, instances, and uses – were individually administered. Children were given the Wechsler Preschool and Primary Scale of Intelligence-Revised (WPPSI-R) to measure their cognitive functioning. Teachers rated children's social competence ("sociable," "hesitant," or "difficult" described above) and completed the Teacher Temperament Questionnaire, which rates children's behavioral style on 15 items ("task orientation," "reactivity," and "personal-social adaptability"). Mothers completed a play questionnaire (as described in the foregoing toddler studies) and rated their child-rearing attitudes toward "creativity," "play," and "teaching" in the home, need for "control" over their children, and "frustration" on the Parents as a Teacher Inventory. The Korean mothers also completed an acculturation measure (as described previously).

Similar to the findings from our previous two studies, European-American children engaged in more social pretend play and negative social interaction than did the Korean-American children. Korean-American children engaged in more positive social interaction, were rated by their teachers as being more "personally socially adaptable," and had higher scores on the WPPSI-R than did the European-American children. The Korean-American mothers also had more positive attitudes toward teaching and learning in the home, indicated a greater need for control over their children, and expressed more frustration in parenting than the European-American mothers. In contrast, European-American mothers held more positive attitudes toward children's play and reported more frequent play in the home than did the Korean-American mothers.

Two different predictive patterns for the Korean-and European-American children's play were identified. For the Korean-American children, being socially adaptable and engaging in positive social interaction with peers was associated with social pretend play, whereas for the European-American children, social adaptability, as well as creativity, and parent–child home play were associated with social pretend play.

The Activity Setting Analyses: Preschoolers' Education in Cultural Contexts. To interpret the quantitative differences we found in our three studies of Korean- and European-American children's play behavior, we used the activity setting analysis to situate play within children's daily experiences in their preschool environments. Features of European- and Korean-American activity settings, derived from the research literature and validated by our observations in the respective preschools (Farver et al., 1995; Farver & Lee, 1997), are elaborated in this section.

Analysis of the *personnel available* showed that all the preschool settings were similar in terms of adult–child ratios, group sizes, frequency and length of outdoor free-play periods, and the matching of teacher and child socioeconomic status and ethnicity. In all settings, there were three 30-minute outdoor free-play periods, and we observed few differences in the outdoor preschool environments. During outdoor free play, children rode bikes, dug in sandboxes, played on climbing structures, and played run-chase.

There were, however, clear differences in the *nature and purpose of the indoor activities being performed*. Observations made inside the Korean-American settings indicated that children spent much of their indoor periods seated at tables working quietly and independently with flash cards; copying dittoed numbers, English letters, and Korean characters; constructing block designs from printed cards; coloring "theme-related" figures (i.e., hearts, Santa Claus, Easter bunnies, etc.); and building structures with *Leggo* blocks. Classroom materials (crayons, paper, pencils, manipulatives, puzzles, etc.) were not child accessible but were distributed by the teacher. If children left their seats or began loudly to interact with peers, they were gently encouraged to return to their tables. Daily "circle time" consisted of singing in English or Korean, listening quietly to stories read aloud, and answering teacher-initiated questions in rote memorization fashion. In general, when directly asked, teachers said that play was basically an outdoor activity for children to release excess energy and helped them to concentrate better on their studies. None of the teachers that were interviewed believed play was important or that it related to helping children learn. At the end of each day, children were given homework assignments to complete in the evening with their parents' help.

In contrast, we observed in the European-American preschools that children were free to choose from a variety of activities that were set up on the classroom perimeters, to play with toys, to interact with classmates, or to participate in a teacher-directed activity such as cooking food, recording story narratives, or creating puppet shows, if they desired. Classroom materials and toys were generally child accessible in all settings. "Circle times" involved "show-and-tell" periods and stories read aloud. In implementing the DAP guidelines, each preschool incorporated play into their daily programs. Teachers who were interviewed said that play was "children's work" and that during play children experimented with the world, developed their creative abilities and cognitive skills, and learned how to get along with other children.

There were also differences in the *cultural goals, values, and beliefs* and in *the scripts governing children's social interaction*. As discussed previously, with some variation, American society maintains an individualistic orientation, whereas traditional Korean culture is collectivistic (Triandis, 1989). Although after immigration Korean families begin "acculturating" to the American lifestyle, most continue to retain values that stress social harmony, cooperation, group identity, and emotional control (Holt, 1989). Accordingly, Korean culture also holds a different view of the self, others, and the interdependence of the two (Kim & Choi, 1994). Although Americans often focus on the individuated self, or the "I," Koreans generally emphasize the relatedness and interdependence among individuals, or the "we" (Maday & Szalay, 1976). The Korean interdependent view of the self is expressed as *Chong*, which is the affective bond uniting Korean families and social groups. It is associated with being attentive to others' needs, attempting to "read" their minds, and maintaining harmonious shared experiences (Choi, Kim, & Choi, 1993). In contrast, the American independent view of the self is generally expressed through a preoccupation with one's self, an emphasis on individuality and self-assertion, and "saying" what is on one's mind (Markus & Kitayama, 1991).

These differences in orientation are reflected in child-rearing practices and parental ethnotheories. For example, in American society, it is expected that children will develop an autonomous sense of self, and parents reward displays of self-reliance and self-confidence with praise (Hoffman, 1988; Levine, 1980). In contrast, Korean parents disapprove of children engaging in behaviors that call attention to themselves and instead encourage the development of a sense of self that is interdependent with others, not separate (Strom, Park, & Daniels, 1986). Thus, among Koreans, a person is often referred to as someone's father, someone's son, someone's brother, and so on, but seldom as just someone (Kim, 1995).

Similarly, the pragmatics or the implicit rules for using language effectively and appropriately are also different in the Korean and American cultures. In Korean culture, social status is displayed in language use. Based on Confucianism, Korean individuals are assigned a hierarchical social position reflecting their age, role, and gender, which are acknowledged in an honorific form of communication (Chu, 1978; Kim, 1995). Thus, a person of lower status uses a different form of the Korean language when addressing someone of higher status.

Styles of communication are also different. In Korean culture, where harmonious relationships are valued, communication is rarely direct or confrontational. Instead, one talks "around an issue" and relies on the other's sensitivity to understand the point of the conversation (Chu, 1978;

Kim, 1995). Korean child-rearing practice also discourages children from expressing their own opinions or asserting themselves, especially when their ideas differ from those of family or friends (Kim & Choi, 1994). Korean children are taught to control the display of emotion, to value group harmony, and to reduce conflict in social interaction (Kim, 1995). In contrast, in American culture, where parents encourage the development of self-expression and independent action, children's style of communication is direct, but their social interaction is also often conflictual.

In summary, the activity setting and quantitative analyses of our preschool studies suggest that there were distinct culturally defined social environments that determined children's opportunities for social interaction and play. Adult beliefs about play, the emphasis they placed on the development of particular skills, and the kinds of early experiences they provided for young children produced differences in children's play behavior and in their educational outcomes. In the Korean-American preschools, where school-readiness skills were emphasized and play was not considered important for early childhood education, teachers provided a highly structured daily schedule centered on academic-related activities, and children had few opportunities to interact socially with their peers. In contrast, consistent with their beliefs about the benefits of play and their goals to develop children's social as well as cognitive skills, Euro-American teachers provided child-centered, play-oriented curricula, and children had many opportunities for social interaction and play. When adults are highly involved in structuring children's settings, preschoolers' activities resemble "work" more than "play," and children also learn different skills. For example, in the Korean-American settings, children scored high on the PPVT-R and the WPPSI-R, and in the Euro-American settings, children perfected social skills and play.

It is also important to note that parents' reports about play activities in the home and their child-rearing attitudes were consistent with the teachers' behavior and educational goals and values in the respective preschools. The Korean-American mothers' reports of frustration with parenting, their need for control over their children's behavior, confidence in their ability to foster teaching and learning in the home, and infrequent parent–child play in the home may be related to their level of acculturation and the difficulties they experience in reconciling Korean traditional values with American lifestyles. Research with Korean immigrants has shown that parents who play with their children experience less frustration with parenting and that the length of residency in the USA was positively related to how much time they reported playing with their children (Park, 1983). Moreover, research has also shown that in very traditional and relatively unacculturated Korean households, playing with children is considered culturally inappropriate adult behavior because it entails a loss of parental respect (Kim, 1995; Strom et al., 1986).

Differences in the social conventions, communication styles, and the norms governing self-expression in the two cultures also influenced how children socially interacted during outdoor free play and how they coordinated social pretend play with a partner. Korean-American children whose culture emphasizes a relational mode, characterized by group interdependence and sensitivity to others, responded in a cooperative fashion to peers' play initiations, were nonconfrontational in their dyadic play, and were rated by their teachers as being more "socially adaptable." They avoided using communicative strategies that required them to direct another child's behavior, to set and enforce rules, or to decide roles or scripts. On the other hand, European-American children, whose culture emphasizes an aggregate mode, characterized by independence and a preoccupation with the self and its expression, were frequently aggressive and negative in their responses to peer initiations and rejected their partner's contributions; their play was often conflictual. Similarly, the thematic differences found in children's pretend play may also be related to variations in the social goals of the two groups. For example, consistent with their culture's emphasis on harmonious interpersonal relationships, the Korean-American children may have reduced social conflict by enacting familiar and realistic themes that required little negotiation and were easily shared with their play partners. On the other hand, consistent with their cultural values, the European-American children may have been more interested in pursuing their own interests rather than promoting shared realities by enacting fantastic and dangerous play themes.

The results suggest that facets of the preschool activity settings cannot be separated from culture. Children develop context-specific abilities, which are tied to the content and structure of their daily activities and are shaped by adults with particular developmental goals in mind. Therefore, the extent to which social competence, cognitive skills, creative abilities, and child-rearing attitudes may influence the frequency, complexity, and expression of children's play, depends on the extent to which a cultural group emphasizes and structures the development of these skills and attributes, as well as the extent to which play is considered beneficial for young children.

Conclusions

The notion that the social settings around children are powerful influences on their development is a longstanding one in the social sciences (Bronfenbrenner, 1979). One way to examine this idea is using activity setting analysis, which is derived from the work of Vygotsky, the Whitings, Super and Harkness, and Weisner and his colleagues. In my discussion and illustration of this model, I have proposed that despite differences in culture and ecology across communities, comparative research can generate principles about human development.

Overall, the activity setting analysis revealed the different kinds of activities that are available to toddlers and preschoolers in the various settings. In addition, our findings also suggest that social pretend play is a universal facet of early childhood. However, culture highly influences the frequency, expression, and social contexts in which children's play occurs. The activity setting analysis was useful in examining how variations in household demography, sibling caregiving, social conventions, communication styles, and the construal of the self influenced children's social behavior and self-expression, as well as how they engaged in social pretend play with different partners. This model also provided the means for clarifying how broad cultural factors become translated into specific developmental contexts and helped to broaden our current understanding about the role of culture in children's development. The activity setting analysis supported our efforts to uncover the specific elements of sociocultural contexts that contribute to different patterns of preschool education, which are shaped by what adults believe are important experiences for young children.

Although there has been growth of interest in cross-cultural research, we are only beginning to address the relationships among environmental influences, cultural practices, and developmental outcomes. Moreover, because the data base is expanding to include culturally diverse populations, which will in turn force a reconsideration of our developmental theories, there remains a need to refine our methods for conducting comparable cultural research. Generally, when we conduct cross-cultural studies, we take our established, and often Western-biased, methods into the new setting. In addition, the physical demands of fieldwork, language differences, and the norms toward participation in research exhibited by members of different communities also contribute to making cross-cultural research problematic (Triandis, 1984). These fundamental problems can be overcome by shifting our unit of analysis from the individual to the developmental context, and by examining the relationships between the developing person and facets of their ever-changing world. The activity setting approach is a promising alternative to current cross-cultural research paradigms.

References

Alba, F. (1982). *The population of Mexico: Trends, issues, and policies.* Trenton, NJ: Transaction.

Beizer, L. & Howes, C. (1992). Mothers and toddlers: Partners in early symbolic play. In C. Howes, O. Unger, & C. Matheson (Eds.), *The collaborative construction of pretend* (pp. 25–43). Albany, NY: SUNY Press.

Betancourt, H., & Lopez, S. R. (1993). The study of culture, ethnicity, and race in American psychology. *American Psychologist, 48*, 629–37.

Bronfenbrenner, U. (1979). *The ecology of human development.* Cambridge, MA: Harvard University Press.

Choi, S. C., Kim, U., & Choi, S. H. (1993). Korean culture and collective representation. In U. Kim & J. W. Berry (Eds.), *Indigenous psychologies: Experience and research in cultural context* (pp. 23–43). Newbury Park, CA: Sage.

Chu, H. (1978). The Korean learner in an American school. In *Teaching for cross-cultural understanding.* Arlington, VA: Arlington Public Schools.

Curry, N. E., & Arnaud, S. (1984). Play in developmental settings. In T. Yawkey & A. Pelligrini (Eds.), *Child's play: Developmental and applied* (pp. 65–72). Hillsdale, NJ: Erlbaum.

Developmentally Appropriate Practice (1994). National Association for the Education of the Young Child, Washington, DC.

Dunn, J., & Dale, N. (1984). I, a daddy: 2-year-olds' collaboration in joint pretend play with sibling and with mother. In I. Bretherton (Ed.), *Symbolic play* (pp. 131–57). New York: Academic.

Edwards, C. P., & Whiting, B. (1993). Mother, older sibling, and me: The overlapping roles. In K. Macdonald (Ed.), *Parent–child play: Descriptions and implications* (pp. 317–48). New York: SUNY Press.

Farver, J. M. (1992a). An analysis of young American and Mexican children's play dialogues. In C. Howes, O. Unger, & C. Matheson (Eds.), *The collaborative construction of pretend* (pp. 55–66). New York: SUNY Press.

Farver, J. M. (1992b). Communicating shared meaning in social pretend play. *Early Childhood Research Quarterly, 7*, 22–35.

Farver, J. M. (1993). Cultural differences in scaffolding play: A comparison of American and Mexican mother– and sibling–child pair. In K. MacDonald (Ed.), *Parent–child play: Descriptions and implications* (pp. 349–66). Albany: SUNY Press.

Farver, J. M., & Howes, C. (1993). Cultural differences in American and Mexican mother–child pretend play. *Merrill-Palmer Quarterly, 39*, 344–58.

Farver, J. M., & Kim, Y. (under review). Within cultural differences: Predicting social pretend play in Korean- and Anglo-American preschoolers.

Farver, J. M., Kim, Y., & Lee, Y. (1995). Cultural differences in Korean- and Anglo-American preschoolers' social interaction and play behavior. *Child Development, 66*, 1089–99.

Farver, J. M., & Lee, Y. (1997). Social pretend play in Korean- and Anglo-American preschoolers. *Child Development, 68*, 544–36.

Farver, J. M., & Wimbarti, S. (1995). Indonesian toddlers' social play with their mothers and older siblings. *Child Development, 66*, 1443–513.

Fiese, B. (1989). *Creating the zone of proximal development: Lessons from the study of symbolic play.* Paper presented at the biennial meeting of the Society for Research in Child Development, Kansas City, MO.

Garvey, C. (1990). *Play.* Cambridge, MA: Harvard University Press.

Gauvain, M. (1995). Thinking in niches: Sociocultural influences on cognitive development. *Human Development, 38*, 25–45.

Geertz, H. (1961). *The Javanese family.* New York: Glencoe.

Gottfried, A. E., & Brown, C. C., (Eds.). (1986). *Play interactions: Contributions of play materials and parental involvement to children's development.* Lexington, MA: Heath.

Glaser, B., & Strauss, A. (1967). *The discovery of grounded theory.* New York: Aldine.

Haight, W., & Miller, P. (1993). *Pretending at home.* Albany, NY: SUNY Press.

Harkness, S., & Super, C. (Eds.). (1996). *Parents' cultural belief systems: Their origins, expressions, and consequences.* New York: Guilford.

Hoffman, L. (1988). Cross-cultural differences in child rearing goals. In R. LeVine, P. Miller, & M. Maxwell (Eds.), *Parental behavior in diverse societies* (pp. 99–122). San Francisco: Jossey-Bass.

Holt, D. D. (1989). *The education of Korean-American youth: Achievements, problems, and mental health issues.* Sacramento: California Department of Education.

Howes, C. (1988). Peer interaction of young children. *Monographs for the Society of Research in Child Development, 53* (1, Serial No. 217).

Kim, S. J. (1995). *The effects of parenting style, cultural conflict, and peer relations on academic achievement and psychological adjustment among Korean immigrant adolescents.* Unpublished doctoral dissertation, Department of Educational Psychology, University of Southern California, Los Angeles.

Kim, U., & Choi, S. H. (1994). Individualism, collectivism, and child development: A Korean perspective. In P. Greenfield & R. Cocking (Eds.), *Cross-cultural roots of minority child development* (pp. 227–58). Hillsdale, NJ: Erlbaum.

Koentjaraningrat, R. (1985). *Javanese culture.* Oxford: Oxford University Press.

Leont'ev, A. N. (1981). The problem of activity in psychology. In J. Wertsch (Ed.), *The concept of activity in Soviet psychology.* New York: Academic Press.

LeVine, R. A. (1980). Anthropology and child development. In C. Super & S. Harkness (Eds.), *Anthropological perspectives on child development* (pp. 23–35). San Francisco: Jossey-Bass.

Macdonald, K. (Ed.). (1993). *Parent–child play: Descriptions and implications.* New York: SUNY Press.

Maday, B. C., & Szalay, L. B. (1976). Psychological correlates of family socialization in the United States and Korea. In T. Williams (Ed.), *Psychological anthropology* (75–92). Hague: Mouton.

Markus, H. R., & Kitayama, S. (1991). Culture and self: Implications for cognition, emotion, and motivation. *Psychological Review, 98,* 224–53.

O'Connell, B., & Bretherton, I. (1984). Toddlers' play alone and with mothers. In I. Bretherton (Ed.), *Symbolic play* (pp. 335–68). New York: Academic Press.

Park, S. H. (1983). *The identification of factors related to child rearing expectations of Korean-American immigrant parents of preschool children.* Unpublished doctoral dissertation, North Texas State University.

Richman, A., Miller, P., & Solomon, M. (1988). The socialization of infants in suburban Boston. In R. LeVine, P. Miller, & M. Maxwell (Eds.), *Parental behavior in diverse societies* (pp. 12–22). San Francisco: Jossey-Bass.

Rogoff, B., & Gardner, W. (1984). Guidance in development. In M. E. Lamb & A. L. Brown (Eds.), *Advances in developmental psychology* (pp. 206–26) (Vol. 2). Hillsdale, NJ: Erlbaum.

Rogoff, B., Gauvain, M., & Ellis, S. (1984). Development viewed in its cultural context. In M. Bornstein & Michael Lamb (Eds.), *Developmental psychology: An advanced textbook* (pp. 533–71). Hillsdale, NJ: Erlbaum.

Roopnarine, J., Johnson, J., & Hooper, F. (Eds.). (1994). *Children's play in diverse cultures.* New York: SUNY Press.

Strom, R., Park, S. H., & Daniels, S. (1986). Adjustment of Korean immigrant families. *Educational and Psychological Research, 6,* 312–27.

Suárez, E. (1978). *Social stratification and social mobility in Mexico City.* Mexico City: National Autonomous University of Mexico Press.

Super, C., & Harkness, S. (1986). The developmental niche: A conceptualization at the interface of child and culture. *International Journal of Behavioral Development, 9,* 545–69.

Tapia-Uribe, F., LeVine, R., & LeVine, S. (1994). Maternal behavior in a Mexican community: The changing environments of children. In P. Greenfield & R. Cocking (Eds.), *Cross-cultural roots of minority child development* (pp. 41–54). Hillsdale, NJ: Erlbaum.

Tharp, R., & Gallimore, R. (1988). *Rousing minds to life: Teaching, learning, and schooling in social context.* Cambridge: Cambridge University Press.

Triandis, H. (1984). Cross cultural psychology. *American Psychologist, 39,* 1006–16.

Triandis, H. (1989). Cross cultural studies of individualism and collectivism. *Nebraska symposium on motivation.* Lincoln: University of Nebraska Press.

Vygotsky, L. (1978). *Mind in society.* Cambridge, MA: Harvard University Press.

Weisner, T. (1984). Ecocultural niches of middle childhood: A cross-cultural perspective. In W. A. Collins (Ed.), *Development during middle childhood* (pp. 335–69). Washington, DC: National Academy Press.

Weisner, T. (1989a). Cultural and universal aspects of social support for children: Evidence from the Abaluyia of Kenya. In D. Belle (Ed.), *Children's social networks and social supports* (pp. 290–310). New York: Wiley.

Weisner, T. (1989b). Comparing sibling relationships across cultures. In P. Zukow (Ed.), *Sibling interaction across cultures* (pp. 1–15). New York: Springer-Verlag.

Weisner, T., Gallimore, R., & Jordan, C. (1988). Unpackaging cultural effects on classroom learning: Native Hawaiian peer assistance and child-generated activity. *Anthropology and Education Quarterly, 19,* 327–53.

Weisner, T., Matheson, C., & Bernheimer, L. (1995). American cultural models of early influence and parent recognition of developmental delays: Is earlier always better than later? In S. Harkness & C. Super (Eds.), *Parents' cultural belief systems: Their origins, expressions, and consequences* (pp. 496–531). New York: Guilford.

Wertsch, J. V. (1985). *Vygotsky and the social formation of mind.* Cambridge, MA: Harvard University Press.

Wertsch, J. V. (1991). *Voices of the mind: A sociocultural approach to mediated action.* Cambridge, MA: Harvard University Press.

Whiting, B. B. (1976). The problem of the packaged variable. In K. F. Riegel & J. A. Meacham (Eds.), *The developing individual in a changing world* (pp. 303–9) (Vol. 1). Chicago: Aldine.

Whiting, B. B. (1980). Culture and social behavior: A model for the development of social behavior. *Ethos, 8,* 95–116.

Whiting, B. B., & Edwards, C. (1988). *Children of different worlds: The formation of social behavior.* Cambridge, MA: Harvard University Press.

Williams, W. (1991). *Javanese lives: Men and women in modern Indonesian society.* New Brunswick, NJ: Rutgers University Press.

5 The Pragmatics of Caregiver–Child Pretending at Home: Understanding Culturally Specific Socialization Practices

Wendy L. Haight

Understanding cross-cultural variation and constancy in caregiver–child interaction requires examination of the broader contexts in which specific practices are embedded. In the following excerpt, 2½-year-old Angu and her caregiver are playing school in the living room of their compact apartment in Taipei (translation from the Mandarin):

> **Caregiver:** (*smiling*) Stand up, bow, sit down, teacher is going to deliver a lesson. (*Angu, smiling, moves closer to her caregiver.*)
> **Caregiver:** Teacher is coming to the classroom. What should the class monitor say?
> **Angu:** Stand up!
> **Caregiver:** OK. Stand up. (*Angu stands up and bows.*)
> **Caregiver:** Sit down. . . . (*They read the story.*)
> **Caregiver:** We have finished the story. (*She claps her hands.*) . . . Before we dismiss the class, the class monitor should say: 'Stand up! Bow! Sit down!' Stand up! (*Angu stands up.*)
> **Caregiver:** Bow! (*Angu bows*). . . .
> **Caregiver:** Class is dismissed. Go play on the slide (*indicates imaginary sliding board in the living room.*) . . . Class is dismissed and you are happy. (Haight, Wang, Fung, Williams, & Mintz, 1995)

Halfway around the world, 3-year-old Nancy and her caregiver also are pretending together in their house in Chicago. Nancy's caregiver is preparing decorations for a Halloween party when Nancy begins to show signs of boredom. Her mother suggests that she drive her car:

The research program described in this chapter was generally supported by grants from the Spencer Foundation.

> Nancy retrieves a childsized red plastic dashboard with steering wheel and seatbelt, and positions herself for driving. "Be sure to fasten your seat belt, right?" reminds her mother, "Buckle up for safety!" Nancy fastens her seatbelt, turns the steering wheel, and pushes the horn. To her mother's queries, "Where are you going? Are you taking a trip?" Nancy replies, "To Havana." . . . Nancy continues to steer the car while demonstrating how to drive. "You drive a car like this. Like this. OK?" She explains that Havana is far away and discusses with her mother how many stops will be needed en route, and how old one has to be to get a driver's license. (Haight & Miller, 1992, p. 1)

Angu, Nancy, and their caregivers display a variety of similarities in their interactions. Both Angu and Nancy frequently engage in pretend play with their caregivers, and both children develop into skillful pretenders. Furthermore, both caregivers encourage their children's pretending within such mundane contexts as caregiving, cooking, and cleaning. Sometimes they even use their children's interest in pretend play to encourage cooperation and to teach. For example, Nancy's caregiver is able to complete her Halloween preparations by simultaneously alleviating her daughter's boredom with a pretend game. She even manages to insert a safety lesson into the play ("Be sure to fasten your seat belt, right? . . . Buckle up for safety!")

Despite their similarities, however, there are also substantial variations in the ways in which Angu and Nancy interact with their caregivers, and in the social functions of these interactions. In contrast to Nancy's caregiver, Angu's caregiver frequently uses her child's interest in pretending to rehearse appropriate conduct such as formal interactions with a teacher ("Before we dismiss the class, the class monitor should say: 'Stand up! Bow! Sit down!") Furthermore, she leads the interaction throughout the play, introducing topics and providing instructions. Nancy's caregiver also initiates the play, but then she allows her child to lead the interaction, supporting and elaborating upon Nancy's ideas.

How can one understand and interpret these intercultural similarities and differences? The styles of interaction and functions of caregiver–child pretend play in Angu's and Nancy's homes seem to reflect caregivers' sensitivity both to children's development and to broader, culturally specific socialization beliefs and goals. Angu's caregiver is concerned with teaching her child proper conduct during hierarchically organized adult–child interactions. Nancy's caregiver is concerned with supporting her child's individuality and self-expression. Both caregivers apparently use caregiver–child pretend play to support their children's development of culturally valued characteristics, and they do so through developmentally and culturally appropriate communicative practices.

In this chapter, we use caregiver–child pretend play to illustrate the centrality of culture to understanding the significance of particular socialization practices for children's development. Following Garvey (1990), we define *pretend play* as a subcategory of play in which objects, actions, persons, places, or other aspects of the here and now are transformed or treated nonliterally. For example, a stuffed animal is animated, a sibling transformed into a lion, or behaviors conventionally associated with one context are enacted in a different context, as in a child's enactment of her bedtime routine on the kitchen floor after breakfast. By *culture*, we mean a dynamic system of shared meanings (e.g., Quinn & Holland, 1987) instantiated through common practices. For example, within European-American middle-class culture, play generally is viewed as important for children's development, and parents generally engage in play with their children and provide them with abundant time, space, and materials (toys) for play (e.g., Haight & Miller, 1992, 1993). By psychological *development*, we refer to individuals' active construction of meaning from a variety of cultural resources and personal experiences. For example, a parent's emerging understanding of caregiver–child play is constructed from complex experiences involving the media and "experts" such as pediatricians and teachers, and from personal experiences including those occurring within particular families (Haight, Parke, & Black, 1997).

Understanding the development of pretend play in cultural context requires analysis of pretend play as it spontaneously occurs in everyday life, and as it relates to other socialization beliefs and practices. Thus, we begin this chapter with a discussion of the social context of spontaneously occurring pretend play in the home. In particular, we focus on the extent of caregiver participation in young children's pretending, and on the potential role of such interactions in shaping the development of pretend play. Second, we describe our strategy for understanding pretend play in cultural context. More specifically, we discuss a basic premise of our research that the development of pretend play is a dialectical process of socialization and acquisition, as well as our strategies for studying caregiver–child pretend play and interpreting our research findings. Third, we present an example from our work: namely, the cross-cultural variation and constancy within Chinese and U.S. families in the pragmatics of caregiver–child pretend – that is, the use of pretend play within social interactions including the communicative conventions for conducting pretend play with a partner. We conclude with suggestions for future research, including investigation of possible longer-term developmental outcomes of caregiver participation in pretend play on the emergence of children's creativity.

Caregiver Participation in Children's Spontaneous Pretend Play at Home: Prevalence and Significance

Recent evidence from naturalistic, home observations indicates that young children's spontaneous pretend play is predominantly social (e.g., Haight & Miller, 1992, 1993) and that in many communities, adult caregivers (Beizer & Howes, 1992; Göncü, Mistry, & Mosier, 1991; Haight & Miller, 1992, 1993; Haight et al., in press) or sibling caregivers (e.g., Farver, 1993) are important participants. Furthermore, the pretend play of young, Western, middle-class children with their caregivers is more sustained, more complex, and more diverse than their solo pretending, and young children incorporate their mothers' pretend talk into their own pretending (Dunn & Wooding, 1977; Fiese, 1987; Haight & Miller, 1992, 1993; O'Connell & Bretherton, 1984; Slade, 1987).

Given recent descriptions of caregiver participation in children's pretend play, as well as its apparently facilitory effects on children's concurrent pretend play, it is important to consider its relevance to the development of pretending. According to the prevailing Piagetian view, others do not play a significant role in the emergence and early development of pretend play, where such development primarily is considered to be the level of sophistication of children's independent symbol use. Rather, pretend play arises spontaneously from the structure of individual thought and does not become sufficiently "socialized" to permit symbols to be shared until several years later (i.e., collective symbolism) (Piaget, 1962).

Recently, researchers have examined this Piagetian position by relating the extent and quality of caregiver participation in social pretend play with their young children to children's emerging use of symbols in their independent pretend play. Consistent with a Piagetian position, existing evidence is weak regarding the facilitory role of caregiver participation on the level of symbol use in children's solo pretend play (see Fein & Fryer, 1995; Bornstein & Tamis-LeMonda, 1995). Of course, evidence that caregiver participation is not strongly associated with children's symbolic competence does not mean that caregivers have no significant role in the development of pretend play. Indeed, the development of children's symbolic competence may be supported in multiple social contexts – for example, pretend play with older siblings, and oral narrative and book reading with parents. Hence, one would not necessarily expect that individual variation in caregiver participation in pretend play per se necessarily would relate to individual variation in children's symbolic competence, even within pretend play.

A parallel strategy for investigating caregivers' potential contributions to the development of children's pretend play is to focus on unique characteristics of pretend play. Competent *social* pretend play requires more than the ability to perform increasingly complex symbolic transformations; it requires the ability to communicate appropriately with another about those symbolic transformations. Recent researchers who take a communicative view of pretending (Garvey, 1990; Garvey & Kramer, 1989; Göncü, 1993; Miller & Garvey, 1984) argue that coordinating a pretend performance with another requires that partners mark the nonliteral orientation, negotiate and assign roles, and jointly transform objects, locations, and so forth. Indeed, Garvey and Kramer (1989) present evidence that communication within pretend play is not simply an outcome of ordinary language development but represents a unique, specialized use of language that develops over the preschool period.

In addition, others (e.g., Haight, Masiello, Dickson, Huckeby, & Black, 1994; Haight & Miller, 1992, 1993) have argued that social pretend play requires that players appropriately insert communications about pretend play into ongoing events and interactions, and that the circumstances under which such communications are appropriate may vary. Indeed, Haight et al. (in press) present evidence of cross-cultural variation in the contexts and social functions of spontaneous pretend play in the home. This growing evidence of the conventionalized form of pretend communications, as well as their culturally specific functions in ongoing social interactions, strongly suggests that they are learned through interaction with more experienced players such as caregivers.

In summary, although the study of caregiver–child pretend play traditionally has not been prioritized, increasing evidence indicates that caregivers do participate in their young children's pretend play. Such participation may provide critical support for the emerging pragmatics of children's pretend play – that is, the culturally appropriate coordination of pretend performances with a partner, and the use of pretend play within naturally occurring social contexts.

Studying the Pragmatics of Caregiver–Child Pretend Play in Cultural Context

A number of scholars (e.g., Beizer & Howes, 1992; Farver, 1993; Garvey, 1990; Göncü et al., 1991) are making important contributions to our emerging understanding of the pragmatics of pretend play in various cultural contexts. In this chapter, however, I elaborate upon contributions to this research trend from my own laboratory. My colleagues and I have described adult caregiver–child pretend play in and around the home in middle-class families in three separate longitudinal data sets. The first data set (Haight & Miller, 1992, 1993) includes extensive, longitudinal, naturalistic observations of nine middle-class, European-American children videotaped at home from the ages of 12 to 48 months. The second data set (Haight et al., 1997) includes longitudinal, videotaped observation of 29 middle-class, European-American children playing at home with their parents over the third year of life, and extensive interviews with parents regarding beliefs about children's development, including pretend play. The third longitudinal study (Haight et al., in press; from a larger data set, see Miller, Fung, & Mintz, 1996) involves extensive naturalistic home observations, interviews, and other ethnographic data from middle-class families: nine Chinese, five European-American, and four African-American. In this section, we explore the basic premises and methodological and interpretive strategies of this ongoing research program.

Basic Premises

A basic premise of our research is that individuals develop in relation to their environments, and hence development can be understood only by situating children in their cultural contexts (e.g., see Gaskins, Miller, & Corsaro, 1992). In general, development occurs through the dialectical processes of socialization and acquisition. *Socialization* is the process by which caregivers structure the social environment and display patterned meanings for the child (Haight & Miller, 1993; Miller & Sperry, 1988; Wentworth, 1980). It may be direct, as when caregivers actively contribute ideas and structure children's pretend play, or indirect, as when caregivers provide miniature replicas (e.g., Pocahontas and Meeko dolls, which communicate that pretend play is a sanctioned activity), as well as suggest particular themes. Socialization may be intentional, as when parents choose to enroll their young children in a preschool program emphasizing learning through play, or unintentional, as when children observe their parents engrossed in play.

Socialization is a dynamic process informed by parents' belief systems – that is, their "taken-for-granted ideas" about the nature of children's development, which provide a frame of reference within which to interpret experience and to formulate goals and strategies for socializing children within the constraints of culture (Harkness & Super, 1996; also see Farver, Gaskins, Göncü et al., and Tudge et al., this volume). Parental belief systems result both from cultural resources and from parents' own individual experiences and resources. More specifically, as members of a particular community, parents are presented with "social representations," "cultural models" (Goodnow, 1988), or "folk psychologies" (Bruner, 1990) of play by the media and through face-to-face interactions with others, including "experts" such as teachers and pediatricians (see Harkness & Super, 1996). In addition, every parent has individual interests and resources and unique life experiences, including the patterns of acquisition displayed by his/her own specific children.

Acquisition is the process by which children interpret, respond to, and ultimately embrace, reject, accept, ignore, or elaborate upon the social patterns to which they are exposed (Miller & Sperry, 1988; Wentworth, 1980; also see Guberman, this volume). Acquisition and socialization are dialectical processes. Caregivers alter the content and structure of their socialization messages in response to the various stances toward those messages assumed by their individual children, and children adjust their understanding and behavior in relation to caregivers' socialization. For example, a 3-year-old boy was given a set of large building blocks for Christmas by his parents, who are college professors interested in promoting his cognitive development and in discouraging his aggressive play. He eagerly incorporated the blocks into his play but, to the dismay of his parents, as pretend guns. His parents, who had refused to buy him any toy guns, subsequently reflected upon why their efforts to discourage pretend fighting were unsuccessful. They concluded that some of their son's play fighting was an expression of exuberance and a desire for strength. They subsequently purchased for their son brightly colored plastic squirt guns for water play. Although this young boy maintained his interests in power relations, these interests also were shaped by his parents' passivism. For example, as an 8-year-old, he enthusiastically participates in Aikido, a Japanese form of defensive martial arts.

Methodological Strategies

Consistent with our basic premise that the socialization and acquisition of pretend play can be understood only in relation to the contexts in which they occur, our studies share two key methodological features: microscopic descriptions of spontaneous pretend play, and holistic descriptions of the broader contexts of practices and beliefs in which pretend play is embedded. Our interpretations are grounded within detailed examinations of both the specifics of everyday life and participants' reflections on those events (see Gaskins, Miller, & Corsaro, 1992). Throughout, we prioritize issues of accuracy and consistency – for example, through reliability checks on individual coding categories. We also prioritize issues of cultural validity (see Corsaro, 1985; Harding, 1992) – for example, through the triangulation of data as we relate multiple levels of data from multiple sources (e.g., interviews with parents about their children's play, and direct observations of parents playing with their children).

Microscopic Descriptions of Spontaneous Pretend Play in Context. A hallmark of our research program is its observational approach. Our observations share several key features. First, our observations are *naturalistic*. In all of our studies, we observe pretending under the conditions in which it ordinarily occurs – at home, on the playground, on the way to the grocery store – with family members and friends near at hand. This approach allows us not only to study children's development within environments that are meaningful to them but also to embed pretend play within a range of other activities.

Second, our observations are *sustained*. To provide in-depth coverage of each child's pretending, we obtain lengthy samples of play (2 to 4 continuous hours per observation session) from a relatively small number of children. For example, in my work with Peggy Miller (Haight & Miller, 1992, 1993), we analyzed the mundane contexts from which pretending emerged, who initiated the episodes and how they were sustained, prolonged episodes of pretending in their entirety, and sequences of related episodes.

Third, our observations are *repeated over time*. Our studies entail successive longitudinal samples of behavior. For example, by observing caregiver participation in pretend play with children from 1 to 4 years of age (Haight & Miller, 1992, 1993), we were able to juxtapose stable individual differences with normative patterns of developmental change, to consider the cultural bases of socialization patterns, and to relate variation in socialization patterns to children's development.

Fourth, *rapport building* is an important and ongoing process in our naturalistic observations. To sample relatively natural behavior, and to elicit full responses to interviews, it is extremely important that the families feel comfortable with the observer. In our cross-cultural study of caregiver–child pretend play in Asian and U.S. families (Haight et al., in press), our observers visited informally with family members prior to each observation session or interview. Furthermore, the process of rapport building was facilitated through our use of members of the cultural community under study as observers (i.e., African-American, European-American, and Chinese) who were familiar with the language/dialect of the families and with local customs.

Holistic Descriptions of the Broader Context. We embed our observations of spontaneous pretend play within an ethnographic overview of the social and physical contexts in which children develop constructed from extensive fieldwork within the communities under study. Field notes from diverse contexts and interviews of participants provide a broader context in which to place microscopic observations within families. For example, in our cross-cultural study of pretend play in Asian and U.S. families (Haight et al., in press), we participated in a variety of community activities involving families with young children such as school carnivals. In addition, we conducted in-depth interviews to understand the meaning of events to the participants themselves. Multiple, in-depth interviews with parents allowed us to seek clarification of caregivers' responses and allowed caregivers to reflect and elaborate upon their earlier responses.

Strategies for Interpretation

Our studies have yielded descriptions of intra- and intercultural variation and constancy in caregiver–child pretend play. Understanding the meaning and significance to development of these play practices requires consideration of the broader context of beliefs and practices. For example, to interpret *intracultural constancy* in middle-class, European-American caregivers' supportive participation in their toddlers' pretend play (Haight & Miller, 1992, 1993; Haight et al., 1997), we considered the broader context of ideological, ecological, and development factors. We found that middle-class, European-American caregivers expressed the beliefs that cognitive development is a priority in early childhood, that such development is facilitated through interaction with adults, and that caregiver–child interaction in pretend play, as well as in other contexts such as book reading and construction play, facilitates children's cognitive development (Haight et al., 1997). In addition, we observed young children participate in social pretend play with partners other than caregivers, such as siblings and peers, when they were available, but such opportunities were relatively infrequent in middle-class, European-American urban homes where siblings were not close in age and other children were not easily accessible (Haight & Miller, 1992, 1993). Our data also suggest that caregiver participation in young children's pretend play may be developmentally based in young children's need for substantial scaffolding during their initial forays into social pretend play. Before the age of 3 years, play with peers was not as elaborate or extended as caregiver–child pretend play (Haight & Miller, 1992, 1993).

Interpretive frameworks also must account for diversity within a particular cultural case including any cultural bases for differences (e.g., see Palacios & Moreno, 1996; and Harkness & Super, 1996). *Intracultural variation* may reflect differences in contact with a cultural knowledge base; with culturally facilitated experiences; with individual experiences, characteristics, and preferences (Harkness & Super, 1996); and/or with broader cultural factors such as parental roles (Haight et al., 1997). For example, in our in-depth study of parents' beliefs and behaviors related to pretend play (Haight et al., 1997), we found intracultural variation in the relations between middle-class, European-American parents' beliefs about pretend play and their spontaneous pretend play with their young children. More specifically, we found stronger and different belief-behavior relations for mothers than for fathers. For example, we found that "affective" components of beliefs – that is, the extent to which parents viewed the activity as enjoyable – were related to the frequency of spontaneous father–child pretend play. "Cognitive" and "motivational" components – that is, the extent to which parents viewed pretend play as important to children's development and their own participation as facilitory – were related to the frequency of spontaneous mother–child pretend play.

We interpreted these differences in belief-behavior relations within a broader context of culturally based gender roles for parents (Haight et al., 1997). Particularly with respect to caregiving and interaction in early childhood, maternal roles in European-American, middle-class communities tend to be more culturally mandated while paternal roles are more discretionary (Parke, 1996). We argued that mandated roles may be relatively more affected by controlled (or rational) processing, and discretionary roles by automatic (or experiential) processing (see Epstein, 1994). In our studies, mothers generally took primary responsibility for the care and development of young children. Perhaps, mothers who viewed pretend play as important to their children's development also felt relatively more responsible than fathers to ensure, personally, that their children participated in this developmentally stimulating activity. A more deliberate or controlled approach to play would allow greater use of existing beliefs, as opposed to situational cues and demands (e.g., initiations from the child), as a guide to action. This interpretation is consistent with prior descriptions of fathers as more spontaneous and unpredictable in their play, whereas mothers are more modulated and deliberate in their play (Parke, 1996).

Interpreting *intercultural variation* also requires that specific practices be related to the broader patterns of socialization beliefs and practices in which they are embedded. Cross-cultural variation in caregiver–child pretend play may reflect cultural differences in those competencies into which children are being socialized – for example, success in oral or literate communities. Such variation also may reflect caregivers' diverse adaptations to universal features of child development – for example, support of children's emerging symbolic competencies primarily through dance and ritual rather than pretend play. In particular, there is considerable variability in the ways in which caregivers and young children are involved together in pretend play related to larger cultural systems, and such variation has consequences for children's development (e.g., Farver & Howes, 1993; Göncü et al., 1991; Haight & Miller, 1992, 1993; Haight et al., 1997; Haight et al., in press). Such variation provides an important opportunity to observe the culturally specific social practices through which meanings are created and re-created in relation to development. For example, consistent with a cultural emphasis on ownership, U.S. caregivers provide a large number of specialized objects (miniature replicas such as dolls and trucks) for their children's pretend play, and U.S. children's pretend play revolves around, and may be scaffolded by, such toys. In contrast, consistent with principles of filial piety in which a high value is placed on social harmony, Chinese caregivers provide children with relatively few objects but relatively extensive exposure to explicit models of proper conduct during pretend play, and Chinese children's pretend play may be scaffolded by their growing understanding of social routines (Haight et al., in press).

Similarly, *intercultural constancy* requires consideration of broader patterns of beliefs and practices. Cross-cultural constancy may reflect universal aspects of human development to which parents are responding – for example, the acquisition of communicative competence. On the other hand, cross-cultural constancy also may be culturally based in diverse underlying socialization goals. For example, both African-American and Chinese mothers emphasized impeccable conduct while pretending with their children. However, Chinese mothers viewed impeccable conduct as an index of virtue, whereas African-American mothers viewed impeccable conduct as a survival skill in a sociocultural context perceived to be hostile (Haight et al., 1995).

In summary, a basic premise of our research is that development can be understood only in relation to the contexts in which it occurs. Development results from the dialectical processes of socialization and acquisition – that is, the interactive processes through which adults and children are structuring and responding to the social environment. Accordingly, our strategy for investigating the pragmatics of caregiver–child pretend play includes sustained, naturalistic, longitudinal observations conducted by familiar adults of children's everyday routines in and around their own homes. These "microscopic" observations are embedded within a "holistic" description of the broader context of socialization beliefs and practices developed from observations in a variety of contexts, and from multiple, in-depth interviews with caregivers. Embedding specific socialization practices within a broader context of beliefs and practices provides a basis for the meaningful interpretation of intra- as well as intercultural constancy and variation in caregiver–child pretend play.

An Example: The Pragmatics of Caregiver–Child Pretend Play in U.S. and Chinese Families

In this section, we provide a detailed example of intercultural variation. In particular, we consider broader, culturally specific patterns of beliefs and practices in relation to the ways in which caregivers and children in middle-class Chinese and U.S. families conduct their social pretend play, and we consider the functions of pretend play within their social interactions. In general, pretend play is sanctioned in both middle-class Chinese and U.S. families, where caregivers participate extensively with their young children (Haight et al., in press). There is, however, substantial variation in the ways in which caregiver–child pretend play is socially conducted and functions within interactions. These variations are related to broader patterns of socialization beliefs and practices within which caregiver–child pretend play is embedded.

Middle-class, European-American caregivers in our sample generally endorse a "child-centered" approach to socialization in which they strive to adapt an appropriate environment for their uniquely developing children (e.g., Chow, 1994; Fung, 1994). Relative to Chinese caregivers, they value individuality, independence, and self-expression (e.g., Chow, 1994; Fung, 1994; Greenfield, 1994). In contrast, filial piety is a guiding principle of socialization in Confucian societies. Filial percepts include obeying and honoring one's parents and conducting oneself so as to bring honor rather than disgrace to the family (Ho, 1994). A high value is placed upon social harmony, which is obtained through obeying, respecting, and submitting to elders; adherence to rules; and cooperation (see Chow, 1994; Fung, 1994; Ho, 1994; Pan, 1994).

Confucian principles require not only that children control their impulses and show loyalty and respect to their elders but also that elders responsibly teach or "govern" their children (Chow, 1994). Indeed, Confucian societies place relatively greater emphasis than U.S. society on the power of socialization practices over the child's innate, genetically determined characteristics in accounting for developmental outcomes (Wang, Goldin-Meadow, & Mylander, 1995). For Chinese mothers, teaching their children is a role responsibility, an indicator of parenting success, and a primary expression of maternal love, care, and involvement (e.g., Chow, 1994; Ho, 1994).

Consistent with these beliefs, caregiver–child relations in middle-class Chinese families are more hierarchically determined and didactic than in middle-class European-American families. For example, Chinese caregivers initiate a relatively greater proportion of episodes of interaction with their young children than U.S. caregivers (Fung, 1994; Wang et al., 1995), and relatively fewer caregiver–child interactions are characterized by mutuality (Miller et al., 1996). Furthermore, Chinese caregivers provide children with extensive exposure to explicit models of proper conduct and are heavily didactic relative to U.S. caregivers in interactions with their young children (e.g. Fung, 1994; Miller et al., 1996; Wang et al., 1995).

In general, the social conduct of caregiver–child pretend play in U.S. and Chinese families is related to these more general socialization beliefs and practices in which the play is embedded. Middle-class, U.S. caregiver–child pretend play reflects a "child-centered" approach to socialization through a pattern of mutuality. By the time children are pretending fluently at around age 2, caregiver–child pretend play is initiated approximately equally by caregivers and children (Haight & Miller, 1992, 1993; Haight et al., in press), and both mothers and children are responsive to one another's initiations of pretend play, responding with further pretending. Furthermore, mothers elaborate upon and prompt young children's pretend contributions (Haight & Miller, 1992, 1993). Consistent with filial percepts, caregiver–child pretend play in Chinese families is both initiated and led primarily by caregivers. Children in both Chinese and U.S. families, however, become increasingly active in their initiations of pretend play over the toddler and preschool age range, perhaps reflecting their common gains in communicative competence (Haight et al., in press).

The social functions of caregiver–child pretend play also are related to broader socialization beliefs and practices. We found that both middle-class U.S. and Chinese caregivers initiate pretend play for purposes of socialization, but they do so to achieve diverse socialization goals through culturally appropriate practices. Middle-class, European-American caregivers initiate pretend play in a variety of contexts including negotiating problematic interpersonal interactions. For example, they initiate pretend play while encouraging the child in new or chronically problematic behaviors, such as wearing a bicycle helmet, or while redirecting the child's behavior from dangerous, annoying, or forbidden activities such as tantruming (Haight et al., 1994). In contrast, Chinese caregivers more frequently than U.S. caregivers initiate pretend play with their children in the contexts of teaching proper conduct, especially routine interactions with non-kin adults (Haight et al., in press). For example, a Chinese caregiver initiated pretend play to practice appropriately greeting a guest.

A word of caution is in order here: As Miller et al., (1996) state, it is important not to overstate cross-cultural variation in caregiver–child interactions. The processes of socialization and acquisition are dialectical even in cultures where adult–child relations are relatively hierarchical. Not only do Chinese children accommodate their elders, Chinese mothers accommodate their children's immaturity. In particular, they discuss the importance of "opportunity education" – that is, utilizing everyday activities and ongoing interactions of interest to the children as a context of instruction (Fung, 1994). Opportunity education is contrasted with "lecturing," a practice viewed as ineffective with young children. Chinese caregivers' use of pretend play to practice explicitly proper conduct supports Confucian socialization goals in a manner that is engaging to young children, an example of opportunity education in action.

In summary, understanding the significance of particular socialization practices to children's development requires that they be placed within the broader context of beliefs and practices. We focused on the role of caregivers in children's emerging abilities to use pretend play in ongoing social interactions and to conduct pretend play with a partner. We assumed intercultural constancy in the overall process of acquiring a pragmatics of pretend play. More specifically, the conventionalized nature of communication within social pretend play suggests that children will develop a pragmatics of pretending in interaction with more experienced partners in U.S. and Chinese families. We then explored intercultural diversity in the specific conventions that children acquire in relation to broader patterns of culture-specific socialization beliefs and practices.

Conclusions

Our data support several themes advanced in this book. First, patterns of intercultural variation in social practices coupled with constancy in the development of pretend play suggest that diverse cultural practices may serve similar developmental functions. We found that despite variation in the physical ecology of pretend play, there were no differences in the frequency with which young Chinese and U.S. children pretended. We suggested that the practice of providing special objects for children's pretend play in U.S. families is culturally based and serves a variety of functions, including the scaffolding of young children's early pretend play. Although Chinese families provide their children with fewer toys, shared knowledge of social routines may scaffold their young children's emerging pretend play.

Second, intercultural constancy in caregiver–child pretend play coupled with intercultural variation in more general socialization beliefs and practices suggests that apparently similar cultural practices may serve diverse social functions. Both Chinese and U.S. caregivers initiated pretend play and used some initiations to manage children's behavior. Consistent with filial precepts, however, Chinese caregivers initiated pretend play to rehearse appropriate conduct. Such functions were noticeably absent from the initiations of U.S. caregivers.

Third, our description of the relationship between U.S. mothers' and fathers' beliefs about pretend play and their spontaneous participation in their young children's pretend play illustrates the importance of considering the cultural bases of intracultural variation. In particular, we found more and different relations between parental beliefs about pretend play and their spontaneous play behaviors for mothers than for fathers. We related this intracultural variation to broader patterns of gender roles in parenting – specifically, the relatively mandatory nature of maternal roles and the more discretionary nature of paternal roles (Parke, 1996).

Directions for Future Research

Future, more extended, longitudinal research should consider longer-term developmental outcomes of caregiver–child pretend play. In particular, cultural context is important not only to understanding the development of pretend play but to understanding the development of other culturally valued activities of which pretend play may be a precursor. For example, a number of developmentalists have argued that pretend play is an early childhood precursor to creativity (e.g., Singer & Singer, 1990; Smolucha & Smolucha, 1987). Like more mature forms of creativity, pretend play requires individuals to imagine "what if" – to mentally explore, change, comment upon, exaggerate, elaborate, and poke fun at the "real" world. Like other forms of creativity, pretend play also has a particular structure – for example, communicative conventions for marking the activity as nonliteral and negotiating transformations. Thus, variation in the ways in which caregivers pretend with their young children may have implications for both the immediate development of play and the longer-term development of related activities involving creativity.

To understand the significance of variation in caregiver–child pretend play to the development of creativity, however, culturally appropriate definitions of creativity must be considered. All creating, including artistic, scientific, business, and more mundane pursuits, takes place within sociocultural contexts that vary not only in the products they define as creative but also in the materials and structures provided for the development of new ideas (Baker-Sennett, Matusov, & Rogoff, 1992). In conceptualizing creativity, researchers traditionally have emphasized divergent thinking, individuality, and self-expression. The middle-class, European-American caregivers in our studies, as well as progressive, U.S. early-childhood educators, do seem to excel at enhancing these dimensions of creativity. For example, the practice in some progressive schools of allowing children to use "invented spelling" allows even very young children to participate in creative writing of their own stories. On the other hand, Chinese socialization practices have been criticized as controlling, overly structured, and not facilitory of the development of creativity (Ho, 1994), where ''creativity'' primarily is conceived of as divergent thinking.

Successful participation in creative endeavors, however, also involves knowledge of specific structures and the development of specific skills. Our ethnographic and observational data suggest that Chinese caregivers excel in providing their children with structures for creativity and that Chinese children receive relatively extensive experience in developing skills within these structures. For example, Chinese caregivers tended to initiate and lead pretend play. Chinese caregivers also provided children with extensive exposure to other cultural frameworks for creativity. For example, a common activity for Chinese fathers in our study was reading poems to their young children (Fung, 1994). Through the memorization of many (3,000) Tsang poems, Chinese parents believed not only that the meaning of children's daily lives would be enhanced but also that the children would learn to write poetry (Haight et al., 1995). On the other hand, progressive U.S. educators have been criticized for failing to explicate to children the cultural frameworks necessary for appropriate participation during ''creative'' activities such as sharing time or story narrations (see Tobin, 1995), which may result in decreased motivation. For example, children who have not been taught to hold a pencil, or some simple phonics rules, eventually may become frustrated in writing their stories.

In short, both Chinese and U.S. caregivers apparently support their children's participation in pretend play and other creative activities, but they do so in ways consistent with broader patterns of culturally specific beliefs and related practices. An important question for future research is the extent to which diverse socialization practices within pretend play and other contexts are related to the immediate acquisition of a pragmatics of pretending, and to longer-term outcomes including children's acquisition of other forms of creativity.

References

Baker-Sennett, J., Matusov, E., & Rogoff, B. (1992). Social cultural processes of creative planning in children's playcrafting. In P. Light & G. Butterworth (Eds.), *Content and cognition: Ways of learning and knowing* (pp. 93–114). Hertfordshire, England: Harvester-Wheatsheaf.

Beizer, L., & Howes, C. (1992). Mothers and toddlers: Partners in early symbolic play: Illustrative study # 1. In C. Howes (Ed.), *The collaborative construc-*

tion of pretend play (pp. 25–44). Albany: State University of New York Press.

Bornstein, M., & Tamis-LeMonda, C. (1995). Parent–child play: Three theories in search of an effect. *Development Review, 15,* 382–400.

Bruner, J. (1990). *Acts of meaning.* Cambridge, MA: Harvard University Press.

Chow, R. (1994). Beyond parental control and authoritarian parenting style: Understanding Chinese parenting through the cultural notion of training. *Child Development, 65,* 1111–19.

Corsaro, W. A. (1985). *Friendship and peer culture in the early years.* Norwood, NJ: Ablex

Dunn, J., & Wooding, C. (1977). Play in the home and its implications for learning. In B. Tizard & D. Harvey (Eds.), *Biology of play* (pp. 45–58). London: Heinemann.

Epstein, S. (1994). Integration of the cognitive and psychodynamic unconscious. *American Psychologist, 49,* 709–24.

Farver, J. (1993). Cultural differences in scaffolding pretend play: A comparison of American and Mexican mother–child and sibling–child pairs. In K. Mac-Donald (Ed.), *Parent–child play: Descriptions and implications* (pp. 349–66). Albany: State University of New York Press.

Farver, J., & Howes, C. (1993). Cultural differences in American and Mexican mother–child pretend play. *Merrill-Palmer Quarterly, 39,* 344–58.

Fein, G. (1981). Pretend play: An integrative review. *Child Development, 52,* 1095–1118.

Fein, G., & Fryer, M. (1995). Maternal contributions to early symbolic play competence. *Development Review, 15,* 367–81.

Fiese, B. (1987, April). *Mother–infant interaction and symbolic play in the second year of life: A contextual analysis.* Paper presented at the meeting of the Society for Research in Child Development, Baltimore.

Fung, H. (1994). *The socialization of shame in young Chinese children.* Unpublished doctoral dissertation, University of Chicago.

Garvey, C. (1990). *Play.* Cambridge, MA: Harvard University Press.

Garvey, C., & Kramer, T. (1989). The language of social pretend play. *Developmental Review, 9,* 364–82.

Gaskins, S., Miller, P., & Corsaro, W. (1992). Theoretical and methodological perspectives in the interpretive study of children. In W. Corsaro & P. Miller (Eds.), *Interpretive approaches to children's socialization: New directions in child development* (pp. 5–24). San Francisco: Jossey-Bass.

Göncü, A. (1993). Development of intersubjectivity in social pretend play. *Human Development, 36,* 185–98.

Göncü, A., Mistry, J., & Mosier, C. (1991, April). *Cultural variations in the play of toddlers.* Paper presented at the meeting of the Society for Research in Child Development, Seattle.

Goodnow, J. J. (1988). Parent's ideas, actions, and feelings: Models and method from developmental and social psychology. *Child Development, 59*, 286–320.

Greenfield, P. (1994). Preface. In P. Greenfield & R. Cocking (Eds.), *Cross-cultural roots of minority child development*. Hillsdale, NJ: Erlbaum.

Haight, W., Masiello, T., Dickson, L., Huckeby, E., & Black, J. (1994). The everyday contexts and social functions of spontaneous mother–child pretend play in the home. *Merrill-Palmer Quarterly, 40*, 509–22.

Haight, W., & Miller, P. (1992). The development of everyday pretend play: A longitudinal study of mothers' participation. *Merrill-Palmer Quarterly, 38*, 331–49.

Haight, W., & Miller, P. (1993). *Pretending at home: Development in sociocultural context*. Albany: State University of New York Press.

Haight, W., Parke, R. D., & Black, J. E. (1997). Mothers' and fathers' beliefs about and spontaneous participation in their toddlers' pretend play. *Merrill-Palmer Quarterly, 43*, 271–90.

Haight, W., Wang, X., Fung, H., Williams, K., & Mintz, J. (1995, April). The ecology of everyday pretending in three cultural communities. Paper presented at the meeting of Society for Research in Child Development, Indianapolis, IN.

Haight, W., Wang, X., Fung, H., Williams, K., & Mintz, J. (in press). Universal, developmental, and variable aspects of children's play: A cross-cultural comparison of pretending at home, *Child Development*.

Harding, S. (1992). After the neutrality ideal: Science, politics and "strong objectivity." *Social Research, 59*, 567–87.

Harkness, S., & Super, C. (1996). Introduction. In S. Harkness & C. Super (Eds.), *Parents' cultural belief systems: Their origins, expressions, and consequences* (pp. 1–26). New York: Guilford.

Ho, D. (1994). Cognitive socialization in Confucian heritage cultures. In P. Greenfield & R. Cocking (Eds.), *Cross-cultural roots of minority child development* (pp. 285–314). Hillsdale, NJ: Erlbaum.

Miller, P., Fung, H., & Mintz, J. (1996). Self construction through narrative practices: A Chinese and American comparison. *Ethos, 24*, 1–44.

Miller, P., & Garvey, C. (1984). Mother–baby role play: Its origins in social support. In I. Bretherton (Ed.), *Symbolic play: The development of social understanding* (pp. 101–30). Orlando, FL: Academic Press.

Miller, P., & Sperry, L. (1988). Early talk about the past. The origins of conversational stories of personal experience. *Journal of Child Language, 15*, 293–315.

O'Connell, B., & Bretherton, I. (1984). Toddlers' play alone and with mother: The role of maternal guidance. In I. Bretherton (Ed.), *Symbolic play: The development of social understanding* (pp. 337–68). Orlando, FL: Academic Press.

Palacios, J., & Moreno, M. (1996). Parents' and adolescents' ideas on children: Origins and transmission of intracultural diversity. In S. Harkness & C. Super (Eds.), *Parents' cultural belief systems: Their origins, expressions, and consequences* (pp. 215–53). New York: Guilford.

Pan, H. W. (1994). Children's play in Taiwan. In J. Roopnarine, J. Johnson, & F. Hooper (Eds.), *Children's play in diverse cultures* (pp. 31–50). Albany: State University of New York Press.

Parke, R. (1996). *Fatherhood.* Cambridge, MA: Harvard University Press.

Piaget, J. (1962). *Play, dreams and imitation in childhood.* New York: Norton.

Quinn, N., & Holland, D. (1987). Culture and cognition. In D. Holland & N. Quinn (Eds.), *Cultural models in language and thought* (pp. 3–40). New York: Cambridge University Press.

Singer, D., & Singer, J. (1990). *The house of make-believe.* Cambridge, MA: Harvard University Press.

Slade, A. (1987). A longitudinal study of maternal involvement and symbolic play during the toddler period. *Child Development, 58,* 367–75.

Smolucha, L., & Smolucha, F. (1987). Vygotsky's theory of creative imagination. *Siegen Periodical of International Empirical Literature, 5,* 299–308.

Tobin, J. (1995). The irony of self-expression. *American Journal of Education, 103,* 233–58.

Wang, X., Goldin-Meadow, S., & Mylander, C. (1995, March). *A comparative study of Chinese and U.S. mothers interacting with their deaf and hearing children.* Paper presented at the meeting of the Society for Research in Child Development, Indianapolis.

Wentworth, W. M. (1980). *Context and understanding: An inquiry into socialization theory.* New York: Elsevier.

6   Children's Play as Cultural Activity

*Artin Göncü, Ute Tuermer, Jyoti Jain, and
Danielle Johnson*

Research on children's play has shed light on many psychological dimensions of children's play. (For reviews, see Fein, 1981; Rubin, Fein, & Vandenberg, 1983.) However, previous research also raised challenging questions for subsequent work. One of these questions is how to account for cultural variations in children's play. In this chapter, we discuss how cultural differences in children's play emerged as an important area of inquiry and how we developed our program of research to address this question.

The chapter is organized into four sections: We first provide a brief summary of how children's play is conceptualized in dominant development theories to illustrate that these theories do not adequately address cultural differences in children's play. Second, we propose A. N. Leont'ev's activity theory as an appropriate framework to guide cultural studies of children's play. Third, we present five principles that we constructed as an extension of Leont'ev's theory to guide our work on children's play as a cultural activity. We argue that understanding children's play requires:

1. understanding how the economical structure of children's communities determines the availability of play as one type of activity;
2. identification of the beliefs of children's communities about the value of play;
3. analysis of how the community values about play are conveyed to children;

Play studies reported in this chapter were supported by the Spencer Foundation. We are grateful to Eugene Matusov and Joe Becker for their comments on an earlier version of this chapter. Portions of this work were presented at the meetings of the Society for Research in Child Development (1991; 1995) and the American Educational Research Association (1992).

4. examination of how children represent their worlds in play; and
5. adoption of an interdisciplinary methodology involving multiple data-gathering and analysis techniques.

In the fourth section of the chapter, we give examples from our program of research as illustrations of our effort to describe children's play as a cultural activity. We end with recommendations for future research.

Conceptualization of Children's Play in Western Developmental Theories

The efforts to understand children's play have been guided by two assumptions of dominant developmental theories that are based on the play of middle-class children in the Western world.[1] These assumptions are that play is a universal activity and that play promotes development. In the following paragraphs, we trace the history of how previous research used these assumptions uncritically and in support of one another, leading to unfounded judgments about the play of children who are not Western or middle class. We conclude this section with a summary of efforts (e.g., McLoyd, 1982; Schwartzman, 1978) that criticized such research and tried to guard against cultural misinterpretations in psychological research.

With regard to the assumption that play is a universal activity, two points are worth noting: First, a conviction shared by most prominent developmental theories (e.g., Parten, 1932; Piaget, 1945; Vygotsky, 1978) is that the origins, frequency, and development of children's play follow more or less the same patterns in different parts of the world (Gaskins & Göncü, 1988). For example, most theorists appear to believe that all children in the world engage in pretend play. Second, the specific characterizations of play proffered in these theories are assumed to apply to all children. For example, Piaget, Parten, and Vygotsky each noted that social pretend play emerges around 3 years of age as a result of explicit play negotiations in which children engage (Göncü, 1993).

With regard to the second assumption, developmental theorists believed that play is an activity that is necessary for the optimal development of children. Furthermore, developmental theorists emphasized that children's play is valuable only in the service of understanding the development of the psychological phenomena that it promotes rather than that

---

[1] Unless otherwise stated, our discussion is limited to pretend play.

play is a valuable activity of childhood which is worthy of study in its own right. Some theorists referred to children's play only in their discussions about the representation of experiences with affective significance. For example, Freud (1961) referred to play as a repetition compulsion, a therapeutic activity in which children relive painful past experiences at their own will in order to work through the feelings caused by the experiences. In a similar vein, Piaget (1962) conceptualized children's play as an extreme pole of assimilation where children re-create the emotionally significant experiences in their effort to test their mastery over them.

Another group of theorists focused on play as part of their discussions of the development of communication and cognition. For example, Bateson (1955) focused on play as part of his theory of metacommunication. For Bateson, play is one of several important activities that require metacommunication (i.e., exchanging messages which indicate that actions and utterances should be interpreted at a representational level rather than at face value [Garvey, 1990; Göncü & Kessel, 1984, 1988]). In turn, metacommunication about play enables children to distinguish play communication as one class of events from nonplay communication as another, leading children to grasp the notion of category.

Finally, Vygotsky (1978) was the most notable of theorists who emphasized the developmental significance of children's play by referring to it as the "leading activity." Vygotsky made two related points in advancing his theory. First, Vygotsky referred to pretend play as the zone of proximal development in which the imagined situation enables children to function beyond their existing level of competence (Gaskins & Göncü, 1988, 1992). Second, Vygotsky emphasized play as a mechanism necessary in the acquisition of language. He claimed that the ability to represent an experience (e.g., riding a horse) through a symbolic means (e.g., riding a stick) enables children to grasp the notion that words can be used to represent the meaning of experience (Göncü & Becker, 1992).

The common and explicit focus of these developmental theories that play promotes development received implicit support from the first assumption that play is universal in guiding researchers to focus on the developmental functions of children's play rather than on play itself. Once it was assumed that play is universal, the research focus on the "serious" consequences of play could be justified more easily than a focus on play itself, which perhaps was considered a frivolous activity (cf. Göncü, Mistry, & Mosier, 1991; Sutton-Smith, 1983). As a result, research of the last two decades examined almost exclusively the role of play in children's development.

Such research efforts can be classified into two categories. The first category includes work that examined the correlates and developmental consequences of play. These efforts sought to establish relationships between play and other areas of development such as language, perspective taking, and problem solving, arguing that similar abilities were involved in play and in these activities (for reviews, see Fein, 1981; Rubin et al., 1983). In addition, some scholars stated that play is an appropriate therapeutic medium (e.g., Winnicott, 1971), and others argued that play is an educationally valuable activity for young children (e.g., DeVries & Kohlberg, 1987).

The second category of efforts used play as a means of intervention for those children whose play appeared not to fit the developmental norms established by the dominant developmental theories. Given the assumption that play is a universal activity with a specific description, any difference between the theoretical claims and the observations were interpreted as an idiosyncrasy, if not a deficit, of the play group under question. Often low-income children from the U.S. and non-Western children were identified as those who needed play intervention (also see Farver, Gaskins, Haight, this volume).

Different reactions to the intervention research brought culture and social class to the attention of play researchers, whose roles in children's development have not been adequately addressed in the dominant theories. One reaction came from McLoyd (1982) and another from Schwartzman (1978), both of whom appeared to remain loyal to the two assumptions of these play theories but took issue with the methodology of intervention research. Primarily, McLoyd focused on research on social class differences addressed in psychological research, and Schwartzman focused on cultural differences addressed in anthropological research. Both scholars reached similar conclusions, claiming that the reported or assumed social class and cultural differences were due to the methodological problems rather than reflecting the realities of children's play. For example, Schwartzman stated and McLoyd concurred that the lesser frequency of sociodramatic play of low-income, ethnic, and linguistic minority children in a strange environment such as a mobile research laboratory may be due to the fear of a strange environment rather than the lack of ability.

We regard the contributions of McLoyd and Schwartzman as critical to the advancement of play research. However, we believe that even if the previous work had not had any methodological problems, it still would not have provided an accurate characterization of the play of children who come from low-income or non-Western communities. Focusing on methodological considerations alone presumes that the norms established by Western theorists (e.g., Piaget, 1945) based on the play of middle-income children provide absolute universal criteria against which the play of children from diverse cultures should be judged (Gaskins & Göncü, 1992). Instead, as we argue in this chapter, the development of play characterized in Western theories is only one of many possible cultural models of children's play. Social class and cultural differences may be due to varying cultural norms of development rather than children's deficit. Thus, an adequate examination of children's play in a given community can be accomplished only by taking into account the unique cultural milieu in which play is embedded (see also Goldman, 1998).

In summary, during the last two decades, the developmental theorists' priority has become the researchers' value that understanding play's developmental functions is more important than understanding play itself. This value justified instituting intervention programs for children whose play did not fit the commonly accepted characterizations of Western theories. However, such efforts may not have enriched the play of low-income or non-Western children. Rather, intervention efforts simply may have taught these children to play just like their middle-income or Western counterparts. The value of this effort is an important one to address, but it is beyond the scope of our chapter. For us, the immediate issue is that interventions prohibited the emergence of efforts to understand the play of children in low-income or non-Western communities, which may not be deficient but may simply be different from the play described in the dominant literature. In the following section, we make an effort to remedy this situation by directing our attention to the work of Leont'ev.

A Theory of Children's Play as a Cultural Activity: A. N. Leont'ev's Activity Theory

Our search to account for cultural variations in children's play led us to the theory of Leont'ev for three major reasons: First, Leont'ev (1981a, b) conceptualized human development as becoming conscious of skills as a result of participation in and appropriation from activities by using the tools of their culture, thus making culture an integral part of children's development. Leont'ev claimed that a culture's economical structure determines the availability of activities for its members. As a function of varying economical structure and labor relations from one culture to another, the activities available to individuals vary also. Consistently, Leont'ev stated that his theory reflects the conditions of the Soviet Union at the time it was developed, and it should be taken as such. Therefore, looking for the same activity in different cultures of varying labor relations may prove meaningless. Instead, an adequate comparison of children from different cultures should involve first an examination of children's development on the basis of what is required from them within their own culture, and then a comparison of this with the requirements for children from other cultures.

Second, Leont'ev claimed that depending on the unique requirements of each activity, the skills and the ways in which they are appropriated may vary from one activity to another. For example, schooling and pretend play may contribute to children's development in different ways due to unique requirements of each activity within the same culture. Alternatively, and as an extension of Leont'ev, we suggest that the same activity may serve different developmental functions across cultures (also see Haight, this volume). Thus, acknowledging variability both in the availability and in the development function of activities directs us to gain an understanding of why an activity is present (or absent) in different cultures, as well as why and how the developmental function of activities may vary across cultures.

Third, Leont'ev proposed a theory of children's play that focuses not only on the contribution of play to children's development but also on what children do in play, encouraging research efforts to understand this activity. We return to Leont'ev's ideas on children's play after we lay out his notions of appropriation, activity, and the development of consciousness (also see Cole, 1997; Engeström, 1987; Martin, Nelson, & Tobach, 1995; Wells; 1993; Wertsch, 1981.)

Appropriation, Activity, and Consciousness

In elaborating his notion of appropriation, Leont'ev drew from Vygotsky's central thesis of development as a process of internalization of skills that first exist on the interpsychological plane before they exist on the intrapsychological plane (i.e., they become the individual's own). Leont'ev (1981a) defined appropriation as a "process that has as its end result the individual's *reproduction* of historically formed human properties, capacities, and modes of behaviour" (p. 422). For Leont'ev, this is possible only as a result of participation in social activity and becoming conscious of skills involved in accomplishing it.

An activity is a unit of life that is historically determined and social in origin. An individual engages in an activity to satisfy a need such as grocery shopping for food. Leont'ev (1981a) stated that "by activities we mean processes that are psychologically characterised by what the process as a whole is directed to (its object) always coinciding with the objective that stimulates the subject to this activity, i.e., the motive" (pp. 399–400) For Leont'ev, then, each activity has an existence of its own, involving a subject, an object, and a motive. Variations across activities in any of these components lead to variations in the appropriation of skills specific to each activity.

Leont'ev proffered a three-level system to explain the development of consciousness. *Activity* and its *motive* exist at the most global level. An activity such as grocery shopping is driven by its motive, such as the need for food. Therefore, before she engages in it, a shopper is aware of what she needs but is not fully conscious of what activity will involve.

This fuller consciousness occurs at a second level involving *actions* and *goals*. By participating in what Leont'ev called "practical activity through the use of cultural tools," a person develops consciousness or awareness of actions. Only at this stage is the shopper conscious of her actions, which are goal-directed (e.g., going to the produce section to pick up vegetables). Furthermore, it is at this stage that the shopper uses the tools of the culture, such as language, in the service of accomplishing her goals (e.g., asking for directions to the produce department). As a result of participation in an activity such as shopping, an individual appropriates aspects of the historically formed system of meanings about trade relations that have relevance to her experience.

The third level is parallel to goals and actions. This level involves *conditions* and *operations*. Operations are automated actions that no longer require conscious attention. For example, after the shopper becomes familiar with the store, turning the cart at the end of an aisle to move it into another one becomes automated. Conditions refer to the specific features of the environment, such as length of the aisles in which the operations are carried out.[2]

In summary, Leont'ev conceptualized development of the individual

---

[2] It is worth noting that depending on the purpose and the degree of consciousness associated with it, the same unit of life can be classified under either activity, action, or operation.

as actively participating in social activity. Participation enables the individual to learn how to use the tools of the culture, which is necessary to accomplish an activity as well as to appropriate the skills necessary to function in the society.

Play as Activity

Following Vygotsky, Leont'ev considered some activities as "leading types of activities." These activities lead individuals to appropriate skills that are necessary to accomplish an activity, and they also give birth to other activities. Leont'ev stated that the leading activity during infancy is mastery of the object environment, imaginative play during preschool years, schoolwork during middle childhood, and economical work during adolescence and adulthood. Imaginative play is a leading activity because it allows children to appropriate from a given imagined situation in question as well as enabling children to rehearse adult roles in which they must engage in the future.

Leont'ev's explanation of why children play is similar to that of Vygotsky, who believed that children engage in play in order to realize tendencies that they normally cannot in real life. For Leont'ev (1981a) a preschool-age child engages in play as a result of his or her desire to act like an adult. For example, pretending to ride a stick as if it were a horse is the result of a child's desire to be like an adult (p. 373).

Leont'ev (1981a) claimed that the only activity in which such a desire can find its reality is play, because play is not an economical activity. The motive for play is not in its objective result of actually riding a horse. The motive is in the practice of adult roles, such as riding a horse, enabled by the play action (p. 368). Leont'ev called this relationship between a goal for play action and a unit of consciousness that is associated with it *personality sense*.

Leont'ev maintained that actions and operations in play correspond to the adult actions and operations that the child desires to acquire. When a child rides a stick as if it were a horse, the act of riding the stick corresponds to riding a horse. What the child does in play is the *real* action for the child. The goal for play is not arbitrary or imaginary.

According to Leont'ev, imagination in play arises as a result of the discrepancy between the child's real desire to be like an adult and the conditions under which such a desire is accomplished. To emphasize this point, he stated that "it is not imagination that determines the play action but conditions of the play action that make imagination necessary and give rise to it" (p. 374). Leont'ev introduced *meaning sense* and *play sense* to explain the emergence of imagination in play. Meaning sense refers to the unit of consciousness that is associated with certain operations, such as the possible uses of a stick. Play sense, on the other hand, refers to how such uses gain idiosyncratic meaning for the child in the service of understanding adult roles. For example, play sense emerges when running with a stick between the legs becomes riding a horse.

Leont'ev (1981a) stated that play contributes to the development of imagination, personality, and abstract thinking during preschool years. Like Vygotsky, he emphasized imaginative play as an activity of instruction. He stated that "the child begins to learn by playing" (p. 396). The child creates a world of instruction by realizing actions (i.e., specific play roles) through different operations (i.e., actual play acts), creating and resolving problem situations all by herself.

Principles of a Cultural Approach to the Study of Children's Play

Following the theory of Leont'ev, we proffer five principles that guide our work on cultural variations in children's play.

1. The economical structure of children's communities determines the availability of play as one type of activity. Following Leont'ev's thesis that activities in a culture are determined by its economical structure, we state that children's activities vary from one community to another depending on how children's communities are structured. The emerging descriptive data support this premise by indicating that the school and home life of an urban middle-income child involves an abundance of play opportunities. In these communities, parents make provisions for children's play (see Haight, this volume; Haight & Miller, 1993) and engage in play with their children (Dunn & Dale, 1984; Farver, Kim, & Lee, 1995; Haight & Miller, 1993). In contrast, in small villages with subsistence economy, parent–child play is rare (Farver & Howes, 1993; Gaskins, 1990; Rogoff, Mistry, Göncü, & Mosier, 1993). Possibly, adults do not have the time to play with children due to demanding work life in small villages. Also, young children contribute to the economical welfare of their families in communities relying on subsistence economy and do not have time to play (Gaskins, 1990, and this volume). In light of these findings, we argue that a fuller understanding of children's play requires a closer study of the economic structure of children's communities than has been done in developmental psychological research to date.

2. Understanding children's play requires identification of the beliefs of children's communities about the value of play. As other scholars have noted (e.g., Goodnow, in press; Harkness & Super, 1996), values about children's activities vary across communities, influencing the type of opportunities provided for children's development. As an extension of this literature, we offer that values about play may vary across different communities. To follow the previous example, it is plausible that in middle-class communities where parents have formal education and are familiar with scholarly literature indicating the developmental benefits of play, parents value adult–child play and create opportunities for it (also see Haight, this volume). However, in low-income urban communities and in small villages with subsistence economy, parents may not value play because they need children's help in maintenance and work activities. It is also possible that parents may value play but cannot engage in it due to their time and work constraints. As we illustrate in the following pages, in some village communities, parents value play but delegate it to children (also see Gaskins, this volume).

3. Understanding children's play requires analysis of how community values about play are conveyed to children. In order to find out how children learn whether play is acceptable or what type of play is acceptable, we must examine how adults, siblings, and peers in a community establish intersubjectivity or shared understanding with children (Göncü, 1993; Matusov, 1996; Sawyer, 1997). (For further discussion, see Goodnow, in press.) In principle, values can be communicated to children in two ways. One possible way is to inform children explicitly whether or not play is a desirable activity. This can occur by simply engaging (or not engaging) in the activity with them or informing them of the value (e.g., telling children that they can play after they do their homework).

A second way of communicating the value about play is tacit and implicit. This can be accomplished through "curriculum design" by making only certain activities and tools of the culture available. For example, adults may value play, but they may communicate this value to their children by providing toys, space, and time instead of engaging in play with them. Examples of this can be seen in preschools (cf. Fitzgerald & Göncü, 1993; Göncü & Weber, 1992).

4. Understanding children's play requires an examination of how children represent their worlds in play. Following Leont'ev and others (e.g., Bretherton, 1984; Fein, 1981; Garvey, 1990; Göncü, 1987, 1993; Piaget, 1962; Slaughter & Dombrowski, 1989; Sutton-Smith, 1983; Vygotsky, 1978), we propose that the study of children's play include an examination of the kinds of adult roles adopted by children, the type of events represented in children's play, and the ways in which the physical environment is used in the service of children's play desires, as well as the communicative context in which play desires are developed.

Such an approach to children's play would enable us to understand the development of personal sense (i.e., children's understanding of adult roles and possibly why certain roles gain signifiance in children's lives). Examination of how adult roles are represented will indicate ways in which children transform the meaning of the immediate environment in the service of such representation. Most importantly, it will reveal valuable information about the development of creativity by its focus on how children can express play actions through different operations (also see Haight, this volume).

5. Understanding children's play requires adoption of an interdisciplinary methodology involving multiple data-gathering and analysis techniques. Following our belief that children's play develops as an extension of community structure, adult values, and communication between children and other members of their community, as well as what children imaginatively practice, we argue that an adequate study of children's play requires an interdisciplinary approach. This not only means studying children's play in view of its economical, cultural, educational, and psychological contexts; it also calls for expanding the common methods of data gathering and interpretation in developmental psychology. For example, understanding economic structure and labor relations will require historical and archival analysis, whereas understanding the representation of adult life in play will require narrative methods, both of which are uncommon in developmental psychology.

In summary, examining children's play in view of these five principles will enable us to understand the specific occurrance of this activity in a given community. In turn, this understanding will prevent researchers from making unfounded judgments about the play of children from other communities. However, if we need to make one, our judgment will be informed by our understanding of a culture developed on the basis of these principles.

Studies of Children's Play as Cultural Activity

In this section, we outline the progression of our program of research. We first report two studies which focused on the play of toddlers and then report a third study on the play of preschool-age children.

Cultural Variations in Toddlers' Play

In keeping with the first principle, the first study that brought the significance of community structure in children's play and led us to a search for a theory that integrated culture and activity was conducted with toddlers. In collaboration with Jayanthi Mistry and Christine Mosier (Göncü et al., 1991), we examined whether or not the occurrence and frequency of social play and the nature of play partners of toddlers varied as a function of children's communities. We also looked at whether or not there were differences across the communities in the kinds and themes of children's play.

Data analyzed to address these questions were collected for a study of how toddlers and their caregivers from four communities collaborate in shared activities (Rogoff et al., 1993). Caregivers and their 1- to 2-year-old toddlers from four communities participated in the study – an urban middle- to upper-income community in the United States (Salt Lake City), an urban middle-income community in Turkey (Kecioren), a Mayan peasant community in Guatemala (San Pedro), and a tribal peasant community in India (Dhol-Ki-Patti). With each family, we conducted a child-rearing interview in which we asked caregivers to engage in play and games, dressing, feeding, and exploring novel objects with their toddlers. (For a detailed discussion of the communities, access to the communities, and the interview procedures, see Rogoff et al., 1993).

Our first question – that there would be community differences in children's play partners – was motivated by parental reports during our interviews, which became the bases of our expectations. In keeping with the second and third principles, we asked caregivers who the toddlers' play partners were. Based on their answers, we expected that there would indeed be community differences in children's play partners. Caregivers in San Pedro reported that they did not play with children; rather, they delegated such roles to other children. Also, caregivers in Dhol-Ki-Patti did not see the interview context as conducive to adult–child play, possibly due to perceiving the researchers as having higher status and acting with reservation before them. Furthermore, the Dhol-Ki-Patti caregivers may have interpreted the exploration of novel objects as playing with toys, an activity typically delegated to toddlers while adults take care of chores.

However, parents in Kecioren and Salt Lake City reported providing toys for and playing with their children, and they did not see the interview context as inappropriate for this activity. In fact, parents from Kecioren and Salt Lake City engaged in discourse with their toddlers as playmates more than the San Pedro and Dhol-Ki-Patti caregivers during the exploration of novel objects (cf. Rogoff et al., 1993), conveying to their children that they valued adult–child play. With this information, we expected that there would be more instances of adult–child play during the interview in Kecioren and Salt Lake City than in San Pedro and Dhol-Ki-Patti. We also expected that San Pedro and Dhol-Ki-Patti children would serve as play partners for the toddlers more often than in Kecioren and Salt Lake City, where adults would serve this role to a greater extent.

We found that all of the children from Salt Lake City, Kecioren, and Dhol-Ki-Patti, and most of the children in San Pedro engaged in social play. Community variations occurred in the partners and frequency of social play. Children in Salt Lake City and Kecioren engaged in social play with significantly more frequency than children in Dhol-Ki-Patti and San Pedro. Children's partners in Salt Lake City and Kecioren were adults significantly more frequently than in Dhol-Ki-Patti and San Pedro. However, Dhol-Ki-Patti and San Pedro children engaged in play with child partners with significantly greater frequency than those in Salt Lake City and Kecioren.

In keeping with the fourth principle, our second goal was to examine the kinds of play and themes that were likely to occur during our interviews. Based on our experience about the kinds of play activities that were present in the communities included in the study, as well as definitions provided in the existing play literature, we included object play (i.e., using an object or a toy to have fun), language play (i.e., having fun with words and sounds), physical play (i.e., having fun in terms of sensory and motor actions), pretend play (i.e., using an idea or an object to represent the meaning of something else with the purpose of having fun), and games (i.e., routinized activity of having fun, in which actions of the partners are coordinated by rules).

Our findings indicated that larger numbers of toddlers in Salt Lake City and Kecioren engaged in pretend and language play as well as games while exploring novel objects than in Dhol-Ki-Patti and San Pedro. In addition, there were community differences in the themes of these kinds of play. Some of the differences were in the play themes commonly found in the Western world. For example, the kind of pretend play that occurred only in Salt Lake City and Kecioren involved adopting pretend roles, where parents entered into play as actors with their children. This was most apparent in the roles of Salt Lake City parents, who pretended to be wild animals and monsters. Also, participants in Salt Lake City and Kecioren engaged in making up words, mimicking children's vocalizations, and labeling games more often than their counterparts in Dhol-Ki-Patti and San Pedro.

However, we also found that caregivers in the non-Western communities (i.e., Kecioren and Dhol-Ki-Patti) engaged in play themes that have not been the focus of research on the play of Western middle-income children. One of these play themes was fun-filled teasing of children (e.g., pretending that an animal such as a millipede is "coming to get" the child), which was observed only in the play of low-income Western children (e.g., Miller, 1986).

In a second study, Göncü and Jain (in progress) are examining how pretend play occurs in mother–toddler interaction in Kecioren. This study was designed to address two questions. First, the decision to focus on pretend play with this middle-class Middle-Eastern community was based on the fact that we do not have extensive knowledge of mother–child play in a non-Western community, although detailed descriptions of mother–child pretend play in Western communities exist (e.g., Dunn & Dale, 1984). Because the Kecioren mothers reported that they provided toys for children's play and that they engaged in play with their children, and because we found that pretend play occurred during the interviews, we decided to investigate further the nature of such play. Second, we questioned whether or how pretend play occurs in different activities such as dressing, feeding, and exploration. What are the relative contributions of mothers and their children to the construction of pretend-play episodes, and what themes of day-to-day living do mother–toddler dyads represent in their pretend play?

Our preliminary findings indicate that pretend play occurs across a wide spectrum of activities. However, consistent with our reading of Leont'ev, pretend activities can be used for different purposes depending on the context. Similar to their middle-class Western counterparts, Kecioren mothers engaged in pretend play with their children with the sole purpose of having joint fun, as in doll play, which occurred in the context of exploring the toy. Also, Kecioren mothers used pretend play as a means of getting chores accomplished, as in pretending that a plane (i.e., a spoon full of food) is arriving at a hangar (i.e., the child's mouth).

Our analyses of pretend-play communications indicate that both mothers and children contribute to the construction of their pretend play. For example, mothers and children alike initiate pretend play. Just like their Western counterparts, the Kecioren mothers supported children's pretend activities in terms of providing suggestions, but they also engaged in play as co-actors, adopting a host of roles, such as having a toast by lifting a glass of tea in the air as if it were a glass *raki* and saying "cheers" in response to the son's initiation. Finally, in support of Göncü and Becker (1992), our analyses reveal that "pretend-world activities" (e.g., having a toast) derive from "real-world activities" (e.g., a family dinner). In addition, they indicate that pretend-world activities are put back into the context of real-world activities such as feeding the toddler in accomplishing the real-world activities.

In summary, our work focusing on the play of toddlers supports our Leont'ev-inspired thesis that children's play varies from one community to another depending on how children's communities are structured, how play is defined, and the kind of significance attributed to children's play in their communities. Furthermore, through our analyses of play communications, themes, and roles, as well as the activity context in which play occurs, we are beginning to understand how children's play sense develops (cf. Leont'ev, 1981a). Observation of variations across communities in these aspects of play is enabling us to understand differences in meanings that children appropriate in their communities (e.g., expression of humor through teasing vs. animation of exaggerated animal gestures). Finally, examination of the way in which play meanings are expressed is revealing important information about how children's motives find their reality in play actions and operations (e.g., pretending to be an adult through having a toast).

Cultural Variations in the Play of "Preschool-Age Children"

Carried out by the authors of the present chapter, the goal of this study is to describe the play of 4- to 6-year-old children from three different low-income communities – two U.S, one African-American and one European-American, and the third from a peasant community in Turkey, a part of the world that has not been the focus of much cross-cultural research (LeVine, 1980). Our specific purpose in summarizing this ongoing study is to illustrate that adequate descriptions of children's play require a methodology that is interdisciplinary in nature and should involve a multiplicity of data-gathering and analysis techniques in children's natural environments.

With respect to understanding and describing the structure of the communities in which we worked, we relied on demographic information from census data, information we gathered from community representatives, and information we obtained from participating families. The African-American children came from an economically impoverished urban community in Chicago, where only half of the adults over the age of 25 have a high-school or higher degree. The European-American children came from an almost exclusively European-American semirural community outside of Chicago, with the participants in our study being the poorest families in this community. The educational level of the parents ranged from eighth grade to college degrees. The peasant Turkish sample was drawn from a small village community in western Turkey, where most parents had some elementary-school education.

We chose to work with these three particular communities due to our ongoing collaboration with them and through connections with community leaders. Our access to the African-American community was possible because of our decade-long collaboration with a community organizer and children's teacher whose work with Göncü varied from mentoring student teachers in the Early Childhood Program (ECP) at the University of Illinois to co-authoring papers (e.g., Göncü & Cannella, 1996). Our access to the European-American community was possible as a result of one of the ECP graduate's involvement in the Head Start program in Chicago. Finally, we had access to the Turkish village due to our connections with the local community leaders/activists such as the village mayor.

In keeping with the second and third principles that understanding children's play requires understanding the significance attributed to children's play and how adults communicate their values to children, we conducted interviews with adults who played significant roles in children's development and education. In all communities we interviewed the caregivers of children. In addition, we interviewed the teachers of children in the U.S. communities, for the African-American children were attending a State pre-kindergarten program and the European-American children were attending a Head Start program. No preschool education was available for the Turkish children.

Our questions inquired about what kinds of activities were available to children, whether or not the parents and teachers valued children's play, to what extent play was available to children, who children's play partners were, where children played, what types of objects children used when they played, and whether or not children had toys. In addition, we made an effort to infer how adults communicated their notions about play to children by observing their interactions with children.

In keeping with the fourth principle that understanding children's play requires examination of how children represent their worlds in play, we videotaped children as they engaged in play in their natural environments. We followed caregivers' and teachers' reports in deciding where to video-tape children at play. This meant videotaping U.S. children in school during their free-activity period and in the community either at home or on a playground. The Turkish children were videotaped as they engaged in free play in the village.

Afterward, we transcribed children's videotapes in a narrative fashion, describing children's play events in the sequence in which they occurred. The transcripts included the description of verbal and nonverbal behaviors of all the target children as well as the behavior of adults and other children who happened to be either playing with or in the vicinity of the target children. In addition, we noted the affective tone of the players. We transcribed the videotapes in such a way that the finished product looked like a screenplay to a reader who would be able to enact the scene by reading the transcriptions.

We are in the beginning stages of our data analyses where we are identifying the *instances* of responses to our interview questions about children's play and *instances* of children's play in view of our five principles (e.g., Göncü, Tuermer, Jain, & Johnson, 1995). With respect to the first principle, we are finding that community structure directly influences children's play and that such influence is evident in many aspects of children's play. For example, community play of the African-American children is highly supervised due to violence involved in this inner-city community, some Turkish parents do not play with their children due to time constraints, and play interaction with peers is scarce for some of the European-American children because homes are farther apart in this semi-rural community.

With regard to the second principle on adult values, parents often expressed positive feelings about children's play across the three communities. For example, one European-American parent reported, ''I think it's one of the most important things kids can have growing up, because once you get to be an adult, you don't get it anymore.'' One African-American parent reported, ''He's a child, that's why he's 'posed to be playin'.'' Similarly, one Turkish grandmother reported that "playing with mud is good; children learn how to cultivate the earth that way."

With respect to the third principle on constructing intersubjectivity with children about the significance of play, adults convey their values to children in several ways. To date, our analyses of parent–child communication reveals two ways in which such communication occurs. Some of the parents convey their approval of children's play by encouraging children to engage in play. For example, one Turkish father told the children, "Come on, tidy up your house now," referring to the pretend house of his two daughters. One of the girls began to organize the objects under a stairwell leading to their house, while her younger sister observed her. The father then invited the younger daughter by saying, "Go ahead, you play house, too."

Sometimes adults convey their values about play by actively engaging in play with their children when their schedules allow it. Following is an example of an African-American child and her mother's pretend play taking place on a playground with no toys whatsoever.

Mother: ". . . pretend like you washin' dishes . . . Huh?"
Child: "The dishes right here."
Mother: "The dishes right here?"
Child: "And our house up here?"
Mother: "O.K., sit down here. Wash the dishes. O.K."
Child: "Yeah, yeah."
Mother: ". . . wash the thing . . . soap. You want a, you want a dish water. You make some dish water."
Child: "O.K."
Mother: "Go ahead make dish water. Squeeze the soap out, turn the water on. Test the water, test a little water to see if it's warm."
Child: "It's warm."
Mother: "It's warm, warm. O.K., when you, when the water, stop, you gotta turn the water off."

With regard to the fourth principle, our analyses aim to address several different dimensions of children's play activities. Primarily, we have been focusing on the social structure, kinds, and thematic features of children's play. We are finding that similarities exist between the play of children included in our study and the previous studies of Western middle-income children, but there are also significant differences. The most obvious differences emerge in the kinds and themes of play. For example, the low-income U.S. and Turkish children included in our study engage in many different kinds of play, such as teasing and playing with music, that have not been identified or reported as commonly occurring with middle-class Western children (Göncü et al., 1995). In a similar vein, we are finding specific themes, such as having a pretend conversation with a real rooster and singing and dancing while pretending to be in church, that have not been reported in prior research.

In our future work, we will move on to identifying quantitative patterns in each community as we also perform qualitative analyses of children's play roles and themes as expression of their understanding of adult life. After having completed the description of play in each community we will then move on to comparisons across communities in order to identify similarities and differences across cultures.

Summary and Conclusions

We adopted Leont'ev's theory as a guide for our search to understand children's play and argued that Leont'ev's theory includes culture as an integral part of human development. Leont'ev guides our work in two critical ways. First, he brings to our attention the significance of community structure, which influences the activities in which adults and children engage. Such an emphasis drives us to focus on the economic (e.g., family income), physical (e.g., toys and play settings), and social-ecological (e.g., adult beliefs and adult–child communication) aspects of children's lives to understand what developmental opportunities a community provides for its children. This emphasis, valuable in its own right, also welcomes the integration of other psychological theories with Leont'ev's ideas. For example, to address how ecological features affect children's play, we can easily draw from Barker and Wright (1955); to address how adults' theories of child development guide their practice, we can draw from Heider (1958) and Whiting and Edwards (1988); to understand culture as an evolving system of meaning transformed from one generation to the next, we can draw from Bruner (1990), Cole (1997), and Shweder (1989).

The second important way in which Leont'ev guides our work is in the conceptualization of children's play as an activity. Extending the work of Vygotsky, Leont'ev saw play as a unit of life in which children try to be like adults in their community. For one thing, this conceptualization of children's play encourages thematic analyses of children's play in an effort to understand how children express their interpretation of adult roles in their community. For another, Leont'ev's conceptualization of play encourages us to explore how a real-life action becomes an operation of children's play, leading to the development of abstract thinking and humor.

When we see children's play as an interpretive cultural activity, it becomes clear that variations in play reflect larger similarities and differences across children's cultures. This means that efforts to understand play in one community through the lenses of a theory developed in another community will be limited to the similarities between the two communities. Differences will be overlooked or possibly misunderstood.

We believe as researchers that our theories are interpretive devices just like children's play and that our devices are bound by our own cultural milieu. Consequently, we maintain that understanding play in a given community is possible only in terms of local theories that are in existence in that community. Therefore, we claim that understanding children of different cultures is possible only by engaging in dialogue with the researchers and the community members of children's cultures. Such collaborations will productively reveal unique cultural descriptions and also enable identification of possible universals.

References

Barker, R. G., & Wright, H. F. (1955). *Midwest and its children.* New York: Harper & Row.

Bateson, G. (1955). A theory of play and fantasy. *Psychiatric Research Reports, 2,* 39–51.

Bretherton, I. (1984). *Symbolic play: The development of social understanding.* New York: Academic.

Bruner, J. (1990). *Acts of meaning.* Cambridge, MA: Harvard University Press.

Cole, M. (1997). *Cultural psychology: A once and future discipline.* Cambridge, MA: Harvard University Press.

DeVries, R., & Kohlberg, L. (1987). *Programs of early education: The constructivist view.* New York: Longman.

Dunn, J., & Dale, N. (1984). I, a daddy: Two-year-olds' collaboration in joint pretend play with sibling and with mother. In I. Bretherton (Ed.) *Symbolic play* (pp. 131–57). New York: Academic.

Engeström, Y. (1987). *Learning by expanding: An activity theoretical approach to developmental research.* Helsinki: Orienta-Konsultit.

Farver, J., & Howes, C. (1993). Cultural differences in American and Mexican mother–child pretend play. *Merrill-Palmer Quarterly, 39,* 344–58.

Farver, J. A. M., Kim, Y. K., & Lee, Y. (1995). Cultural differences in Korean-and Anglo-American preschoolers' social interaction and play behaviors. *Child Development, 66*, 1088–99.

Fein, G. (1981). Pretend play in childhood: An integrative review. *Child Development, 52*, 1095–1118.

Fitzgerald, L., & Göncü, A. (1993). Parent involvement in urban early childhood education: A Vygotskyan approach. In S. Reifel (Ed.), *Advances in early education and day care: Vol. 5. Perspectives on developmentally appropriate practice* (pp. 197–212). Greenwich, CT: Jai Press.

Freud, S. (1961). *Beyond the pleasure principle.* New York: Norton.

Garvey, C. (1990). *Play.* Cambridge, MA: Harvard University Press.

Gaskins, S. (1990). *Exploratory play and development in Mayan infants.* Unpublished doctoral dissertation, University of Chicago.

Gaskins, S., & Göncü, A. (1988). Children's play as representation and imagination: The case of Piaget and Vygotsky. *The Quarterly Newsletter of the Laboratory of Comparative Human Cognition, 10*, 104–7.

Gaskins, S., & Göncü, A. (1992). Cultural variation in play: A challenge to Piaget and Vygotsky. *The Quarterly Newsletter of the Laboratory of Comparative Human Cognition, 14*, 31–35.

Göncü, A. (1987). Toward an interactional model of developmental changes in social pretend play. In L. Katz (Ed.), *Current topics in early childhood education* (pp. 108–25). Norwood, NJ: Ablex.

Göncü, A. (1993). Development of intersubjectivity in social pretend play. *Human Development, 36*, 185–98.

Göncü, A., & Becker, J. (1992). Some contributions of a Vygotskyan approach to early education. *International Journal of Cognitive Education and Mediated Learning, 2*, 147–54.

Göncü, A., & Cannella, V. (1996). The role of teacher assistance in children's construction of intersubjectivity during conflict resolution. In M. Killen (Ed.), *Children's autonomy, social competence, and interactions with adults and other children: Exploring connections and consequences. New Directions for child development* (pp. 57–69). Vol. 73. San Francisco: Jossey-Bass.

Göncü, A., & Kessel, F. S. (1984). Children's play: A contextual-functional perspective. In F. Kessel & A. Göncü (Ed.), *Analyzing children's play dialogues.* No. 25. San Francisco: Jossey-Bass.

Göncü, A., & Kessel, F. S. (1988). Preschoolers' collaborative construction in planning and maintaining imaginative play. *International Journal of Behavioral Development, 11*, 327–44.

Göncü, A., Mistry, J., & Mosier, C. (April, 1991). *Cultural variations in the play of toddlers.* Paper presented at the meeting of the Society for Research in Child Development, Seattle.

Göncü, A., Tuermer, U., Jain, J., & Johnson, D. (1995). *Pretend play in a low-*

income African-American community. In A. Göncü & A. Nicolopoulou (Chairs), *The pretend play of cultures: Cultures of pretend play.* Symposium conducted at the biennial meeting of the Society for Research in Child Development, Indianapolis, IN.

Göncü, A., & Weber, E. (1992). *Preschoolers' classroom activities and interactions with peers and teachers.* Paper presented at the meeting of the American Educational Research Association, San Francisco.

Goldman, L. R. (1998). *Child's play.* Oxford: Berg.

Goodnow, J. J. (in press). Parenting and the ''transmission'' and ''internalization'' of values: From social-cultural perspectives to within family analysis. In J. Grusec & L. Kuczynski (Eds.), *Parenting strategies and children's internalization of values: A handbook of theoretical and research proposal.* New York: Wiley.

Haight, W., & Miller, P. (1993). *Pretending at home: Early development in sociocultural context.* Albany: SUNY Press.

Harkness, S., & Super, C. (1996). *Parents' cultural belief systems: Their origins, expressions and consequences.* New York: Guilford.

Heider, F. (1958). *The psychology of interpersonal relations.* New York: Wiley.

Leont'ev, A. N. (1981a). *Activity, consciousness and personality.* Englewood Cliffs, NJ: Prentice-Hall.

Leont'ev, A. N. (1981b). The problem of activity in psychology. In J. V. Wertsch (Ed.). *The concept of activity in Soviet psychology* (pp. 37–71). Armonk, NY: M. E. Sharpe.

LeVine, R. (1980). Anthropology and child development. In C. Super & S. Harkness (Eds.), *Anthropological perspectives on child development* (pp. 23–35). San Francisco: Jossey-Bass.

Martin, L., Nelson, K., & Tobach, E. (Eds.). (1995). *Sociocultural psychology.* New York: Cambridge University Press.

Matusov, E. (1996). Intersubjectivity without agreement. *Mind, Culture, and Activity: An International Journal, 3*(1), 25–45.

Miller, P. (1986). Teasing as language socialization and verbal play in a white, working-class community. In B. B. Schieffelin & E. Ochs (Eds.), *Language socialization across cultures* (pp. 199–212). Cambridge: Cambridge University Press.

McLoyd, V. (1982). Social class differences in sociodramatic play: A critical review. *Developmental Review, 2,* 1–30.

Parten, M. B. (1932). Social participation among preschool children. *Journal of Abnormal Psychology, 27,* 243–69.

Piaget, J. (1962). *Play, dreams and imitation in childhood.* New York: Norton.

Rogoff, B., Mistry, J., Göncü, A., & Mosier, C. (1993). Guided participation in cultural activity by toddlers and caregivers. *Monographs of the Society for Research in Child Development, 236,* 58(8). Chicago: University of Chicago Press.

Rubin, K. H., Fein, G., & Vandenberg, B. (1983). Play. In E. M. Hetherington (Ed.), *The handbook of child psychology: Social development* (pp. 693–774). New York: Wiley.

Sawyer, R. K. (1997). *Pretend play as improvisation: Conversation in the preschool classroom.* Mahwah, NJ: Erlbaum.

Schwartzman, H. (1978). *Transformations: The anthropology of children's play.* New York: Plenum.

Shweder, R. (1989). Cultural psychology: What is it? In J. W. Stigler, R. A. Shweder, & G. Herdt (Eds.), *Cultural psychology: Essays on comparative human development* (pp. 1–43). New York: Cambridge University Press.

Slaughter, D., & Dombrowski, J. (1989). Cultural continuities and discontinuities: Impact on social and pretend play. In M. N. Bloch & A. D. Pellegrini (Eds.), *The ecological context of children's play* (pp. 282–310). Norwood, NJ: Ablex.

Sutton-Smith, B. (1983). Piaget, play, and cognition, revisited. In W. Overton (Ed.), *The relationship between social and cognitive development* (pp. 229–49). Hillsdale, NJ: Erlbaum.

Vygotsky, L. S. (1978). *Mind in society: The development of higher mental processes.* Cambridge, MA: Harvard University Press.

Wells, G. (1993). Reevaluating the IRF sequence: A proposal for the articulation of theories of activity and discourse for the analysis of teaching and learning in the classroom. *Linguistics and Education, 5,* 1–37.

Wertsch, J. V. (1981). (Ed.). *The concept of activity in Soviet psychology.* Armonk, NY: M. E. Sharpe.

Whiting, B. B., & Edwards, C. P. (1988). *Children of different worlds: The formation of social behavior.* Cambridge, MA: Harvard University Press.

Winnicott, D. W. (1971). *Playing and reality.* New York: Basic Books.

PART FOUR

Children's Engagement in Planning, Math, and Literacy

7   Everyday Opportunities for the Development of Planning Skills: Sociocultural and Family Influences

Mary Gauvain

In recent years, psychologists have become increasingly interested in the development and organization of cognitive skill in everyday context. The underlying assumption of this approach is that cognitive development relies in critical ways on children's participation in the activities and practices of the community in which growth occurs. For instance, more opportunity to plan activities with others may help promote and organize the development of children's skill at planning. This chapter examines this premise by discussing children's everyday activities with particular attention to the role that context, as defined by sociocultural processes and experiences, has on children's opportunities to develop one type of intellectual skill: the ability to plan (i.e., to anticipate and organize future activities).

Much of the chapter examines the development of planning skills in one particular social context, the family. The role of the family, especially parents, in facilitating the development of children's cognitive competence from early childhood to adolescence is an important focus for researchers studying the developmental trajectory of intellectual skills. Although there has been extensive research on the role of the family in organizing and supporting children's social and emotional development, there has been less attention devoted to how experiences in the family contribute to cognitive socialization and development, especially within specific domains of cognitive functioning. Because the family is one of the key settings in which cultural values and goals are modeled and transmitted to children, it is an ideal arena for studying cognitive development in context. (For similar discussions, see Haight, and Tudge et al., this volume.)

Ruth Duran Huard, Tiffany Lee, Susan Savage, Jennifer de la Ossa, and Maria Hurtado are thanked for their participation in much of the research described in this chapter.

173

The chapter concentrates on two different but related levels of psychological functioning that contribute to the development of planning skills. It discusses how social interaction helps prepare children to become competent planners. It presents the view that children learn about planning by interacting with others as they coordinate and discuss future actions. It also examines how culture helps children learn about planning. I argue that the cultural context of development helps steer children toward ways of planning that are valued and expected in the community in which development occurs. Although these two contributions to planning and its development are discussed separately, it is important to remember that the social and cultural aspects of development are interdependent influences on human growth. Together, they define the opportunities and constraints that children have in everyday life to develop intellectual skills like planning.

This approach to the development of cognitive skills draws upon the perspective of activity theory (Leont'ev, 1981; Vygotsky, 1978; Zinchenko, 1981). It also extends the concept of "developmental niche" (Super & Harkness, 1986) as a framework for analyzing cognitive development within sociocultural context (Gauvain, 1995; also see Göncü et al. for discussion of activity theory, and see Farver for developmental niche, this volume). Central to a sociocultural approach is the idea that human behavior and thinking occur within meaningful contexts as people conduct purposeful, goal-directed activity. Cultural subsystems, or niches, can be used to analyze the ways that meaningful activities are derived from the larger sociocultural context of development and are linked to individual cognitive growth. Cultural subsystems include activity goals and values of the culture and its members; historical means, such as material and symbolic tools, that satisfy cultural goals and values; and organized social structures that instantiate cultural values and goals in everyday routines and practices. These subsystems help compose the framework for intellectual development as it occurs in sociocultural context. In this chapter, the cultural subsystems of activity goals and everyday routines that are relevant to planning and its development are of primary concern.

Before we discuss the development of planning from this perspective, a brief review of the development of planning skills from laboratory research is presented. This review provides a summary of age-related changes in planning that have been observed to date. This research provides us with an understanding of children's planning competence at certain ages under particular contextual conditions. Such information is useful when observing children's planning-related behaviors in everyday contexts, where less control is possible but similar behaviors or future-oriented concerns may occur.

Following this, the role of the social and cultural context in the development of these skills are addressed. Illustrations from Western and non-Western communities are presented to show commonalities and differences that appear across sociocultural contexts. Two types of research from my own laboratory are presented. One direction of study investigates planning opportunities that rely directly on social participation, such as coordinating activities with others, and planning that is guided in either design or execution by more experienced societal members. Much of this research examines parent–child interaction involving future-oriented behaviors. The other direction of research concentrates on less interpersonally direct but still fundamentally social processes that contribute to the acquisition and organization of individual planning skills. Less direct social processes, such as the determination of children's daily routines, play materials, activity settings, and companions, may compose a substantial portion of the planning-related opportunities that children encounter in their everyday lives, especially in the family context. In fact, the primary influence that parents exert over their children's cognitive development from middle childhood to adolescence may not be in direct dyadic exchanges with their children. Rather, during these years, parents may be most influential through their control over the network composition and boundaries of their children's social and mental life (Parke & Bhavnagri, 1989). This section also describes a method, derived from anthropological research, for examining the development of children's planning within the context of routine activities. This approach offers one way of exploring the hypothesis that a gradual transfer of responsibility from adults to children for planning everyday activities is characteristic of development during middle childhood.

The central purpose of this chapter is to trace the connections between children's cognitive competence in the domain of planning and how opportunities for the development of these skills are part of everyday socialization in a cultural context, most specifically in the family system. By introducing sociocultural and family experiences into the analysis of the development of planning skills, I hope to provide a more complete picture of the development of planning than when these contributions are examined separately.

The Development of Planning Skills

Planning is the deliberate organization of a sequence of actions oriented toward achieving a specific goal. Planning is the focus of this chapter because of its importance in human development. Planning is essential to mature cognitive and social functioning. In fact, a basic assumption of development is that with age children will have greater regulation of their own activities, a process that relies in important ways on the ability to plan.

With development, children show increasing competence at planning actions and in other metacognitive skills and strategies such as organizing task materials and remembering the steps of a plan that are required for effective planning (Friedman, Scholnick, & Cocking, 1987; Haith, Benson, Roberts, & Pennington, 1994). There is evidence that children can plan as early as 12 months of age (Benson, Arehart, Jennings, Boley, & Kearns, 1989; Rogoff, Mistry, Radziszewska, & Germond, 1991; Willatts, 1990). Beyond the first years, children's planfulness increases, with preschoolers capable of devising and executing simple plans in advance of action (Besevegis & Neimark, 1987; Cocking & Copple, 1987; Wellman, Fabricius, & Sophian, 1985). By 5 years of age children: (1) have a fairly good conceptual understanding of planning and when it is needed (Gauvain, 1989; Krietler & Krietler, 1987; Pea, 1982), (2) are capable of planning longer sequences of steps (Klahr & Robinson, 1981; Krietler & Krietler, 1987), (3) are able to use knowledge of familiar events to plan flexibly (Hudson & Fivush, 1991), and (4) consider more alternatives and correct their planning errors more readily during plan execution (Fabricius, 1988). During early to middle childhood, children participate in increasingly complex individual and social activities, many of which rely on the ability to plan, and they show increasing competence in devising elaborate and effective plans in a wide range of cognitive activities (Brown & Campione, 1984; Inhelder & Piaget, 1964; Magkaev, 1977; Szeminska, 1965).

In general, the development of competence at planning is a protracted process, with children able to reach adult levels of performance on certain tasks, such as simple errand planning (Gauvain, 1995), very early. But on more complex tasks, like those requiring complex computation or interpretation, adult-level performance is not reached until adolescence or later (Krietler & Krietler, 1987; Parrila, Aysto, & Das, 1994; Presson, 1987). Even among adults, skill at planning can differ depending on task and experience. For example, experience at the workplace may influence how adults plan on tasks related to their regular work duties. In a study we conducted with employees at the New York City Library, we found that security guards, whose jobs required movement around the building, devised more efficient plans (or routes) of travel for patrons than librarians, whose jobs were mainly in stationary positions (Gauvain & Klaue, 1989).

Explanations for increases in planning with age are twofold. First, with development, children are better able to regulate and suspend voluntary action, which permits greater opportunity for mental consideration of alternative procedures prior to action (Luria, 1976; Vygotsky, 1981). This capability has clear benefits for the development of planfulness and may be related to the development of the forebrain at around 5 years of age (Pribram & Luria, 1973). A second explanation stresses the role of practice in the development of planning. The underlying assumption is that with experience, children come to understand the various components, benefits, and trade-offs of planning and, as a result, show increased incorporation of these skills in their activities.

The social world of adults and other children is one important source of information and practice with planning. The next section discusses how social interaction influences the development of these skills. This is followed by discussion of the ways in which cultural values and practices may foster the development of planning.

Social Interaction and the Development of Planning Skills

Research suggests that social interaction is an important context for the development of planning skills. Much of everyday planning, especially for young children, occurs in social settings as other people elicit and model planning-related behaviors for children. Such experiences may provide a formative base for the development of planning skills (Goodnow, 1987; Rogoff, Gauvain, & Gardner, 1987). Children learn about the process of planning as they coordinate plans with others and as they observe and interact with others who are more experienced planners (Gauvain, 1992; Gauvain & Rogoff, 1989; Gearhart, 1979; Radziszewska & Rogoff, 1988). However, the way in which participants coordinate their mental effort influences what children learn about planning in social context. Cognitive gains from social interaction are more likely when partners share responsibility for decision making, rather than it being divided between partners or dominated by one partner (Gauvain & Rogoff, 1989; Reeve, 1987).

Unlike the planning process studied in psychological laboratories when children work alone on assigned tasks, the process of planning in social context emerges from the social situation. Planning in social context often involves co-construction by the participants as they attempt to coordinate and direct future activities in ways that satisfy their mutual interests and needs. Such exchanges serve as opportunities for cognitive development as children and adults actively participate in the process of organizing and planning the future. It is important to note that the plans that emerge from these transactions are not easily identified as solely the product of the child or the adult. Rather, they involve contributions from all the participants as the planning problem is distributed across their various interests and goals, and they take into account the skills and resources of the participants.

The focus in describing the development of children's planning within social context is not the individual's competence at planning, but the participation of children and adults as the process of planning is initiated and evolves (Rogoff, 1996). In terms of cognitive development, the active role of the child in these interactions is of particular interest. The child's participation is expected to change with time as he or she becomes increasingly skilled at planning. In support of this, evidence suggests that children appropriate knowledge and skill at planning from their joint endeavors with others. For instance, with increasing age, children take on more of the activities involved in joint planning, such as organizing task materials and contributing more strategic information (Gauvain, 1992).

Emphasis on social interaction as a primary focus of cognitive development is central to a sociocultural approach. The ways in which interaction with or observation of more experienced cultural members, such as parents and older siblings, allow for the transmission of culturally valued skills have been described in at least three models. In one model, Rogoff (1990) advances the notion of guided participation, in which caregivers arrange and structure children's participation in activities in order to support and lead cognitive development. By participating in culturally valued activities under the tutelage of more experienced cultural members, children appropriate the understanding and practices necessary for meeting the intellectual challenges of their community.

In contrast to Rogoff's notion of guided participation, which stresses mutual participation as a gateway to cognitive growth, in a second model, Lave and Wenger (1991) emphasize the role of observation in exposing children, or less experienced cultural members, to more experienced members as they participate in valued cultural practices (also see Goodnow, Miller, & Kessel, 1995). This process, which has been labeled legitimate peripheral participation, may be especially important in settings in which explicit adult–child instruction is less common than in Western communities. For Lave and Wenger, the central point is that not all skills are learned by direct guidance or instruction. Rather, much of cultural learning occurs as children live alongside others who are participating in and thereby demonstrating valued cultural skills. This process is similar to the type of social modeling described by Bandura (1986); however, it emphasizes the cultural and goal-directed nature of these transactions.

A third process of social participation directly linked to the development of cognitive skill is apprenticeship (Lave, 1988; Rogoff, 1990). This involves close and active coordination of an expert and a novice (or several novices) in the course of learning an activity. Apprenticeship is task focused, with a particular level of skill as a desired outcome.

Although distinctions exist between the notions of guided participation, legitimate peripheral participation, and apprenticeship, these views share a common thread. They all emphasize the active role of adults in providing culturally based cognitive opportunities and of children (or learners) in procuring or appropriating culturally valued skills as they participate together in the ordinary routines of everyday life. Thus, in all of these interactions, the sociocultural context of development provides the core activities through which children are exposed to and learn about planning.

Culture and the Development of Planning Skills

Connecting the development of planning skills to sociocultural context underscores an important, though often overlooked, component of human planning: its contribution to individual, family, and community vitality. By vitality, I mean the movement of the family, the community, and its members forward, into the future, in order to maintain and extend the values and goals of the group. The process of socialization rests on this tacit, *prospective* commitment. Through cultural institutions and practices, along with the provision of material and symbolic tools (i.e., the stuff of socialization), children become the lifeblood of this move into the future.

Planning allows individuals to move their lives forward in time as they stretch present concerns into future goals (Ochs, Smith, & Taylor, 1989). But plans do not appear out of nowhere. People do not stretch their lives forward in random directions but in patterned ways that reflect the values and goals of the community in which development occurs. This does not mean that there are not individual differences in planning. There are. Individual differences arise from many sources, including intelligence, social opportunity, and socioemotional factors like temperament. However, even when individual contributions are taken into account, people's plans, at least for those within normal ranges of intelligence and mental health, bear a striking resemblance to the plans of others in the cultural community in which they live. This occurs because cultures prescribe socially appropriate and expected ways of participating in and directing human activity. Thus, the common patterns that unite people's plans reflect their shared values and goals, and these are instantiated in cultural practices (Goodnow et al., 1995). Participation in cultural practices through individual activity ensures the continued organization and maintenance of the community, along with the individual's place in it.

This suggests that both the content of what is planned and the overall goals of planning reflect the values and goals of the community. Such values and goals may vary on many dimensions across cultural groups. Cultures that value precision and timeliness direct children toward planning practices that respect these values. These are central values in industrialized societies, and citizens in recently industrialized nations shift their planning goals to include greater concern with these emerging values (Inkeles & Smith, 1974). In cultures in which social status and involvement are central concerns (e.g., native Hawaiian communities), children are socialized to value social cooperation more than individual performance. This influences how children organize and plan their behavior at home and even in school, a setting that typically emphasizes individual goals (Tharp & Gallimore, 1988). Children from cultural groups that do not emphasize cooperative learning norms perceive helping one another in the classroom, even during peer collaborative sessions, as "illegal" (Ellis & Gauvain, 1992). Therefore, they would not be expected to include such arrangements in their plans during class time. In essence, the cultural context of development leads to differences when planning is required. I consider how these differences may be evident in even everyday routines, and how these may be related to the development of planning skills.

Social responsibility is a preeminent feature of intelligence among many African groups (Segall, Dasen, Berry, & Poortinga, 1990). Important for determining a child's intelligence in these communities is the child's willingness to help, especially his or her assumption of responsibility when parents do not ask or tell the child to help. This sociocognitive expectation may be related to the development of planning. Super (1983) recounts the response of a Kipsigi woman when she was asked what an intelligent girl is like. She stated that such a girl would "after eating sweep the house because she knows it should be done. Then she washes the dishes, looks for vegetables, and takes good care of the baby" (p. 202). This example suggests that in the course of everyday activities, children are expected to participate with increasing independence and responsibility in routines that involve identifying and sequencing different events. This process, I argue, is related to the development of planning skills and occurs in many different forms for children throughout the world depending upon the cultural context of development.

What do these observations suggest about how culture, as instantiated in everyday routines and practices, may be incorporated into the study of the development of planning skills? Anthropological research on planning offers some insights to this question (Randall, 1987). In this kind of research, ethnographers have focused on plans created by people in the course of carrying out everyday routines, and results are consistent with those of laboratory work. Both non-Western, nonschooled adults and Western, schooled adults create, modify, and implement plans that are hierarchically complex and involve many steps. For instance, Randall (1977) observed rural fisherman in the Philippines, concentrating on how the fishermen elaborated upon and responded flexibly to the carrying out of their everyday routines. He found that in order to keep the anchor from coming out of the sand on the sea floor, a scad[1] catcher needed to pitch the anchor line at a certain angle with the bottom and keep the line taut. Depending on the strength of the current, the line had to be let out anywhere from 5 to 15 fathoms and be adjusted as conditions changed. To do this, the fisherman procured information available in the setting relevant to his goal. This information could be accessed through observations, by talking to another fisherman or experimenting with environmental conditions, or by searching memory. As a result of these efforts, a particular solution, drawn from a set of alternative solutions, is selected, and the activity continues along this selected path or plan. It is in this way that routines often involve innovative elements, and these elements require a type of planning that resembles the process described by Hayes-Roth and Hayes-Roth (1979) as opportunistic planning or planning-in-action.

Unfortunately for developmentalists, there has been little anthropological research along these lines that concentrates on the development of

---

[1] Kind of spiny ocean fish that is eaten.

planning. However, one study (Geoghegan, 1973) did examine the planning-related routines for selecting name substitutes by 14- to 58-year-old Samalians who live in a traditional, rural community in the Philippines. Whenever a person speaks to another, a form of address is selected from a set of possible forms on the basis of contextual and relational factors – for example, mom, mother, Mrs. Smith, Ms. Smith, Jane, dear, lady, or madam. Although this type of planning does not involve sequencing multiple steps, it does involve a selection within a routine that then influences subsequent discourse. In this way, it is part of a plan-in-action. Consistent with laboratory research on the development of planning, results indicate age-related increases in the complexity of this type of planning-in-action. With age, the number of alternative solution paths and the amount of information that is considered potentially relevant to a selection increases.

In this research, ethnographers have shown that competence at planning in non-Western communities may be understood by studying how people plan during everyday activities. Although they have not studied the generation of novel plans or the development of a plan in response to a task or goal presented by a researcher, approaches that are common in laboratory research, they have demonstrated that planning does occur within familiar, everyday routines as individuals select or create paths of actions to reach their goals. This approach is relevant to research on planning in everyday context in that it suggests that planning is part of many of the routine activities of both Western and non-Western people. Whether the process involves a fisherman catching fish and not losing his line, a suburban commuter driving to work to avoid traffic congestion, or a child deciding how to play on the playground with friends and avoid bullies, there exists a familiar framework within which people identify and select a course of action, a plan that responds to the requirements of the activity and considers the alternatives available in that particular circumstance. Although the steps of the plan are embedded in a routine, the plan itself is selected from a host of alternatives and, therefore, is unlikely to be ritualized or rehearsed in advance. As a result, planning is required in order to select and carry out these actions.

This approach suggests that one way to study planning in everyday context is to examine the planning involved in carrying out complex, routine activities. One way to do this from a developmental perspective is to examine age-related changes in children's participation in and control over everyday activities and routines, an approach we have taken in our research. A first step in this effort, described in more detail in the following section, is identification of the types of routines in which children participate and documentation of how children's involvement in these activities emerges and is supported by others, especially parents.

As a final point on this topic, it is important to point out that although the aforementioned anthropological research indicates commonality in planning across cultural communities, there may also be substantial variation across communities in how and when we plan. Goodnow (1976) discusses how certain features of intellectual performance, such as generalization or completeness of a plan, reflect the goals and values of a culture. For instance, the propensity among Western thinkers to generalize information may hinge upon cultural values that regard a search for universals or principles across events as important and worthy of pursuit. Goodnow (1990) uses Gladwin's (1971) research with Puluwat navigators to illustrate how certain complex mental systems that have been observed in non-Western communities sometimes do not go beyond the problems for which they were developed; they never connect to a more general framework or set of principles. Although the Puluwat system of navigation was well suited to a host of navigational events that the islanders were likely to encounter, it contained several inconsistencies. Gladwin speculated that because the islanders' goal of navigating was met, no further adjustments to the system were needed. In contrast to the Puluwats, participants from cultures that value organizing information into general, rule-based frameworks would more than likely consider this system incomplete or seriously flawed. But such an interpretation itself is flawed because it ignores the connection between human thinking and the culturally organized goals through which thinking is instantiated.

This example also suggests that if someone performs poorly on a task that does not coincide with cultural values or practices, this performance cannot be assumed to reflect individual skill. Thus, in the case of planning, if someone is asked to plan a task that is typically not planned in their community or, if planned, not planned in the way he or she is asked to plan, this person may perform poorly. This does not indicate that the individual lacks the skills involved in planning, such as self-regulation, problem solving, the ability to sequence and order multiple steps, and mental reflection. It simply means that these skills may not have been tapped in this task. Anthropological observations indicate that human beings in all types of communities devise, modify, and enact plans that are complex and involve multiple steps. Yet the deployment of these processes and ways of expressing these skills may differ substantially depending on the goals, values, and practices of the culture in which development occurs. This reasoning suggests that in order to provide a complete picture of the development of planning, it is critical to trace the interdependencies of these future-oriented skills in relation to culture.

Opportunities for the Development of Planning Skills in Children's Everyday Activities in Cultural Context

Every society organizes the environment and routines of children in order to shape development in ways that are beneficial for the community. Because all humans have similar basic needs, the routines of daily life, especially for the young, have much commonality across cultural communities. Despite commonalities, the ways in which routines are carried out varies depending upon socialization goals, and these variations may influence the development of cognitive skills like planning. Yet, despite longstanding interest in the everyday lives of children (Barker, 1968; Bronfenbrenner, 1979; Lewin, 1951), we are still far from understanding the daily lives of children and how these experiences fit with development (Bryant & Djakovic, 1993). As a result, little direct information on opportunities for the development of planning skills in children's everyday lives exists in the developmental literature. However, a few studies have examined children's daily activities and participation in routines more generally and can offer some suggestions as to how to study the development of planning from this vantage.

Goodnow and Burns (1985) interviewed 2,000 school-age children in Australia about their lives in and out of school. Many of the themes that children raised reflected their participation in activities that require planning, and many of these involved social or practical considerations, such as coordinating plans with others or dealing with time constraints. For instance, getting ready for school in the morning on time and completing homework in time to play with other children are but two of the many common, planning-related activities that pose challenges for children during early to middle childhood. By the end of the middle childhood, children are expected to be fairly competent at planning activities such as these, and many of their responsibilities involve some participation in mature practices of the community, such as washing dishes and yard care. It could be argued that with development, children have increasing practice with such routines and become aware of scripts (Nelson, 1981) to guide their behavior during these activities. But scripts are only useful insofar as the scripted procedure is undisturbed. When temporal, social, or material parameters change, planning is once again required. Thus,

Goodnow and Burns's results indicate that with development, children are increasingly skilled, or at least expected to become increasingly skilled, at planning and carrying out routine activities. This study does not explicitly address the role of culture in the organization and implementation of such plans, however. Variation in the everyday planning process and opportunities for the development of planning skills can occur both within and across cultural communities depending on the goals, values, and practices of people.

In order to investigate variation within cultural communities in planning-related practices, we conducted a study of the spatial planning skills of Navajo children (6 to 8 years of age) who were reared in rural versus more urban areas of the reservation (Gauvain & Lee, 1996). We were interested in studying the relation between children's participation in traditional practices involving spatial thinking and their spatial planning skills. The rural children in this study lived in houses that were far from neighbors, the town, and the school. Thus, they needed to walk great distances, even in the course of a single day. In addition, they were likely to participate in traditional practices, such as weaving and herding, both of which require spatial thinking. Such behaviors were less common among the children who lived in and around the reservation towns.

Children's spatial planning was studied by observing them plan a route of travel linking several familiar sites at their school. The types of spatial decisions that children considered and the strategies they used to solve the problem were studied. Children who lived in more rural areas and participated in more traditional practices considered more alternative spatial paths and developed more efficient plans of travel than children who lived in more urban regions and participated little or not at all in traditional activities. By studying children from the same community who had different experiences relevant to the planning activity under study, this research demonstrated the connection between individual planning skills and prior experience in one cultural group. Recently we have extended our study of variations in planning practices within cultural communities by examining one important sociocultural channel through which children have opportunities to develop planning skills: the family context.

The Role of the Family in the Development of Planning

The family is an important social context of cognitive development, especially in complex domains like planning. The family is a sustained socialization context in which family members frequently organize or plan future activities. Parents play an especially important role in helping children develop planning skills by identifying culturally valued goals and helping children organize their actions to meet these goals. And children facilitate this process through their efforts to participate in and observe the skilled activities of others in the family. The different cognitive status of family members allows for the social transmission of cognitive skill through processes like guided participation (Rogoff, 1990), legitimate peripheral participation (Lave & Wenger, 1991), scaffolding (Wood & Middleton, 1975), modeling (Bandura, 1986), and instruction, and such processes are associated with the development of planning skills (Goodnow, 1987; Rogoff et al., 1987). Thus, by its nature and its structure, the family context is a primary site for the development of planning skills.

Research indicates that future-oriented concerns, a central ingredient of the planning process, are commonplace in family discourse. Benson (1994) found that even parents of 9- to 36-month-old children believe that by establishing routines and talking about what will happen, they teach their children about the future. Consistent with this belief, more than three-quarters of observed conversations between mothers and 2-year-olds focused on future-oriented routines and events (Lucarillo & Nelson, 1987). Home observations of families with older children reveal a similar pattern (Ochs et al., 1989). It seems that parents and children are active participants in future-oriented discussions and that concern with planning is woven into the regular family process. Planning in the family involves co-construction by the participants as they attempt to coordinate and direct future activities in ways that satisfy their mutual interests and needs. Such interactions involve contributions from the participants as the planning problem is distributed across their various goals and skills.

My colleagues and I have been studying the linkages between sociocultural context, the family, children's everyday activities, and opportunities for the development of planning skills. In a recent study, 875 schoolchildren (ages 7 to 10 years) in the United States from diverse socioeconomic and cultural communities were asked about their involvement in planning activities during nonschool hours (Gauvain & Huard, 1993). A seven-page, child-oriented survey assessed the nature and extent of children's after-school activities, along with who was responsible (child, parent, or both) for planning these activities. Results indicate that children's responsibility for planning their after-school activities increases with age. However, for many children, there is little free time after school to plan either on their own or with others because this time is often filled with adult-determined and planned obligations.

These results were mediated by cultural and socioeconomic factors. The hectic after-school life of music lessons, soccer practice, playdates, and childcare was most characteristic of the lives of middle-class children of European-American descent. Some children, largely those from Mexican-American families, reported spending their afternoons at home in the company of kin with much free time available. A small but significant portion of children, primarily of Asian-American descent, said they spent their afternoons working alongside their parents in small businesses. The after-school activities of African-American children were less consistent across the group and were largely related to socioeconomic factors.

Another finding was the children's appraisal of how their daily activity schedules affected their emotional experience. Children with full schedules, especially those that were largely adult-determined, reported feeling more stress during the day than children with more free time and more control over their schedules. Also, with increasing age, children reported more feelings of boredom and expressed more complaints about not having enough to do. These results are consistent with research by Dreher and Oerter (1987) in which adolescents' opportunity to plan was associated with their overall coping. Anticipating and organizing future activities apparently enables children and adolescents to cope more effectively with the environment.

In sum, this research suggests that children do have opportunities to develop planning skills in the family context, but that these opportunities are affected in important ways by the cultural values and practices in the community in which development occurs. Results also indicate that planning opportunities change with age and that during early and middle childhood children perceive their parents and other adults as primary influences in determining how their nonschool time is spent.

Despite the formative base provided in this study, it is limited in that the data are from children only. To address this, we conducted a follow-up study of these processes by surveying parents from two ethnic communities, similar to a subset of those studied previously, about their children's lives outside of school (Gauvain & Savage, 1995). Parents of 163 children between the ages of 5 and 12 years participated, with 85 of the families European-American and 78 of the families hispanic. Parents completed a survey that tapped the nature and extent of their children's participation in nonschool activities, the parents' beliefs about the ages when children are able to plan and conduct various activities on their own, and their children's involvement in planning these activities.

Results indicate that both European-American and hispanic children participate in planning various aspects of their daily lives. Consistent with the observations of Whiting and Edwards (1988) for their U.S. sample, even children as young as 5 years of age were reported as having some household responsibilities. They were involved in planning some parts of their daily routines, such as deciding what to wear to school and what to eat for breakfast. With increasing age, they were more involved in planning activities outside the home, including participation in organized social groups, such as team sports and church groups. However, children's involvement in these activities appears to decline as they near adolescence. There were no ethnic differences in these patterns. These data suggest that both European-American and hispanic children participate in planning various aspects of their daily lives, and that these planning opportunities are frequently nested in familiar, everyday routines. However, there were ethnic differences in children's involvement in planning unstructured play, and these mirror findings in the earlier study. Despite similarity in social class, European-American children were more likely than hispanic children to plan indoor activities that involved computers and outdoor activities at playgrounds or at other children's homes.

In terms of parental beliefs about children's developing ability to plan and carry out activities, European-American parents reported that children are able to plan their activities at younger ages than hispanic parents reported. Cognitive socialization in hispanic families may involve a longer period of guided participation than in European-American families, a process that may be supported by the availability of extended kin in hispanic households and neighborhoods (Delgado-Gaitan, 1994). The consequences for children in terms of the development of planning skills as a result of different parental beliefs along these lines is not known. It is reasonable to suspect that some connection between certain parental practices, such as expectations for children's independent performance, and the development of planning exists. Although there are no cross-cultural investigations on this topic, within-culture analysis of parenting practices related to demands for child independence, often referred to as maturity demands, have been conducted. In fact, this is a key issue in the study of parenting style, a topic to which we now turn.

Parental Style and Opportunities for the Development of Planning Skills. Recently we examined children's planning-related experiences in the family in relation to parenting style in order to gain insight into how parental expectations for children's independence or maturity may relate to the development of planning-related skills. To examine parenting style, we adopted the two-dimensional framework suggested by Maccoby and Martin (1983) that characterizes parenting along the dimensions of maturity demands and warmth/responsiveness. These two factors can be used to describe parental promotion of independent planning-related behaviors along with the degree of support they offer. In order to investigate this process with a longitudinal sample, we (Gauvain & Huard, 1998) undertook a reanalysis of data from the Family Socialization and Developmental Competence project (Baumrind, 1966, 1973). The home observations conducted by Baumrind provided a form of ethnographic data useful for investigating how social practices in the family, especially family interaction, may relate to opportunities for children to develop planning skills. Specifically, we were interested in whether children's participation in planning-related discussions at home changed over development, and whether these behaviors were related to parenting style. We operationalized planning by examining children's anticipation of future events as indexed by their talking about these events. Although this operationalization differs from prior research efforts, especially those developed in relation to solitary problem-solving tasks, we argue that much of planning in social context occurs as individuals make their future interests and goals public by talking about them. Such communicative junctures may serve as opportunities for devising, refining, coordinating, or adjusting plans in relation to information from others.

Using Baumrind's records from her home observations conducted when the target children were 4, 9, and 15 years of age, we found that earlier participation in planning-related discussions in the family fostered increased participation in these interactions over the years of childhood and into adolescence. We also found that of the parenting styles identified – namely, authoritative, directive, permissive, and uninvolved – certain styles supported this development better than others. Of these four styles, directive had the highest rate of planning-related discussions in the family when the children were 9 years of age, but they had the lowest rate of planning-related initiations by the target children at adolescence. Thus, even though there are high-level maturity demands in directive households, the accompanying low level of warmth/responsiveness apparently does not encourage children's initiation of planning-related discussions in this family context. This result is consistent with other research that shows that directive parenting does not foster autonomy in children, and that parents with this style are more likely to make decisions on their own rather than involve their children. In contrast, children in families with an authoritative parenting style, which has medium-to high-level maturity demands coupled with high rates of warmth/responsiveness, had higher rates of planning-related initiations in adolescence than children in families with a directive style.

We also found that parenting styles with low-level maturity demands promoted high rates of children's planning-related initiations in adolescence. This may reflect a different process than that which occurs in families with an authoritative parenting style, however. Permissive parenting may be related to higher rates due to the tendency of these parents to defer decision making to the adolescent (Lamborn, Mounts, Steinberg, & Dornbusch, 1991). Uninvolved parenting was also related to relatively high rates of this behavior, perhaps for similar reasons. In general, children in families with low-level maturity demands may need to learn to plan their future activities because their parents may be less likely to do this for them.

In sum, authoritative, permissive, and uninvolved parenting styles all appear to facilitate the development of children's planning-related skills, as assessed by their planning-related initiations, more than a directive parenting style. The roles that scaffolding, modeling, or some other form of social transmission play in this process is important to consider. The consistently high rate of planning-related initiations in authoritative families when children were 4 and 9 years of age indicates that modeling is occurring. We have no direct assessment of guided participation due to the nature of the data, but the increased participation of children between 9 and 15 years of age in these same families suggests that some support for the development of these skills, such as guided participation, has occurred. This conclusion is consistent with laboratory results that have shown greater sensitivity in guided participation among authoritative parents (Pratt, Kerig, Cowan, & Cowan, 1988). For permissive and uninvolved households, we saw lower rates of planning-related interactions in the family when the children were ages 4 and 9. However, child initiations of these discussions were fairly high when the children were 9 and 15 years of age. It appears that as early as age 9, children in these families may assume a fair amount of responsibility for this type of behavior. Because children at this age experience an expansion in social involvements, especially outside the home, active participation in planning-related behaviors may be crucial if they want to have a certain quality of social life. Thus, some modeling appears to be occurring in these families, but we suspect that not much in the way of guided participation is – certainly not as much as we suspect occurs in authoritative households. Finally, the combination of high rates of planning-related discussions in directive households when children were 9 years of age and low rates of child initiations of planning-related discussions at adolescence indicates that modeling may be insufficient, at least in this family context, for promoting the development of this type of skill.

In general, our research and that of others indicate that children in different social circumstances grow up with different opportunities to develop planning skills. Social interactions, especially within the family, along with related cultural practices, help set the stage for how children learn about and practice planning. To date, the processes of social transmission of these skills have not been studied very systematically, and further investigation along these lines is warranted. Finally, it is important to note that despite variation in social and cultural experience, many of the preadolescents in the Gauvain and Huard (1998) study reported that they were less engaged in activities than they would like to be. They also reported high levels of boredom, much higher than younger children. This is interesting in relation to the high rates of activity reported by younger children from these same groups, and it raises questions about the practical implications of these findings.

Practical Implications

Implicit in a social-experiential or practice model of the development of planning skills is the idea that children have the opportunity both to develop and implement plans with others and to practice these newfound skills on their own in the course of their everyday lives. But do young children in Western societies have opportunities to develop and refine these skills? During school hours, children have limited opportunity to plan activities on their own, although much planning may occur as children devise their own ways of carrying out scheduled classroom activities. This topic merits further study, and some of the ideas presented earlier, especially regarding planning during routine activities, may be a useful starting point.

Beyond the classroom, what opportunities do young children have to develop planning skills? According to our research, young children today are busy and overcommitted. This conclusion is consistent with that expressed by David Elkind in his book *The Hurried Child* (1981). When Elkind's book first appeared, it aroused professional and public attention because psychological stressors identified with adulthood, such as scheduling one's day and pressure to achieve, were associated with youth. This circumstance seems to have resulted from several societal trends, trends that have made everyday life for children markedly different from that experienced by the post–World War II generation: Increased numbers of single parents and dual–wage-earning families necessitate long hours in after-school care for many children; parental anxiety about maximizing future options for their children has led to an upsurge in various apprenticeship programs outside of school; parental dissatisfaction with educational quality has led to an increase in compensatory after-school tutorials for children; and heightened concern about child safety has led to increased privatization of play and regulation of playtime by parents. Although these experiences differ in many ways, they are similar in that they all leave children with little time outside of school that is not controlled or supervised by adults. Recall that this is the very type of experience that children in our study reported as stressful. Also note that this leaves children with little time outside of school to be with small groups of children in unstructured activities where relationships and activities may be developed and negotiated by the children themselves. And these are the very types of experiences that have been shown by developmental psychologists to benefit children in developing intellectual skills, including planning, during middle childhood.

In contrast to the caricature of the "hurried child" of middle childhood, our findings indicate that with increasing age children are less involved in socially organized and adult-controlled activities. This suggests that as children get older they have more time to plan on their own. But it is not clear from our data what, or even if, they are planning. At these same ages, children report fewer activities and more boredom. These reports are consistent with the findings of the Carnegie Council on Adolescent Development (1992) from a study of how adolescents spend their time outside of school. Their data indicate that close to 50% of adolescents are mired in boredom with little to do either at home or in their communities. Of course, it could be argued that, at least for adolescents, planning of a sort is occurring. Goals that are important to adolescents, such as affiliation with peers and openness to opportunity, may be best met by planning an "open schedule." However, this conclusion is difficult to reconcile with the fact that a majority of preadolescents (Medrich, Roizen, Rubin, & Buckley, 1982) and adolescents (Carnegie Council on Adolescent Development, 1992) report a lack of purpose and direction in their daily and long-range involvements.

Lack of involvement or direction for so many youth is worrisome. The

Carnegie report contends that this pattern of unproductive activity places adolescents at risk for healthy development. Although the report acknowledges that there have always been some youth in our society at risk of not achieving productive adulthood, it argues that this number has reached epidemic proportions. Attention by professionals toward these issues has largely focused on the social and emotional consequences for children. Clearly, this is where overcommitment and underinvolvement exhibit their most obvious toll. But from a cognitive-developmental perspective, another question can be asked. What is the effect of these experiences on intellectual opportunities and development, such as the development of planning skills? In the experience of both the overcommitted child and the underinvolved adolescent, there appears to be a lack of planning on the part of the youngster to organize his or her time in constructive, goal-directed ways. One conclusion, perhaps too easily drawn, is that children and adolescents lack the planning skills to do this. However, this conclusion is challenged by laboratory findings that show a fairly high level of planning competence, at least on relatively constrained tasks, at these same ages.

Are children and adolescents simply unable to extend the planning skills they demonstrate in the laboratory into their everyday practices? Perhaps planning everyday activities, which tend to be open-ended and entail multiple social and practical considerations, is markedly different from many of the planning tasks studied in the laboratory. Recall that when more complex tasks have been used in this setting, adolescents, and sometimes adults, have difficulty devising effective plans (Krietler & Krietler, 1987; Parrila et al., 1994; Presson, 1987). Planning in the everyday social world, especially for a young adolescent, may be more akin to planning on these more complex tasks. This suggests that in order to understand this developmental process, perhaps especially beyond the years of early childhood, careful task analysis is needed.

But in addition to task analysis, sociocultural analysis is required. This chapter presents the view that the experiences of childhood, especially children's interactions with and guidance from more experienced cultural members, influence the planning skills that children develop. However, as results from our reanalysis of Baumrind's data suggests, in certain sociocultural contexts, preadolescents may have less guidance in developing these skills than they need. And, as a result, the gradual transference of responsibility for this cognitive activity, a practice considered important for learning and development (e.g., see Rogoff, 1990; Vygotsky, 1978), may not occur.

This is an interesting observation, though it is in some ways perplexing, especially in relation to Western cultures. In these communities, the transition to adulthood (i.e., adolescence) is a lengthy process. This would seem to leave much time for guided participation in the development of mature skills like planning. However, depending on parental practices and expectations, a gradual transition in this particular domain may not occur. Expectations for independent performance in planning one's time may, for many young adolescents, arise rather abruptly. The days of parental orchestration are past, but the skills, knowledge, and resources needed for planning in the everyday social world may not yet be in place. In addition, the timing of this may coincide with other pressing developmental demands, including social, physical, and motivational factors.

Poor understanding of the precursors of this adolescent experience – that is, in the ways in which children participate in the construction and organization of their time during middle to late childhood – leaves psychologists unable to explain how these adolescent patterns arise. At present, developmental psychologists do not have the data to answer many of the questions raised here. Research that attends to children's opportunities and support for planning in everyday life, and the relation of these opportunities to the development of planning skills, may provide better understanding of how children learn to organize and direct their time at different points of development. This, in turn, may help us make sense of how the busy child becomes the bored, restless adolescent.

Summary and Conclusions

The development of planning involves learning to set goals and then identifying means and coordinating actions to reach these goals. Children appear to learn much about planning in the course of everyday activities. With increasing age, children show greater engagement in and initiation of future-oriented activities. The years of middle childhood appear to be a particular growth point for these skills. Children's emerging intellectual capabilities together with their expanding social life appear to contribute to substantial growth in planning skills during these years.

Laboratory research shows that children benefit from planning with others, especially more competent individuals like parents and other adults. Much of children's planning in everyday life tends to occur in the company of more experienced cultural members, and this may enhance children's learning about and practice with planning during these years. The nature of social input appears to change over the course of childhood, however. Early in childhood, much of what children learn about planning seems to occur in the family context, with different approaches to parenting leading to different opportunities for children to develop these skills. The picture changes during middle childhood as children move away from social activities planned mostly by adults to more time that the children can plan themselves. This transition is marked by a paradox, however. At the same time that children are given more opportunity to exercise their planning skills, evidence of their planning is sketchy. The "hurried child" appears to give way, all too quickly, to the bored, relatively unengaged adolescent. Because children of these ages show increasing competence on laboratory planning tasks, this raises questions about how the planning skills demonstrated in the lab map onto children's planning behaviors in the everyday world. Examination of cultural practices that encourage, support, and undermine children's planning in everyday contexts may be helpful in addressing this question. Not only will this information expand understanding of human development; it may also benefit practitioners and educators who rely on children's planning skills as they attempt to introduce change and direction to children's lives.

This chapter advances the study of the development of planning in three respects. First, it broadens the scope of research on the development of planning by focusing on how participation in everyday activities and routines, especially within the family context, may contribute to this type of cognitive competence. Second, by studying planning-related behaviors in a sociocultural context, we have identified some ways that the social and cultural world may contribute to the development of these skills. Finally, by drawing attention to everyday practices that may foster children's development in specific domains of intellectual functioning, this chapter contributes to current efforts to understand how everyday opportunities provided by the community in which growth occurs are related to the development of cognitive competence in the domain of planning. This, in turn, may assist us in understanding and addressing the ways in which children in our own communities develop and deploy this important life skill.

References

Bandura, A. (1986). *Social foundations of thought and action: A social-cognitive theory.* Englewood Cliffs, NJ: Prentice-Hall.
Barker, R. (1968). *Ecological psychology.* Stanford: Stanford University Press.
Baumrind, D. (1966). Effects of authoritative parental control on child behavior. *Child Development, 37,* 887–907.

Baumrind, D. (1973). The development of instrumental competence through socialization. In A. Pick (Ed.), *Minnesota symposium on child psychology* (Vol. 7), pp. 3–46). Minneapolis, MN: University of Minnesota Press.

Benson, J. (1994). The origins of future orientation in the everyday lives of 9- to 36-month-old infants. In M. M. Haith, J. B. Benson, R. J. Roberts, & B. Pennington (Eds.), *The development of future-oriented processes* (pp. 375–407). Chicago: University of Chicago Press.

Benson, J. B., Arehart, D. M., Jennings, T., Boley, S., & Kearns, L. (1989, April). *Infant crawling: Expectation, action-plans, and goals.* Paper presented at the meeting of the Society for Research in Child Development, Kansas City.

Besevegis, E., & Neimark, E. (1987, April). *Executive control at an early age: Advance planning in solitary play.* Paper presented at the meeting of the Society for Research in Child Development, Baltimore.

Bronfenbrenner, U. (1979). *The ecology of human development: Experiments by nature and design.* Cambridge, MA: Harvard University Press.

Brown, A. L., & Campione, J. (1984). Three faces of transfer: Implications for early competence, individual differences, and instruction. In M. E. Lamb, A. L. Brown, & B. Rogoff (Eds.), *Advances in developmental psychology* (pp. 143–92) (Vol. 3). Hillsdale, NJ: Erlbaum.

Bryant, B., & Djakovic, M. (1993, March). *How do we capture daily life? A methodological look at the study of "the child-in-context."* Paper presented at the meeting of the Society for Research in Child Development, New Orleans.

Carnegie Council on Adolescent Development. (1992). *A matter of time: Risk and opportunity in the nonschool hours.* New York: Carnegie Corporation.

Cocking, R. R., & Copple, C. E. (1987). Social influences on representational awareness: Plans for representing and plans as representations. In S. Friedman, E. Scholnick, & R. R. Cocking (Eds.), *Blueprints for thinking: The role of planning in cognitive development* (pp. 428–65). New York: Cambridge University Press.

Delgado-Gaitan, C. (1994). Socializing young children in Mexican-American families: An intergenerational perspective. In P. M. Greenfield & R. R. Cocking (Eds.), *Cross-cultural roots of minority child development* (pp. 55–86). Hillsdale, NJ: Erlbaum.

Dreher, M., & Oerter, R. (1987). Action planning competencies during adolescence and early adulthood. In S. Friedman, E. Scholnick, & R. R. Cocking (Eds.), *Blueprints for thinking: The role of planning in cognitive development* (pp. 321–55). New York: Cambridge University Press.

Elkind, D. (1981). *The hurried child: Growing up too fast too soon.* Reading, MA: Addison-Wesley.

Ellis, S., & Gauvain, M. (1992). Social and cultural influences on children's collaborative interactions. In L. T. Winegar & J. Valsiner (Eds.), *Children's development within social context* (pp. 155–80). Hillsdale, NJ: Erlbaum.

Fabricius, W. V. (1988). The development of forward search planning in preschoolers. *Child Development, 59,* 1473–88.

Friedman, S. L., Scholnick, E. K., & Cocking, R. R. (Eds.). (1987). *Blueprints for thinking: The role of planning in psychological development.* New York: Cambridge University Press.

Gauvain, M. (1989). Children's planning in social context: An observational study of kindergartners' planning in the classroom. In L. T. Winegar (Ed.), *Social interaction and the development of children's understanding* (pp. 95–117). Norwood, NJ: Ablex.

Gauvain, M. (1992). Social influences on the development of skill at planning during action. *International Journal of Behavioral Development, 15,* 377–98.

Gauvain, M. (1995). Thinking in niches: Sociocultural influences on cognitive development. *Human Development, 38,* 25–45.

Gauvain, M., & Huard, R. D. (1993, March). *What do children do when they have nothing to do? A study of children's planning in everyday life.* Paper presented at the meeting of the Society for Research in Child Development, New Orleans.

Gauvain, M., & Huard, R. D. (1998). Future talk: The role of the family in the development of competence at planning. In A. Colby & J. James (Eds.), *The development of character and competence over the lifespan* (pp. 31–55). Chicago: University of Chicago Press.

Gauvain, M., & Klaue, K. (1989, June). *Influence of experience in the environment on the organization of directional information.* Paper presented at the meeting of the Jean Piaget Society, Philadelphia.

Gauvain, M., & Lee, T. (1996). *The development of spatial thinking among the Navajo.* Unpublished manuscript, University of California, Riverside.

Gauvain, M., & Rogoff, B. (1989). Collaborative problem solving and children's planning skills. *Developmental Psychology, 25,* 139–51.

Gauvain, M., & Savage, S. (1995, August). *Everyday opportunities for the development of planning skills.* Paper presented at the meeting of the American Psychological Association, New York.

Gearhart, M. (1979, April). *Social planning: Role play in a novel situation.* Paper presented at the meeting of the Society for Research in Child Development, San Francisco.

Geoghegan, W. (1973). *Natural information processing rules.* Monographs of the Language Behavior Research Laboratory, University of California. Berkeley: ERIC Microfiche Files.

Gladwin, T. (1971). *East is a big bird.* Cambridge, MA: Harvard University Press.

Goodnow, J. J. (1976). The nature of intelligent behavior: Questions raised by cross-cultural studies. In L. Resnick (Ed.), *The nature of intelligence* (pp. 169–88). Hillsdale, NJ: Erlbaum.

Goodnow, J. J. (1987). Social aspects of planning. In S. L. Friedman, E. K. Scholnick, & R. R. Cocking (Eds.), *Blueprints for thinking: The role of planning in psychological development* (pp. 179–201). New York: Cambridge University Press.

Goodnow, J. J. (1990). The socialization of cognition: What's involved? In J. W. Stigler, R. A. Shweder, & G. Herdt (Eds.), *Cultural psychology* (pp. 259–86). Cambridge: Cambridge University Press.

Goodnow, J. J., & Burns, A. (1985). *Home and school: A child's-eye view.* Sydney: Allen & Unwin.

Goodnow, J. J., Miller, P. J., & Kessel, F. (1995). *Cultural practices as contexts for development: New directions for child development* (No. 67). San Francisco: Jossey-Bass.

Haith, M. M., Benson, J. B., Roberts, R. J., & Pennington, B. F. (1994). *The development of future-oriented processes.* Chicago: University of Chicago Press.

Hayes-Roth, B., & Hayes-Roth, F. (1979). A cognitive model of planning. *Cognitive Science, 3*, 275–310.

Hudson, J., & Fivush, R. (1991). Planning in the preschool years: The emergence of plans from general event knowledge. *Cognitive Development, 6*, 393–415.

Inhelder, B., & Piaget, J. (1964). *The early growth of logic in the child.* New York: Norton.

Inkeles, A., & Smith, D. H. (1974). *Becoming modern.* Cambridge, MA: Harvard University Press.

Klahr, D., & Robinson, M. (1981). Formal assessment of problem solving and planning processes in children. *Cognitive Psychology, 13*, 113–48.

Krietler, S., & Krietler, H. (1987). Plans and planning: Their motivational and cognitive antecedents. In S. Friedman, E. Scholnick, & R. R. Cocking (Eds.), *Blueprints for thinking: The role of planning in cognitive development* (pp. 205–72). New York: Cambridge University Press.

Lamborn, S. D., Mounts, N. S., Steinberg, L., & Dornbusch, S. M. (1991). Patterns of competence and adjustment among adolescents from authoritative, authoritarian, indulgent, and neglectful families. *Child Development, 62*, 1049–65.

Lave, J. (1988). *Cognition in practice.* Cambridge: Cambridge University Press.

Lave, J., & Wenger, E. (1991). *Situated learning: Legitimate peripheral participation.* New York: Cambridge University Press.

Leont'ev, A. N. (1981). The problem of activity in psychology. In J. V. Wertsch (Ed.), *The concept of activity in Soviet psychology* (pp. 37–71). Armonk, NY: Sharpe.

Lewin, K. (1951). *Field theory in social science: Selected theoretical papers.* New York: Harper & Row.

Lucarillo, J., & Nelson, K. (1987). Remembering and planning talk. *Discourse Processes, 10*, 219–35.

Luria, A. R. (1976). *Cognitive development: Its cultural and social foundations.* Cambridge, MA: Harvard University Press.

Maccoby, E. E., & Martin, J. (1983). Socialization in the context of the family. In P. Mussen (Series Ed.), *Handbook of child psychology* (pp. 1–101) (Vol. 4). New York: Wiley.

Magkaev, V. (1977). An experimental study of the planning function of thinking in young school children. In M. Cole (Ed.), *Soviet development psychology: An anthology* (pp. 606–20). White Plains, NY: Sharpe.

Medrich, E. A., Roizen, J., Rubin, V., & Buckley, S. (1982). *The serious business of growing up: A study of children's lives outside school.* Berkeley: University of California Press.

Nelson, K. (1981). Social cognition in a script framework. In J. Flavell & L. Ross (Eds.), *Social cognitive development* (pp. 97–118). Cambridge: Cambridge University Press.

Ochs, E., Smith, R., & Taylor, C. (1989). Dinner narratives as detective stories. *Cultural Dynamics, 2*, 238–57.

Parke, R. D., & Bhavnagri, N. P. (1989). Parents as managers of children's peer relationships. In D. Belle (Ed.), *Children's social networks and social supports* (pp. 241–59). New York: Wiley.

Parrila, R. K., Aysto, S., & Das, J. P. (1994). Development of planning in relation to age, attention, simultaneous and successive processing. *Journal of Psychoeducational Assessment, 12*, 212–27.

Pea, R. D. (1982). What is planning development the development of? In D. L. Forbes & M. T. Greenberg (Eds.), *Children's planning strategies* (pp. 5–27). San Francisco: Jossey-Bass.

Pratt, M. W., Kerig, P., Cowan, P. A., & Cowan, C. P. (1988). Mothers and fathers teaching 3-year-olds: Authoritative parenting and adult scaffolding of young children's learning. *Developmental Psychology, 24*, 832–9.

Presson, C. C. (1987). The development of spatial cognition: Secondary uses of spatial information. In N. Eisenberg (Ed.), *Contemporary topics in developmental psychology* (pp. 77–112). New York: Wiley.

Pribram, K. H., & Luria, A. R. (1973). *Psychophysiology of the frontal lobes.* New York: Academic Press.

Radziszewska, B., & Rogoff, B. (1988). Influence of adult and peer collaborators on children's planning skills. *Developmental Psychology, 24*, 840–8.

Randall, R. A. (1977). *Change and variation in Samal fishing: Making plans to "make a living" in the Southern Philippines.* Unpublished doctoral dissertation, University of California, Berkeley. (Ann Arbor: University of Michigan, Microfilms No. 77–31511).

Randall, R. A. (1987). Planning in cross-cultural settings. In S. Friedman, E. Scholnick, & R. R. Cocking (Eds.), *Blueprints for thinking: The role of planning in cognitive development* (pp. 39–75). New York: Cambridge University Press.

Reeve, R. (1987, April), *Functional significance of parental "scaffolding" as a moderator of social influences on children's cognition.* Paper presented at the meeting of the Society for Research in Child Development, Baltimore.

Rogoff, B. (1990). *Apprenticeship in thinking.* New York: Oxford University Press.

Rogoff, B. (1996). Developmental transitions in children's participation in sociocultural activities. In A. Sameroff & M. Haith (Eds.), *The five to seven year shift: The age of reason and responsibility* (pp. 273–94). Chicago: University of Chicago Press.

Rogoff, B., Gauvain, M., & Gardner, W. (1987). The development of children's skill in adjusting plans to circumstances. In S. L. Friedman, E. K. Scholnick, & R. R. Cocking (Eds.), *Blueprints for thinking: The role of planning in psychological development* (pp. 303–20). New York: Cambridge University Press.

Rogoff, B., Mistry, J., Radziszewska, B., & Germond, J. (1991). Infants' instrumental social interaction with adults. In S. Feinman (Ed.), *Social referencing and the social construction of reality in infancy* (pp. 323–48). New York: Plenum.

Segall, M. H., Dasen, P. R., Berry, J. W., & Poortinga, Y. H. (1990). *Human behavior in global perspective.* New York: Pergamon Press.

Super, C. M. (1983). Cultural variations in the meaning and uses of children's "intelligence." In J. B. Deregowski, S. Dziurawiec, & R. A. Annis (Eds.), *Expiscations in cross-cultural psychology* (pp. 199–213). Lisse, Netherlands: Swets & Zeitlinger.

Super, C., & Harkness, S. (1986). The developmental niche: A conceptualization at the interface of child and culture. *International Journal of Behavioral Development, 9,* 545–69.

Szeminska, A. (1965). The evolution of thought: Some applications of research findings to educational practice. In P. H. Mussen (Ed.), European research in cognitive development. *Monographs of the Society for Research in Child Development, 30,* 47–57.

Tharp, R. G., & Gallimore, R. (1988). *Rousing minds to life.* Cambridge: Cambridge University Press.

Vygotsky, L. S. (1978). *Mind in society.* Cambridge, MA: Harvard University Press.

Vygotsky, L. S. (1981). The development of higher forms of attention in children. In J. V. Wertsch (Ed.), *The concept of activity in Soviet psychology* (pp. 144–88). Armonk, NY: Sharpe.

Wellman, H., Fabricius, W., & Sophian, C. (1985). The early development of planning. In H. Wellman (Ed.), *Children's searching: The development of search skills and spatial representation* (pp. 123–49). Hillsdale, NJ: Erlbaum.

Whiting, B. B., & Edwards, C. P. (1988). *Children of different worlds: The formation of social behavior.* Cambridge, MA: Harvard University Press.

Willatts, P. (1990). Development of problem solving strategies in infancy. In D. F. Bjorklund (Ed.), *Children's strategies: Contemporary views of cognitive development.* Hillsdale, NJ: Erlbaum.

Wood, D. J., & Middleton, D. (1975). A study of assisted problem-solving. *British Journal of Psychology, 66,* 181–91.

Zinchenko, P. I. (1981). Involuntary memory and the goal-directed nature of activity in Soviet psychology. In J. V. Wertsch (Ed.), *The concept of activity in Soviet psychology* (pp. 300–40). Armonk, NY: Sharpe.

8 Supportive Environments for Cognitive Development: Illustrations from Children's Mathematical Activities Outside of School

Steven R. Guberman

By the time American children begin their formal education, they possess a wide range of mathematical skills. Three- and four-year-olds are capable of counting, comparing, adding, and subtracting sets of objects (Nunes & Bryant, 1996; Saxe & Gearhart, 1988), and, although their solution methods often differ from the methods taught in school, preschoolers demonstrate at least some understanding of basic mathematical principles, such as how to count (Gelman & Gallistel, 1978), one-to-one correspondence (Sugarman, 1983), and relations of equivalence and nonequivalence (Klein & Starkey, 1988). Even 5-month-olds appear to distinguish between appropriate and inappropriate outcomes of adding and subtracting small groups of objects (Simon, Hespos, & Rochat, 1995; Wynn, 1992). The findings of early mathematical competence point to an inborn capacity for human infants to structure certain kinds of environmental information in quantitative ways (Gelman, 1990). But, as with all cognitive propensities, the realization and development of children's mathematical abilities require an environment that provides opportunities to exercise and extend nascent skills and understanding. Although we have learned a great deal about children's mathematical abilities, we are only beginning to study the contexts in which children's skills are used and nurtured.

There are several reasons to study how children use mathematics in their routine activities outside of school. Kessen (1993) noted that "the intellectual reason for the study of everyday behavior is sweet in its simplicity: Everyday behavior is what we want to know about. Somehow

Research reported in this chapter was supported by grants from the National Science Foundation, the Spencer Foundation, and the Graduate School of the University of Colorado. I am grateful to Artin Göncü, Kate Cumbo, Margaret Eisenhart, Debra Menk, and Jrene Rahm for their many helpful comments on drafts of this chapter.

... we lost sight of the core goal, the *understanding of what children do*"
(p. 276; emphasis in the original). The study of everyday behavior takes
on additional significance from a sociocultural perspective, because it is
through participating in everyday activities that social and cultural processes foster and shape children's development. Indeed, children's engagement in everyday activities has become the primary focus of sociocultural analyses of development. For example, Wertsch (1995) has
proposed that "concrete, dynamic human action existing in real spatiotemporal and social contexts" (p. 62) is, appropriately, the common focus
of sociocultural approaches to cognitive development. For Saxe (1991),
cultural activities are contexts for the emergence in children of mathematical goals, which both reflect sociocultural processes and provide
opportunities for children to construct new understanding and skill. Bronfenbrenner (1993) claimed that "the principal engine of psychological,
and especially cognitive, development is engagement in progressively
more complex activities and tasks" (p. 11). And for others, like Rogoff
(1995) and Lave and Wenger (1991), development and learning are the
same as changing forms of participation in sociocultural activities. (For
further discussion of these ideas, see Gauvain, and Tudge et al., this
volume.)

The focus of this chapter is the nature of children's mathematical
activities outside of school. Recent calls for reforming the way mathematics is taught in school (e.g., National Council of Teachers of Mathematics, 1989) are motivated in part by evidence that many American
children have difficulty learning school mathematics and are unable to
apply the mathematics they do learn in school to solve problems that
arise in their everyday lives. In contrast, as Lave, Smith, and Butler
(1989) have noted, "quantitative relations are dealt with inventively and
effectively in everyday situations, without employing school-taught
mathematics in any obvious way" (p. 67). Children across a wide range
of cultures acquire basic, and often sophisticated, mathematical skills
and understanding with little or no formal instruction (Guberman, 1996;
Nunes, Schliemann, & Carraher, 1993; Saxe, 1991). These findings –
success outside of school and failure within – have led to proposals to
use everyday activities that engage children in mathematical problem
solving as models for school instruction (e.g., Fuson, Zecker, Lo Cicero,
& Ron, 1995). For these efforts to be successful, though, we need to
understand better the ways in which children's learning and reasoning
are supported in their everyday endeavors (Heath & McLaughlin,
1994).

In this chapter, sociocultural theory is used to address issues of what constitutes a supportive environment for children's intellectual development. I draw on several studies of children's engagement in mathematical activities outside of school to illustrate characteristics of supportive environments for children's developing mathematical skill and understanding. A central concern is to examine characteristics that may be common across a range of social groups and settings, characteristics that may both inform our understanding of development in social context and be useful in designing instructional programs.

In this chapter, Vygotsky's (1978) conceptualization of the zone of proximal development serves as a framework for understanding how children's developing knowledge is supported and encouraged in teaching interactions between parents and children. Then, borrowing from alternative interpretations of the zone of proximal development, I extend the analysis to include activities that are structured by parents but which take place out of their presence, including learning opportunities in contexts structured specifically for children. Although these analyses highlight the way *adults* design and alter activities so that children are able to join in accomplishing meaningful goals, *children* also contribute to the structure of their environments. I illustrate the ways in which children transform their mathematical tasks by examining children's game play.

What emerges from these studies is that supportive environments permit children to participate meaningfully in activities at a variety of levels of understanding. Although the studies discussed in this chapter vary widely – from poor Brazilian children running errands for their parents to middle-class American teenagers engaged in game play – they point to a central component of supportive environments: a flexibility that makes possible the transformation of activities in ways that encourage children's participation from novice to expert status. In particular, they allow for change: the moment-to-moment changes that occur in face-to-face instructional interactions, as when parents adjust their assistance in response to children's ongoing difficulties (Rogoff, 1990); the age-related and socially organized changes that occur as activities are modified for children by others, as when adults assign children of different ages to distinct settings and tasks (e.g., Whiting & Whiting, 1975); and changes in activities that are brought about by children through their own participation, as when children interpret and transform games in varied ways (e.g., Piaget, 1965). Sometimes, changes are accomplished through negotiation as children interact with more knowledgeable partners, sometimes through the arrangement of appropriate activities for children by adults and social institutions, and sometimes through peer interaction as children bring prior knowledge to their joint participation. In each case, we see that environments are complex emergent constructions that not only shape children's learning and development but also are themselves shaped by the people participating in them.

Children's Engagement in Mathematical Activities

There are many opportunities for American children to engage in mathematical activities. One of the few studies of American children's use of mathematics outside of school was published approximately 75 years ago (Smith, 1924). In that study, teachers in Detroit interviewed 500 first-grade children on 25 consecutive school days. Each child was asked to describe everything he or she had done since leaving school the previous afternoon, and teachers probed for additional information regarding activities they thought might involve mathematics.

The frequency with which children mentioned their uses of mathematics is presented in Table 8.1. The most common activities were commercial transactions – making purchases, depositing and withdrawing money from toy banks, and playing store. The interviews also revealed that 35% of the children's uses of mathematics entailed addition, 23% counting, 12% subtraction, and 8% fractions.

Most of the mathematical uses documented in the 1920s are common among today's children, although any current list surely would include video and computer games prominently. More recent studies (e.g., Guberman, 1992; Medrich, Roizen, Rubin, & Buckley, 1982; Saxe, Guberman, & Gearhart, 1987) have documented abundant opportunities for children, from preschool through high school, to participate in mathematical activities outside of school. These include counting songs and number books, educational television, board and card games, and calculating scores and players' averages in sporting activities. Importantly, children's mathematical activities reflect the cultural values and practices of their society: The types of activities children engage in and the frequency of their engagement vary across cultures (Ginsburg, Posner, & Russell, 1981) and across American ethnic groups (Guberman, 1992) and are related to the knowledge and skills that children develop (Abreu, 1995; Nunes et al., 1993; Saxe, 1991).

Any portrayal of supportive environments must take into consideration how we characterize children's learning and development. From a behaviorist perspective, Smith's (1924) frequency count of the different activi-

Table 8.1. *Relative Frequency with Which Situations Involving Arithmetic Occurred*

Activity	Percent
Transactions carried on in stores	30.0
Games involving counting	18.0
Reading Roman numerals on the clock	14.0
Reading Arabic numerals and finding pages in books	13.0
Dividing food with playmates and pets (fractions)	6.0
Depositing money in and withdrawing money from toy banks	5.0
Playing store	3.0
Measuring distance	2.2
Using calendars	2.0
Running errands	1.2
Setting the table	1.2
Buying and selling tickets	1.1
Acting as newsboy	1.0
Measuring in sewing	1.0
Counting in rhymes and jingles	0.5
Reading house numbers	0.2
Investments (made for them)	0.1
Measuring in manual training	0.1
Measuring height	0.1
Measuring objects	0.1
Reading numbers on hooks in hall	0.1
Reading numbers on tickets	0.1
Total	100.0

Note: From ''An investigation of the uses of arithmetic in the out-of-school life of first-grade children'' by N. B. Smith, 1924, *The Elementary School Journal, 24,* 621–26. Permission granted by the University of Chicago press. Grant #40036.

ties in which children are engaged may be an adequate description of the environment in order to understand children's mathematical learning. But from a constructivist perspective, children's own activity in defining and interpreting their environments also must be considered (Gelman, Massey, & McManus, 1991). Furthermore, a sociocultural (or social constructivist) perspective highlights the social and cultural aspects of children's environments. Of special importance for characterizing supportive environments from a sociocultural perspective are two related notions that comprise the focus of the remainder of this chapter.

First, supportive environments provide opportunities for children to participate meaningfully in cultural activities, to use their prior knowledge and experience in order to achieve a valued goal (Rogoff, 1990; Saxe, 1991). At the same time, environments must challenge children to construct new abilities. Thus, as children develop and acquire new understandings, their participation in everyday activities must also change so that children are provided appropriate uses for their newly acquired knowledge and are challenged toward further development. As Weisner (1984) has noted, "contexts, or scaffolds, for children's development change over time, just as individuals change and develop" (p. 336). There needs to be a reciprocal process between children's developing abilities and the nature of their participation in social life.

The second notion is common to constructivist treatments of development, although sometimes overlooked in sociocultural analyses: Children's own interests and sense-making processes must be central to a formulation of supportive environments. Because environments are neither independent of the actors in them nor imposed on actors, determining which aspects of the environment are relevant and supportive for development depends on how they are attended to and interpreted by children (Gelman et al., 1991). Thus, there is a potential tension between the cultural and social forces that structure children's environments, and embue them with significance, and children's own role in interpreting and transforming their environments.

In order to illustrate these features of supportive environments, I draw from several studies of children's mathematics in which I have been involved. These include analyses of American mothers assisting their preschool children to solve number tasks (Saxe et al., 1987), Brazilian children engaged in commercial transactions (Guberman, 1996), and American children playing a popular board game, MONOPOLY (Guberman & Rahm, 1996; Menk & Guberman, 1996).

Supporting Children's Mathematics Learning in Parent–Child Interactions

One way of characterizing supportive environments for children builds on Vygotsky's (1978) ideas about the zone of proximal development (Brown & Reeve, 1987; Greenfield, 1984). It is through interactions in children's zones of proximal development – defined as the difference between what children are capable of doing on their own and what they can do with the assistance of an adult or more capable peer – that others promote and shape children's cognitive growth. Wertsch (1984) described three key concepts for understanding the zone of proximal development: situation definition, intersubjectivity, and semiotic mediation.

The first notion, *situation definition*, refers to the way that participants represent for themselves the activity or setting in which they are engaged. Wertsch emphasized that the definition of a situation is not given in the setting but is actively constructed by the participants. In the zone of proximal development, each participant defines the situation in a qualitatively different way: "Even though the adult and child are functioning in the same spatiotemporal context, they often understand this context in such different ways that they are really not doing the same task" (Wertsch, 1984, p. 9). Learning in the zone of proximal development occurs when a child modifies his or her situation definition to one that is more in accord with an adult's.

Second, some degree of *intersubjectivity*, or agreement on task definition, must exist among the participants for assistance to be effective. Intersubjectivity is based on a situation definition that differs from both the child's and the adult's initial definitions; it is a third way of defining the situation, a definition that is shared sufficiently among the participants so that they are able to communicate and engage in coordinated action (cf. Matusov, 1996). Intersubjectivity may exist on a variety of levels, from simple agreement on the names of objects to shared definitions and goals.

Third, the shared situation definition is negotiated through *semiotic mediation*, including gestures and language. For instruction in the zone of proximal development to be effective, there must be semiotic flexibility: Adults adjust their presentation of the task in response to children's ongoing behavior. Especially important are the semiotic challenges that adults often provide in their interactions with children, "an invitation to the child to redefine the situation on the adult's terms" (Wertsch, 1984, p. 14).

The notions of task definition, intersubjectivity, and semiotic mediation are helpful for understanding learning within social interaction. In one study, colleagues and I (Saxe et al., 1987) studied how mothers assisted their children to accomplish a series of number tasks. Consider the transcript, in Figure 8.1, of a mother and her 2½-year-old child attempting to count a set of five dots. Although the child knows a great deal about

1	M:	You just count them. Okay, let me hear you count them.
2	C:	(pointing) Three, two, three, two, three, two.
3	M:	What happened to one?
4	C:	(pointing) One, two, one, two, one, two, one, two. (mother begins to point with child) ( )
5	M:	Yeah...Is that how you count? C'mon. (points to a dot)
6	C:	(pause)
7	M:	Count one...
8	C:	One.
9	M:	(points to another dot) What's next?
10	C:	Two.
11	M:	(points to a third dot and waits)
12	C:	(pause)
13	M:	(still pointing) What's next?
14	C:	Three.
15	M:	(points to another dot) And what's next?
16	C:	Two.
17	M:	No. You said one, two, three. What's next? Remember?
18	C:	Four.
19	M:	Right! Very good! (points to another dot) And what's next?
20	C:	(pause)
21	M:	You said one, two, three, four (pointing to the dots). What comes next?
22	C:	Three!
23	M:	No! What happened to five?
24	C:	Five!

Figure 8.1. Transcript of mother and 2½-year-old child counting a set of five dots.

counting, his definition of the task appears to differ substantially from how the mother (and other adults in our culture) understands counting. As can be seen in turns 1 and 2, when asked to count, the child recites number words and points to the to-be-counted objects, but he appears not to understand that each and every object must be assigned a unique number word from a stable order of labels (Gelman & Gallistel, 1978). Without this understanding, the child is engaged in a qualitatively different activity: to recite number words while pointing, actions that are typical of counting, but not to determine the cardinal value of the set. As the mother monitors and responds to the child's activity, the task is transformed, and a third situation definition emerges. Starting at turn 5, the mother takes over pointing to the dots; at this juncture, the task becomes a rote counting activity for the child. The mother and child still may not share the same exact definition of the task – the child's understanding of cardinal value is questionable – but a level of intersubjectivity has been reached that permits them to continue their joint activity. This third situation definition – Vygotsky's (1978) interpsychological plane of functioning – was achieved through semiotic means as the mother used gestures and language to direct the child's attention (e.g., turns 5, 9, and 11).

Especially noteworthy in this interaction are the semiotic challenges provided by the mother. For instance, in turn 7, the mother models appropriate counting behavior by pointing to a dot and stating the correct number word. Once the child successfully accomplishes the intended behavior – repeating "one" – the mother challenges him to redefine the task: It is no longer a repetition task, but through her request for the "next" number (turn 9), the mother suggests to the child that a set sequence of number words is required. Following the child's correct response (turn 10), the mother further reduces the level of assistance she provides, no longer asking for the next number but just waiting for the child to continue; that there is an appropriate "next" number is no longer specified by the mother but becomes a challenge to the child. Indeed, each time the child is successful, the mother follows with a level of assistance that is less specific (or, in one instance [turns 13 and 15], at the same level) than her previous assistance. In contrast, when the child has difficulty responding to his mother's prompts (e.g., turns 12, 16, and 20), the mother responds with greater levels of assistance, such as shifting from just pointing to a dot (turns 5 and 11), to asking for the next number (turns 9, 13, 15, and 19), to repeating part or all of the previous count (turns 17 and 21), to providing the answer (turns 7 and 23).

Through the use of contingent assistance, or "scaffolding" (Wood, Bruner, & Ross, 1976), the child is enabled to continue participating in the task and at the same time is provided opportunities to construct new levels of understanding. In our study of 78 middle- and working-class mother–child dyads (Saxe et al., 1987), scaffolding was common as mothers assisted their preschool children to accomplish counting and number reproduction tasks. Each mother matched her assistance to the type of difficulty, such as counting or pointing, that her child experienced, and she adjusted the specificity of her directives in response to her child's ongoing successes and difficulties. Other studies also have reported scaffolding in parent–child interactions, including analyses of adults assisting infants to use a jack-in-the-box (Rogoff, Malkin, & Gilbride, 1984), language learning (Greenfield, 1984; Zukow, Reilly, & Greenfield, 1982), learning to weave (Greenfield & Childs, 1977), and assembling puzzles (Wertsch, 1984).

In summary, analyses of parent–child interaction in the zone of proximal development point to features of supportive environments. By negotiating a level of intersubjectivity that makes collaboration possible, children contribute to the structure of the tasks in which they engage and at the same time are enabled to complete tasks they could not accomplish on their own. These features are important components of supportive environments, such as the face-to-face parent–child interactions discussed previously and the more distal activities discussed next.

Moving Beyond the Dyad

The tendency of researchers to focus almost exclusively on parent–child teaching interactions as characteristic of supportive environments for children's development has been widely criticized (e.g., Gelman et al., 1991; Lave & Wenger, 1991; Rogoff, Mistry, Göncü, & Mosier, 1993). The focused attention and sensitive adjustments that many parents show in experimental teaching contexts are, most likely, not typical of children's everyday social interactions. Rather, greater attention needs to be given to the social and cultural structuring of activities as children take part in the daily life of their communities. These "more distal arrangements of people's activities that do not require copresence (e.g., choices of where and with whom and with what materials and activities a person is involved)" (Rogoff, 1995, p. 142) may represent the primary way that parents foster and shape their children's development (Whiting & Whiting, 1975).

The need for research on children's learning to move beyond face-to-face interactions was made clear to me in a study of Brazilian children's everyday mathematics (Guberman, 1996). In interviews with parents of children living in shantytown communities in Recife, Brazil, parents almost never reported that they engaged in activities intended to teach their children mathematics. It turned out, though, that their children frequently engaged in activities using mathematics, such as to keep score in soccer and card games. Often it appeared that parents structured children's activities from a distance, thereby contributing to the nature of the mathematics that children would encounter away from home. In the next section, I extend analyses of supportive contexts to include these more distal arrangements of children's environments, focusing on changes in children's engagement in a common everyday task – running errands for their parents to make small purchases.

The Social Organization of Children's Everyday Activities

The zone of proximal development is helpful for understanding the construction of supportive environments like the mother–child interaction discussed earlier. The zone of proximal development may also provide a framework for understanding the structuring of environments that extend beyond "the traditional Vygotskian dyad" (Forman, Stein, Brown, & Larreamendy-Joerns, 1995, p. 6). Lave and Wenger (1991) point out that the "scaffolding" explanation of the zone of proximal development, presented earlier, is just one of three common interpretations. A second, "cultural" interpretation "construes the zone of proximal development as the distance between the cultural knowledge provided by the sociohistorical context, usually made accessible through instruction, and the everyday experience of individuals" (p. 48). A third interpretation, the "collectivist" or "societal" perspective, defines the zone of proximal development as the "distance between the everyday actions of individuals and the historically new form of societal activity" (Engeström, 1987, quoted in Lave & Wenger, 1991, p. 49). This interpretation shifts from a conception of learning as the individual internalization of knowledge to a view of learning as increasing participation in social activity. By doing so, the concern is to move beyond explicitly pedagogical interactions toward understanding how children's learning and development are interwoven with the activities of daily life.

The three interpretations of the zone of proximal development, as described by Lave and Wenger (1991), are closely related. For instance, in the mother–child interaction described previously, the child's and mother's situation definitions may be thought of as the difference between the child's everyday experience and the mother's cultural knowledge, and scaffolding may be viewed as one means by which the mother promotes increasing participation in the task on the child's part. From this perspective, the mother provides a culturally appropriate model of counting for which the child gives up his own spontaneous counting methods. Over the course of participation, regulation of counting behavior shifts from other (i.e., the mother) to self (i.e., the child). These alternative interpretations of the zone of proximal development indicate that a characterization of supportive environments must apply to more than explicitly pedagogical dyadic interactions. Indeed, parents often have a role in structuring children's activities that extend beyond the boundaries of immediate parent–child interactions and into their communities. This was my focus in a study of Brazilian children's engagement in commercial transactions (Guberman, 1996): how children's community activities were structured by their parents and other adults in ways that supported children's use and acquisition of mathematical understanding and skill.

In interviews with the parents of Brazilian children who had little formal mathematics education (Guberman, 1996), parents reported that virtually all their children were sent by them, often several times a day, to make small purchases at local stands, perhaps to buy some rolls, candy, or other small, household provisions. Children from a wide range of ages participated in these commercial transactions, which appeared to entail children's most complex use of mathematics.

Children often relied on resources in the environment, especially other people, as aids in their problem solving. It appeared that other people structured the task differently for children of different ages; as a consequence, the arithmetical problems that emerged in children's transactions varied with age.

For example, while observing at one of the stands in the community, a toddler, about 18 months of age, approached the stand holding a Cr$100 note in her hand. Another customer at the stand held her up to the counter so she could see the merchandise, and she pointed to the type of candy she wanted. The owner of the stand gave her the candy and took her Cr$100 note, and she headed back home having completed a fairly complex commercial transaction without uttering a word and without engaging in any mathematical calculation. The toddler was able to participate in this exchange – a transaction beyond her independent ability – because others had structured the task for her; in this case, her mother knew what candy the toddler would select and had given her the exact amount of money she needed.

This was not an isolated incident. The parents of 105 children were interviewed concerning the responsibilities they assigned to their children when sending them to make purchases at local stands (Guberman, 1996). The interviewers gathered information about how many items parents asked their children to purchase, how much money the parents supplied, whether or not parents reminded their children to expect change, and, if they did, whether or not parents told their children how much change they should receive. Parents' responses were classified as one of four types that differ in the responsibilities they assigned to children and, as a consequence, the complexity of the mathematical problems with which children were engaged.

Consider an example in which a mother asks her child to go to a stand and buy two small loaves of bread, each costing Cr$200. At level 1 ("exact") of the scheme, the mother gives the child the exact amount of money needed for the purchase. All the child needs to do is give the money to the stand owner and receive the two loaves of bread. For the child, using mathematics is neither required nor expected. At level 2 ("wait") of the scheme, the mother gives the child a Cr$500 note and tells her to wait for change but not how much change to expect. Again, the child doesn't need to engage in any calculation but may begin to wonder why after paying with one note she receives not only the loaves of bread but also another note of different appearance; perhaps the child begins to grasp that currency comes in several denominations and to work out their equivalence relations. In level 3 ("check"), the mother tells her child how much change to expect and asks her to count it. At this level, the child must be able to recognize and add different denominations of currency. At level 4 ("calculate"), the child is expected to calculate the cost and change of the purchase, which often entails problems of complex addition and subtraction.

Figure 8.2 contains the percentage of children from each age group at each level of activity complexity. Children under 8 years of age were mostly involved in level 2 transactions: Their parents told them to wait for change but did not expect them to count it. With increasing age, children were engaged in more complex transactions and mathematical problems.

As with the toddler described earlier, many of the children frequently engaged in transactions beyond their independent abilities. In fact, none of the 4- and 5-year-olds and a third of the 6- to 8-year-olds could not even identify the values of currency denominations, although they used them frequently to make purchases.

Analyses revealed that the complexity of the responsibilities parents assigned to children was related to children's mathematical problem-solving abilities (Guberman, 1996). That is, the complexity level of children's commercial transactions correlated with children's performance on a series of problems similar to the ones they encountered in their com-

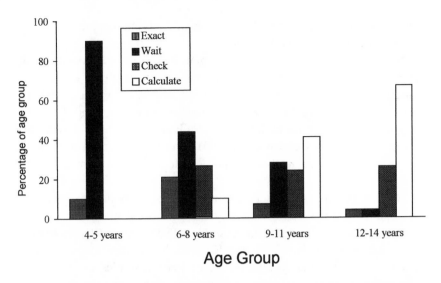

Figure 8.2. Percentage of children at each activity level by age group.

mercial transactions. Moreover, the analyses indicated that the association between children's activities and their arithmetical abilities extended beyond the effects of children's age, grade in school, and years of school attendance. In general, changes in children's mathematical skills were mirrored by changes in the complexity of their everyday mathematical activities.

By adjusting the complexity of the tasks that parents assigned to children, children of many different ability levels could participate in the activity in a meaningful way; they could exercise their existing mathematical skills; observe other, more competent participants; and, perhaps, begin to identify new, more complex mathematical goals. The children and adults constituted a joint problem-solving system, mutually constructing and solving problems instrumental to achieving their goal of purchasing merchandise.

These findings take descriptions of supportive environments beyond laboratory-based parent–child teaching interactions to include the routine activities that comprise children's day-to-day lives. Although parents and other community members were not intentionally *teaching* children about money and mathematics, they structured children's activities in ways that supported children's *learning* as they participated in community activities. Such adjustments, based on children's abilities and interests and on adults' beliefs about what is developmentally appropriate, are ubiquitous in our culture and many other cultures.

Not just parents, but society more generally structures activities and environments in order to facilitate the engagement of children with a wide variety of abilities and interests. Television programs targeted to distinct age groups (e.g., Sesame Street, The Electric Company) and museums designed specifically for children (e.g., Philadelphia's Please Touch Museum, described in Gelman et al., 1991) are two examples of environments structured specifically to support children's involvement and learning.

Another example of the societal structuring of children's mathematical environments in age-appropriate ways comes from a study of children's magazines. Joram, Resnick, and Gabriele (1995) note that "numbers are pervasive in our daily lives" (p. 346), and the abilities to comprehend and read numbers, and to calculate and estimate quantities, are crucial for informed participation in daily life. They found that the uses of numbers in magazines differed according to whether the magazine was intended for children, teenagers, or adults. Only a few difficult numbers are presented in magazines for children, but magazines for adults contain more difficult numbers and more complex uses of number.

In summary, there are parallels between the adjustments that adults make in their problem-solving interactions with children and the community and social arrangement of age-appropriate activities and arenas. In both cases, environments are structured in order to assist children's participation and understanding by providing a range of opportunities for involvement that is intended to match and extend children's abilities. One important difference, though, is the degree of adjustment possible across various contexts. Although parents may continually fine-tune their assistance to meet children's moment-to-moment successes and difficulties, social institutions are less flexible in responding to individual children's abilities and understanding. Rather, to meet a wide range of ability levels, communities and their institutions may provide activities that permit children a large degree of influence in determining their own mathematical environments. For instance, Joram et al. (1995) noted in their study of magazines that the types and uses of mathematics are only *"opportunities for numeracy"* (p. 359); they did not examine how readers made sense of the numbers they encountered. Thus, more attention needs to be addressed to understanding how children, through their participation in cultural activities, interpret and transform mathematical environments in ways that contribute to their own development.

Children's Transformation of Mathematical Activities

Adjusting to children's abilities and interests may be a common component of adults' interactions with children. But, as noted earlier, children are active participants in their own development, shaping and transforming their activities in significant ways. As Engeström (1993) argued, "contexts are easily conceived of as containers of behavior, untouched in themselves by human actions. . . . Such a notion of context beyond our influence is fiction, a fetish" (pp. 65–6). As an example of the way children contribute to defining their mathematical environments, consider "counting-out" games.

At the start of play, children frequently employ counting-out rhymes (e.g., "Eenie-meenie-meinie-mo, Catch a feller by the toe . . .") as a means of assigning participants to a team or selecting who will be "it" in a game. By following the "rules" of counting out, the selection of teams or an individual player to be "it" is intended to be random and therefore fair. In a study of children from 4 to 14 years old, Goldstein (1971) found that 90% of the children he interviewed explained that they used counting out over some other method because it was "democratic," giving everyone an equal chance of being selected. The children, as well as researchers of children's games (e.g., Sutton-Smith, 1959), consider counting out to be a game of chance. But Goldstein found that for many children counting out entailed the use of complex strategies. Children often manipulated the count, such as adding phrases to a rhyme until it landed on the person whom the counter wanted to eliminate. A few of the children had a repertory of several different rhymes and knew which one to employ depending on the size of the group. One 9-year-old, "considered somewhat of a mathematical genius" (Goldstein, 1971, p. 177), had memorized which positions would be "first out" and "last remaining" for all groups consisting of 2 to 10 players. Using his memorized lists, he had complete control over who would be selected when.

Games may be understood as cultural practices, both reflecting and fostering cultural values, skills, and ways of behaving (Cherfas & Lewin, 1980; Parker, 1984; Sutton-Smith & Roberts, 1970). However, as the transformation of counting out from a game of chance to a game of strategy indicates, children often modify the intended or given structure of their games through their active participation.

In order to understand more about the ways in which children transform their activities and thereby contribute to shaping their own environments, colleagues and I videotaped children playing the board game

MONOPOLY (Guberman & Rahm, 1996; Menk & Guberman, 1996). We observed the play of a variety of groups of children who were selected according to criteria that would allow us systematically to compare groups on several dimensions (e.g., age, school achievement, and gender).

There were numerous ways that the activity structure of MONOPOLY, as intended by its manufacturer, was altered in children's play. Some transformations of the rules were so widespread that they appeared to have become part of common knowledge, passed down from one generation of players to another. For instance, when a player lands on an unowned property and decides not to buy it, the intended rule is that the property should be auctioned and sold to the highest bidder; this rule, though, was never followed in any of the games we observed. Similarly, in all games players received a reward when landing on the "Free Parking" space, also contrary to the intended rules. Other transformations, sometimes referred to as "house rules," were intentional and needed to be negotiated among players. For instance, two groups of players decided to reward themselves each time they landed on their own property by taking a specified amount of money from the bank. Another group, ninth-grade students selected by their math teacher as low achievers, agreed to play without using the (play) one-dollar bills that are supplied with the game; they simplified the calculations entailed in play by rounding all values to the nearest five.

From the perspective of supportive environments developed in this chapter, the most interesting transformations pertain to variations in play related to differences in children's mathematical understanding. To examine how the mathematical environments that emerged in play differed as a function of the players' age, we compared the mathematical problems and solutions in the play of groups composed of either 8-, 11-, or 14-year-old girls.

Although all the groups were engaged in the same nominal activity (MONOPOLY), the mathematics that emerged in play differed across them. For instance, the 8-year-old players showed no concern to acquire "monopolies" (all the properties of a specific color), and none had been acquired by the end of their game. In contrast, older children, especially the 14-year-olds, were more likely to acquire monopolies, which allowed them to build houses and hotels and, thereby, to receive higher "rent" payments when another player landed there. As a result, older children's games entailed more complex mathematical problems.

Payments (of play money) from one player to another or to the "bank" occurred frequently during play – over half of each player's turn resulted in a payment to be solved. Most payments required no mathematical calculation other than putting together appropriate units of currency; that is, players frequently needed to determine *how* they would pay their debts but only rarely did they need to calculate the *amount* of their debt. The frequency of calculations, though, varied across games: Calculations were required only 3% of the time in the 8-year-old game, but 16% and 15% in the games of the 11- and 14-year-olds, respectively. Overall, the average payment varied little across the age groups ($163, $156, and $179 for the 8-, 11-, and 14-year-olds, respectively), with one notable exception. Rent payments, which were dependent on the players' interest and success in obtaining monopolies, increased with age: The average rent payment was $26 among the 8-year-old players, $73 among the 11-year-olds, and $97 among the 14-year-olds. In contrast, the frequency of rent payments, which was not affected by whether or not players had obtained monopolies, did not differ between groups (23%–26% of turns across games).

How players chose to make their payments to another player had consequences for the distribution of mathematical work among players and differed across age groups. In the following excerpt from a game of 8-year-old players, the mathematical work is distributed over three players as Amy provides assistance to both Carla and Sarah. At the start of the excerpt, Carla, who throughout the game has been having considerable difficulty calculating monetary values, decides to buy a property that costs $220:

Carla: "Okay, okay. I'll buy it. Wait, two hundred and . . ." (*as she looks through her pile of money*).

Amy: "You just have to take two hundreds (*pointing to Carla's $100 bills*) and . . . or just give a five hundred (*bill*)."

Carla: "Okay." (*She gives Sarah, the banker, a $500 bill.*)

Sarah: (*As banker, Sarah puts the $500 bill in the bank and begins to count out Carla's change, counting down from 500.*) "So, five, four, three (*while taking two $100 bills*) . . . So that's . . . No." (*She takes a third $100 bill from the bank.*)

Amy: "That's three hundred."

Sarah: "Oh! Two hundred . . . (*as she gives Carla two $100 bills*)."

Amy: (*She points to the $20 bills in the bank, indicating that Sarah needs to give Carla more change; she is ignored, and the next player's turn begins.*)

This excerpt illustrates two ways that the mathematical work needed to accomplish the payment is distributed among players. First, Amy provides direct assistance to Carla in determining which bills to use for her payment. Second, after an overpayment is suggested and completed, the work entailed in achieving an accurate payment shifts from Carla (the customer) to Sarah (the banker) – it becomes Sarah's responsibility to determine how much change is due. This second form of assistance is tied to the social roles (e.g., customer and banker) that participants take on in the course of play. Finally, Amy again offers direct assistance – this time to the banker – but is ignored.

The mathematical work entailed in play also shifted from one player to another as a result of how payments were accomplished. The 11-year-olds were most likely to pay the exact amount of money they owed (90% of payments versus 67% and 68% for the 8- and 14-year-olds, respectively), thereby reducing the need to calculate change. In contrast, the 8- and 14-year-olds were more likely to overpay and receive change, shifting much of the mathematical work required for the payment from themselves (as "customer") to another player (as "banker"). The tendency to overpay was related to another indicator of the shifting distribution of work from the player to the opponent, or banker. By overpaying, players typically reduced the number of bills they tendered and, consequently, limited the number of monetary terms included in their calculations. For instance, in the foregoing excerpt, Carla paid with a single $500 bill; an exact payment of $220 would have required a minimum of three bills and the addition of three terms ($100 + $100 + $20). Carla, who appeared to have very weak mathematical skills, often paid her debts using the largest valued bill she had available, a strategy that greatly simplified the mathematical work she needed to accomplish.

In our analyses, we found that the 8- and 14-year-old players were more likely than the 11-year-olds to make their payments with a single bill (36% and 32% of payments in the 8- and 14-year-olds' games, and 23% in the 11-year-olds' games). When 14-year-old players overpaid, they sometimes took into consideration the amount of change they would receive. For instance, in the following excerpt from a game of 14-year-olds, Faye wants to purchase a property costing $260. She looks for $100 bills but, finding that she has only one of them, begins counting her $20 bills. Carla, who is playing as Faye's partner, suggests that Faye "break a 500," which leads to the following exchange:

Faye: "Yeah. We're going to go fifty (*picking up a $50 bill*) plus ten (*adding a $10 bill*) is sixty; then we're going to give her five hundred (*adding a $500 bill*). That means you'll give us two hundred dollars."
Carla: "No, she gives us . . ."

Faye: "Three hundred dollars . . . because we gave her sixty dollars and five hundred dollars."

Unlike the overpayments of younger players, which simplified the player's mathematics, these more complicated overpayments typically increased the mathematical work entailed in determining the payment but reduced the number of bills required for change. As a result, the number of bills given in an overpayment varied with age group: The 8-year-olds averaged fewer than two bills per overpayment (1.7) in contrast to the 14-year-olds, who averaged more than two bills per overpayment (2.1). When 11-year-olds overpaid, which was rare, they always did so using a single bill.

Sometimes a player's attempt to simplify the mathematics entailed in a transaction yielded an unwieldy problem. In the following excerpt, Amanda, another 14-year-old player, has decided to buy a property costing $260. She has in her possession a few $500, $50, and $1 bills, but only one $20 bill and no $5, $10, and $100 bills. Rather than paying with her $500 bill and receiving change, she decides to add to the $500 bill in order to simplify the change she is due. But, because she doesn't have the bills she would need to pay $560 (which would yield $300 change), she pays $570 ($500 + $50 + $20), which leads to the following discussion between Amanda, Brenda (Amanda's partner), and Carla (on the opposing team):

Amanda: "Now, how much do we get back? We put in five hundred and seventy dollars."

Carla: "You are going to get two hundred and thirty dollars."

Brenda: "Are you sure about that?"

Carla: "Yes."

Brenda: "Not if we bought Ventnor."

Carla: "It (costs) two-sixty and you're putting in two-seventy?"

Brenda: "No, we're putting in five hundred."

Carla: "(No, you put in) five-seventy, then you get two hundred and thirty dollars back."

Brenda: (*To Amanda*) "You put in five-sixty . . ."

Amanda: (*Correcting Brenda*) "Seventy."

Brenda: "Oh."

Amanda: (*Takes $230 from the bank, and play continues.*)

Although Amanda originally tried to simplify the change she would receive, she instead complicated the mathematics of the transaction: what could have been $500 minus $260 became $570 minus $260 (or, from Amanda's perspective, $560 + $10 − $260). Additional confusion about what Amanda had paid, and Carla's unproductive efforts to assist, resulted in an error that went undetected.

These complex overpayments were rare: They occurred only three times among the 14-year-olds and never among the 8- and 11-year-old players. We are currently examining other age-related differences in the solution strategies that children use and the mathematics involved in selling and bartering as players attempt to acquire monopolies.

As the excerpts and analyses make clear, the mathematics entailed in play was not determined solely by the structure of the game. Rather, the mathematical environments for these children emerged and were transformed as players jointly participated in the activity, challenging and supporting each other's mathematical understanding in the course of play.

Conclusions

Ackerman (1995) has noted that "we are only too aware that different people need different kinds of support, at different times, in different tasks" (p. 353). The illustrations of supportive environments included in this chapter are only a few of the opportunities in our society for children to learn and use mathematics. A society that values quantitative reasoning skills will naturally provide "redundant opportunities" (Gelman et al., 1991) for children to come in contact with cultural uses of numbers and mathematics, including their interactions with helpful adults and peers, their commercial transactions, the magazines they read, and the games they play.

For environments to support children's cognitive development, they must engage children in meaningful and challenging ways. Csikszentmihalyi (1991) has noted that flow, or intense involvement in enjoyable activities, "is only possible when a person feels [that] the opportunities for action in the given activity (or challenges) are more or less in balance with the person's ability to respond to the opportunities (or skills)" (pp. 127–8). Similarly, for learning to take place in cultural practices, there must be a match between a person's abilities and opportunities for meaningful participation. It is in the zone of proximal development – whether in its scaffolding, cultural, or collectivist guise – that this match is achieved. The notion that instructional activities should be matched to children's abilities has a long history in the study of children's learning and development, although sociocultural theory provides a new lens for understanding how individuals and their cultural environments are intrinsically and reciprocally linked. Sometimes a match between children's abilities and activities is achieved through the negotiation of adults and children in face-to-face interactions (e.g., parents helping children count a set of dots). Other times, parents and the broader community structure activities in ways that allow children with a range of interests and abilities to participate in appropriate ways (e.g., parents assigning distinct responsibilities to children of different ages). And children themselves transform activities in ways that support their own involvement and learning (e.g., children playing MONOPOLY).

The examples in this chapter point to the social nature of learning and development and illustrate the emergent character of children's environments. In each of the examples – counting, shopping, and game playing – it is impossible to define "the task" without knowing how it is interpreted and transformed by those engaged in accomplishing it. Tasks and environments are not unchanging and independent of the people acting in them. Rather, they must be understood as flexible, emergent constructions that reflect both cultural achievements and values and the interpretive, sense-making processes of participants. In this way, sociocultural processes and individual constructive activity are inseparable.

Heath and McLaughlin (1994) have argued that in order to understand fully children's learning and development, it is important to conduct research in a wide range of contexts. They note that attempts to reform school instruction are often based on making the curriculum more "authentic," even though educators have rarely examined how learning takes place in everyday contexts. Although the acquisition of more complex levels of mathematical understanding, or other domains of knowledge, may require alternative forms of support, the examples in this chapter share features that both characterize everyday learning and may be useful for designing formal instruction. Especially important are that activities provide opportunities for change: for children to participate meaningfully as they move from limited knowledge and involvement toward greater understanding and participation; and for activities to change as they are transformed by children who, through their constructive activity, acquire new understanding and encounter new challenges.

References

Abreu, G. de. (1995). Understanding how children experience the relationship between home and school mathematics. *Mind, Culture, and Activity, 2*, 119–42.

Ackerman, E. (1995). Construction and transference of meaning through form. In L. P. Steffe & J. Gale (Eds.), *Constructivism in education* (pp. 341–54). Hillsdale, NJ: Erlbaum.

Bronfenbrenner, U. (1993). The ecology of cognitive development: Research models and fugitive findings. In R. H. Wozniak & K. W. Fischer (Eds.), *Development in context: Acting and thinking in specific environments* (pp. 3–44). Hillsdale, NJ: Erlbaum.

Brown, A. L., & Reeve, R. A. (1987). Bandwidths of competence: The role of supportive contexts in learning and development. In L. S. Liben (Ed.), *Development and learning: Conflict or congruence?* (pp. 173–223). Hillsdale, NJ: Erlbaum.

Cherfas, J., & Lewin, R. (Eds.). (1980). *Not work alone: A cross-cultural view of activities superfluous to survival.* Beverly Hills, CA: Sage.

Csikszentmihalyi, M. (1991). Literacy and intrinsic motivation. In S. R. Graubard (Ed.), *Literacy: An overview of fourteen experts* (pp. 115–40). New York: Hill and Wang.

Engeström, Y. (1987). *Learning by expanding.* Helsinki: Orienta-Konsultit Oy.

Engeström, Y. (1993). Developmental studies of work as a testbench of activity theory: The case of primary care medical practice. In S. Chaiklin & J. Lave (Eds.), *Understanding practice: Perspectives on activity and context* (pp. 64–103). New York: Cambridge University Press.

Forman, E., Stein, M. K., Brown, C., Larreamendy-Joerns, J. (1995, April). *The socialization of mathematical thinking: The role of institutional, interpersonal, and discursive contexts.* Paper presented at the annual meetings of the American Educational Research Association, San Francisco.

Fuson, K. C., Zecker, L. B., Lo Cicero, A. M., & Ron, P. (1995, April). *El mercado in Latino primary classrooms: A fruitful narrative theme for the development of children's conceptual mathematics.* Paper presented at the annual meeting of the American Educational Research Association, San Francisco.

Gelman, R. (1990). Structural constraints on cognitive development: Introduction to a special issue of *Cognitive Science. Cognitive Science, 14,* 3–9.

Gelman, R., & Gallistel, C. R. (1978). *The child's understanding of number.* Cambridge, MA: Harvard University Press.

Gelman, R., Massey, C. M., & McManus, M. (1991). Characterizing supporting environments for cognitive development: Lessons from a children's museum. In L. B. Resnick, J. M. Levine, & S. D. Teasley (Eds.), *Perspectives on socially shared cognition* (pp. 226–56). Washington, DC: American Psychological Association.

Ginsburg, H. P., Posner, J. K., & Russell, R. L. (1981). The development of mental addition as a function of culture and schooling. *Journal of Cross-Cultural Psychology, 12,* 163–78.

Goldstein, K. S. (1971). Strategy in counting out: An ethnographic folklore field study. In E. M. Avedon & B. Sutton-Smith (Eds.), *The study of games* (pp. 167–78). New York: Wiley.

Greenfield, P. M. (1984). A theory of the teacher in the learning activities of everyday life. In B. Rogoff & J. Lave (Eds.), *Everyday cognition: Its development in social context* (pp. 117–38). Cambridge, MA: Harvard University Press.

Greenfield, P. M., & Childs, C. P. (1977). Weaving, color terms, and pattern representation: Cultural influences and cognitive development among the Zinacantecos of Southern Mexico. *International Journal of Psychology, 1*, 89–107.

Guberman, S. R. (1992). *Math and money: A comparative study of the arithmetical achievements and out-of-school activities of Latino and Korean American children.* Unpublished doctoral dissertation, UCLA.

Guberman, S. R. (1996). The development of everyday mathematics in Brazilian children with limited formal education. *Child Development, 67*, 1609–23.

Guberman, S. R., & Rahm, J. (1996, April). *Negotiating Boardwalk: Emergent mathematics in children's game play.* Paper presented at the annual meeting of the American Educational Research Association, New York City.

Heath, S. B., & McLaughlin, M. W. (1994). Learning for anything everyday. *Journal of Curriculum Studies, 26*, 471–89.

Joram, E., Resnick, L. B., & Gabriele, A. J. (1995). Numeracy as cultural practice: An examination of numbers in magazines for children, teenagers, and adults. *Journal for Research in Mathematics Education, 26*, 346–61.

Kessen, W. (1993). Rubble or revolution: A commentary. In R. H. Wozniak & K. W. Fischer (Eds.), *Development in context: Acting and thinking in specific environments* (pp. 269–79). Hillsdale, NJ: Erlbaum.

Klein, A., & Starkey, P. (1988). Universals in the development of early arithmetic cognition. In G. B. Saxe & M. Gearhart (Eds.), *Children's mathematics* (pp. 5–26). San Francisco: Jossey-Bass.

Lave, J., Smith, S., & Butler, M. (1989). Problem solving as an everyday practice. In R. I. Charles & E. A. Silver (Eds.), *The teaching and assessing of mathematical problem solving* (pp. 61–81). Hillsdale, NJ: Erlbaum.

Lave, J., & Wenger, E. (1991). *Situated learning: Legitimate peripheral participation.* Cambridge: Cambridge University Press.

Matusov, E. (1996). Intersubjectivity without agreement. *Mind, Culture, and Activity, 3*, 25–45.

Medrich, E. A., Roizen, J., Rubin, V., & Buckley, S. (1982). *The serious business of growing up: A study of children's lives outside school.* Berkeley, CA: University of California Press.

Menk, D. W., & Guberman, S. R. (1996, April). *To buy or not to buy: Individual and group motives in children's play of a board game.* Paper presented at the annual meeting of the American Educational Research Association, New York City.

National Council of Teachers of Mathematics (1989). *Curriculum and Evaluation Standards for School Mathematics*. Reston, VA: Author.

Nunes, T., & Bryant, P. (1996). *Children doing mathematics*. Oxford: Blackwell.

Nunes, T., Schliemann, A. D., & Carraher, D. W. (1993). *Street mathematics and school mathematics*. Cambridge: Cambridge University Press.

Parker, S. T. (1984). Playing for keeps: An evolutionary perspective on human games. In P. K. Smith (Ed.), *Play in animals and humans* (pp. 271–93). New York: Basil Blackwell.

Piaget, J. (1965). *The moral judgment of the child*. New York: Free Press.

Rogoff, B. (1990). *Apprenticeship in thinking: Cognitive development in social context*. New York: Oxford University Press.

Rogoff, B. (1995). Observing sociocultural activity on three planes: Participatory appropriation, guided participation, and apprenticeship. In J. V. Wertsch, P. del Río, & A. Alvarez (Eds.), *Sociocultural studies of mind* (pp. 139–63). Cambridge: Cambridge University Press.

Rogoff, B., Malkin, C., & Gilbride, K. (1984). Interaction with babies as guidance in development. In B. Rogoff & J. V. Wertsch (Eds.), *Children's learning in the "zone of proximal development"* (pp. 31–44). San Francisco: Jossey-Bass.

Rogoff, B., Mistry, J., Göncü, A., & Mosier, C. (1993). Guided participation in cultural activity by toddlers and caregivers. *Monographs of the Society for Research in Child Development, 58* (8, Serial No. 236).

Saxe, G. B. (1991). *Culture and cognitive development: Studies in mathematical understanding*. Hillsdale, NJ: Erlbaum.

Saxe, G. B., & Gearhart, M. (Eds.). (1988). *Children's mathematics*. San Francisco: Jossey-Bass.

Saxe, G. B., Guberman, S. R., & Gearhart, M. (1987). Social processes in early number development. *Monographs of the Society for Research in Child Development, 52* (2, Serial No. 216).

Simon, T. J., Hespos, S. J., & Rochat, P. (1995). Do infants understand simple arithmetic? A replication of Wynn (1992). *Cognitive Development, 10*, 253–69.

Smith, N. B. (1924). An investigation of the uses of arithmetic in the out-of-school life of first-grade children. *The Elementary School Journal, 24*, 621–6.

Sugarman, S. (1983). *Children's early thought: Developments in classification*. New York: Cambridge University Press.

Sutton-Smith, B. (1959). *The games of New Zealand children*. Berkeley, CA: University of California Press.

Sutton-Smith, B., & Roberts, J. M. (1970). The cross-cultural and psychological analysis of games. In G. Luschen (Ed.), *The cross-cultural analysis of games* (pp. 100–8). Champaign, IL: Stipes.

Vygotsky, L. S. (1978). *Mind in society: The development of higher psychological functions.* Cambridge, MA: Harvard University Press.

Weisner, T. S. (1984). Ecocultural niches of middle childhood: A cross-cultural perspective. In W. A. Collins (Ed.), *Development during middle childhood: The years from six to twelve* (pp. 335–69). Washington, DC: National Academy Press.

Wertsch, J. V. (1984). The zone of proximal development: Some conceptual issues. In B. Rogoff & J. V. Wertsch (Eds.), *Children's learning in the "zone of proximal development"* (pp. 7–18). San Francisco: Jossey-Bass.

Wertsch, J. V. (1995). The need for action in sociocultural research. In J. V. Wertsch, P. del Río, & A. Alvarez (Eds.), *Sociocultural studies of mind* (pp. 56–74). Cambridge: Cambridge University Press.

Whiting, B., & Whiting, J. (1975). *Children of six cultures.* Cambridge, MA: Harvard University Press.

Wood, D. J., Bruner, J. S., & Ross, G. (1976). The role of tutoring in problem solving. *Journal of Child Psychology and Psychiatry, 17,* 89–100.

Wynn, K. (1992). Addition and subtraction by human infants. *Nature, 358,* 749–50.

Zukow, P. G., Reilly, J., & Greenfield, P. M. (1982). Making the absent present: Facilitating the transition from sensorimotor to linguistic communication. In K. E. Nelson (Ed.), *Children's language* (Vol. 3, pp. 1–90). New York: Gardner Press.

9   Becoming Literate in the Borderlands

Christine C. Pappas

This chapter sees literacy as a set of social or *cultural practices* (Green & Dixon, 1994; Reder, 1994). According to Reder (1994), the fundamental issues addressed in this perspective are:

> how individuals in their day-to-day interactions create and recreate the contexts in which written materials are used, how these interactions influence and are influenced by the use of written materials, and how participants interpret and give meaning to the texts and actions involved. (p. 36)

These are clearly significant questions for understanding literacy development. Of course, children engage in, and learn to read and write in, socially patterned activities out of school, but the focus here is on when they cross the school borders to create new identities as readers and writers. Thus, I use the metaphor ''borderlands'' to depict how young urban kindergartners and first-graders who come from diverse ethnolinguistic backgrounds are becoming literate as they participate in the literacy cultural practices in classrooms where their teachers have explicitly attempted to take on collaborative styles of teaching.

The teaching described here is quite different from what is usually

The research reported in this chapter has been supported by grants from the Spencer Foundation and the Center for Urban Educational Research and Development at the University of Illinois at Chicago. The data presented, the statements made, and the views expressed are solely the responsibility of the author.

I want to thank the three teacher researchers, Sonia, Anne, and Pam, whose inquiries I have presented here, for their insights in teaching–learning in urban schools, as well as the support and research assistance of Diane Escobar, Shannon Hart, Jane Liao, Linda Montes, Caitlyn Nichols, Dian Ruben, Hank Tabak, and Liliana Zecker.

I appreciated the critical feedback from Artin Göncü and Liliana Barro Zecker on an earlier draft of this chapter.

provided for low-SES (socioeconomic status) and ethnic minority children. Too frequently, the asymmetrical power relations of society have been reproduced in the schools for these children. As a result, many urban teachers do not value or consider using students' existing knowledge bases when they structure literacy teaching–learning experiences. Instead, what has been pervasive is a pedagogy that reflects a "deficit view of subordinated students" (Bartolome, 1994) where rigid, teacher-directed classroom practices underestimate and constrain what these children can display intellectually (Moll, 1992). Cultural differences are considered as barriers to literacy acquisition, and diversity is seen as something to be reduced or displaced. Due to this deficit view, unchallenging, rote learning has been commonplace, which, in turn, has led to student alienation of much of the curricula and teaching formats operating in schools.

The teachers I present in this chapter have an alternative view of their students' abilities. To them, diversity is recognized and fostered as a strength or asset in learning. The teachers have taken on their own inquiries (Cochran-Smith & Lytle, 1993) to change their literacy curricula so that they reflect the aims of what Willinsky (1990) has called the "New Literacy." More specifically, these teacher-researchers have tried to redefine literacy by *building on* the diversity of their students, by valuing and incorporating their students' local and culturally varied understandings into the curriculum. These efforts have required examination and study of instructional roles and interactions in order to make reading and writing more connected and meaningful to the real lives of their students.

In describing these teacher-researchers' classroom contexts as borderlands, I have drawn on Delgado-Gaitan's (1996) use of the term:

> Borderlands exist as a synthesis of varied worlds. . . . People define and redefine identity, experience, feelings, beliefs and dreams in borderlands. Borderlands transcend rigid ideological and cultural borders which we construct to understand our multiple identities. Within borderlands we create the time, space and context to exchange experiences and learn new identities. As the protean self emerges in the borderlands, people are empowered to experiment with their full potential. (p. 12)

New Literacy ideas represent a movement away from traditional transmission-oriented teaching–learning literacy practices to ones that involve increasing student control of texts and their meanings. The teacher-researchers have attempted to enact literacy curriculum that would capitalize on the linguistic and intellectual capabilities that her "language minority" and other nonmainstream students possess, but they are too frequently ignored and assumed to be in conflict with the demands of schooling (Crawford, 1992; Delgado-Gaitan, 1996; Losey, 1995; Moll & Gonzalez, 1994). Issues of teacher power and authority have been made problematic in their efforts, and it is in these contexts, or borderlands, that we explore how young children become literate – how they become empowered to take on new beliefs, experiences, and identities as readers and writers.

This chapter is organized into three major sections. The first section describes the major role that teacher research plays in developing cultural practices to realize New Literacy ideas. It also sketches the power/knowledge issues that underlie the teachers' instructional literacy endeavors. Because classroom education, to a very large degree, *is* talk (Lemke, 1985a), classroom discourse is a significant topic of discussion to characterize the collaborative talk structures that emerged in the literacy routines due to the efforts of these teacher-researchers. The last part of this first section covers two ideas of New Literacy – the "epistemic" mode of engagement of text, which Wells (1990; Wells & Chang-Wells, 1992) argues is the major feature of what it means to be literate, and how this mode is illustrated in "emergent" literacy, a developmental way to look at early literacy learning (Teale & Sulzby, 1986).

The second section consists of three classroom vignettes – one from a bilingual kindergarten classroom and two from first-grade classrooms – to illustrate how young learners (and their teachers and peers) participate in various reading and writing cultural practices that reflect New Literacy agenda. The first and second vignettes depict whole-class, teacher-led routines; and the third focuses on an individual student–teacher interaction. All three show the ways in which these teacher-researchers provide their expertise as they share power and authority with their students in collaboration, thereby making it possible for young readers and writers to engage in texts epistemically.

Finally, the last section further discusses the significance of the collaborative nature of the literacy cultural practices, or borderlands, that were constructed in the three vignettes. The talk or discourse by which the interactions were accomplished and the power relations that were embodied by them are reconsidered, along with future research and educational implications.

Transforming Literacy Cultural Practices to Enact New Literacy Goals

The data presented in this chapter are part of a larger collaborative school-university action research project[1] in which teacher-researchers from two urban elementary schools have attempted to develop New Literacy practices that are student-centered. Thus, their approaches have involved moving away from the transmission-oriented educational model that Freire (1972) has criticized as the "banking concept of education," where knowledge is seen as deposits into the heads of learners who are thought of as empty vessels. It is this view that is still so prevalent in the urban schools populated by low-SES, ethnic, and linguistic "minority" children and fuels the deficit model. The teacher-researchers here, however, are challenging this traditional teaching–learning relationship of transmission and reception by attempting to establish collaborative interactions with students. In doing so, individualistic conceptions of learning are also questioned by emphasizing that learning activities take place not *within* individuals but in transactions *between* them (Wells & Chang-Wells, 1992). This perspective reflects a sociocultural theory consistent with Vygotskian ideas (see Gaskins, Gauvain, Göncü et al., Guberman, and Tudge et al., this volume; Moll, 1990, 1992; Newman, Griffin, & Cole, 1989; Vygotsky, 1962, 1978; Wells, 1994; Wertsch, 1991).

To understand better the kinds of borderlands that these teacher-researchers were attempting to create, three major, interrelated topics are covered: (1) the rationale and importance of teacher inquiry for creating New Literacy agenda; (2) the kind of classroom discourse that is realized in such an enterprise; and (3) how the "epistemic" mode of engagement of text is an integral feature of the New Literacy for "emergent" literacy learners.

The Role of Teacher Research

Most of traditional educational research has dichotomized "theory and practice" by emphasizing that researchers from the university produce the theoretical background for all and any educational innovation (Altricher,

---

[1] More information about the methodology and other details of this collaborative school – university action research project can be found in Pappas (1997) and Pappas and Zecker (in press a, in press b).

Posch, & Somekh, 1993). This is a hierarchical, "outside-in" stance that sees knowledge for teaching being generated at the university and then used in schools (Cochran-Smith & Lytle, 1993). The voices of teachers, their points of view, have been missing in traditional research because it rarely involves a level of question posing from teachers; as a result, it "strengthens the assumptions that practitioners do not produce knowledge, that their personal knowledge is not useful" (Gitlin, 1990, p. 444).

Teacher research – that is, teachers' own *systematic, intentional inquiry* (Cochran-Smith & Lytle, 1993) on their practices to construct their own theories of teaching and learning – has been part of the larger criticism of traditional educational research that examines different questions: Who owns knowledge in education? Who benefits from research? (Richardson, 1994). (For a more detailed account of this critique and paradigm shift, and the issues involved in doing collaborative work with teacher researchers, see Pappas, 1997.)

Thus, the teachers here have chosen their own questions of inquiry about literacy teaching–learning. There was only one common premise of the research group: that *all* children – humans – construct their own knowledge in social contexts, and as a result, teachers need to consider new roles in their students' learning. Although the teacher-researchers were at different levels in their experience in implementing this perspective in their classrooms, they all began to see themselves more as "facilitators" in supporting their students' literacy understandings. Many, however, questioned what that really meant in their day-to-day practices. Thus, an early, major focus of these teachers' struggles to be agents of change in their classrooms centered around their questions of when and how to share authority and power with their students. That is, as these teacher-researchers had begun to utilize a more collaborative style of teaching, they grappled with how they could fashion instructional interactions so they could share their expertise at the same time they fostered children's active construction of their own expertise (Kreisberg, 1992; Wells & Chang-Wells, 1992). As indicated in the introduction, their inquiries involved their struggles to implement New Literacy curriculum, which consisted of their attempts to hand over a greater locus of meaning of texts to students (Willinsky, 1990).

Creating Collaborative Classroom Discourse

In our project, the study of these changes focused around the analysis of classroom discourse because it is the medium by which most teaching takes place and in which students demonstrate to teachers much of what they have learned (Cazden, 1988). Classroom talk is conceived as "the social use of language to enact regular activity structures and to share systems of meaning among teachers and students" (Lemke, 1985a, p. 1). Thus, this is a social-semiotic perspective (Halliday, 1978, 1993; Halliday & Hasan, 1985; Lemke, 1990; Young, 1992) that focuses on how various educational routines, with their corresponding discourse patterns, are organized during a school day (Erickson & Shultz, 1977; Green & Dixon, 1994; Wells, 1993).

Classroom discourse studies have indicated that most of the talk in many classrooms has properties that makes it quite different from talk in most other settings. First of all, this talk is dominated by teacher questions, typically a certain kind of questions termed "pseudo" questions – ones for which the teacher already *knows* the answers (Edwards & Mercer, 1987; Ramirez, 1988 Young, 1992). Second, these questions are frequently embedded in a characteristic initiate-respond-evaluate (IRE) talk structure that is primarily controlled by the teacher (Cazden, 1988; Edwards & Mercer, 1987; Wells, 1993; Young, 1992). In this IRE pattern, the teacher *initiates* a sequence or interaction by calling a child to respond; then the nominated child *responds* to the initiation or question posed by the teacher; and finally the teacher *evaluates* the correctness of what the child has said, then calls on the next child, and so on. The IRE structure, which has also been characterized as the teacher's controlling monologic script (Gutierrez, Rymes, & Larson, 1995), is the essence of traditional transmission-oriented education and has reflected dominant cultural values. It has been especially prevalent in urban schools, allowing few opportunities for the consideration of students' different culturally and linguistically interactional styles (Cummins, 1994; Foster, 1992; McCollum, 1991). It has made impossible "the joint construction of a new sociocultural terrain, creating spaces for shifts in what counts as knowledge and knowledge representation" (Gutierrez et al., 1995, p. 445).

A central theme throughout all of the teachers' inquiries in the project, then, has been their attempts to develop *alternatives* to teacher-dominated IRE patterns in order to realize New Literacy ideas. By giving their students more control of their own literacy learning, they are attempting to transform literacy cultural practices so that *both* teacher and student "voices" are privileged in collaborative transactions (Gutierrez et al., 1995; O'Connor & Michaels, 1993; Wells, 1993, 1994; Young, 1992). Moreover, because what is valued as knowledge, and the construction of power, are both culture-bound and locally situated (Bartolome, 1994; Cummins, 1994; Gutierrez et al., 1995), such collaborative talk represents discourse for social change (Fairclough, 1992).

Promoting "Epistemic" Engagement of Text for Emergent Literacy Learners

A major facet of the New Literacy perspective sees *"literacy as a social process with language that can from the beginning extend the students' range of meaning and connection"* (Willinsky, 1990, p. 8, emphasis in the original). This fits well with Wells's conception of what it means to be "literate," and the fact that it can be applied to very young, primary-age learners, who may not yet be using adult, conventional forms of written language but who *are* readers and writers nonetheless.

Wells's (1990) definition is:

> To be literate is to have the disposition to engage appropriately with texts of different types in order to empower action, thinking, and feeling in the context of purposeful social activity. (p. 379).

To further explicate this characterization of literacy, Wells proposes and describes several modes of engagement of text. He argues that one of them, the epistemic mode of engagement – where "meaning is treated as tentative, provisional, and open to alternative interpretations and revision" (Wells, 1990, p. 369) – fully exploits the potential of literacy because it empowers the thinking of those who use it. In this sense of engagement, "text" is extended to mean "any artifact that is constructed as a representation of meaning using a conventional symbol system" (Wells & Chang-Wells, 1992, p. 145), which can also include classroom discourse. Of course, children learn to interpret and contribute to oral texts in many ways in the various social contexts that have supported their language development. However, in most of these settings, language accompanied action, and attention was focused only partially on what was said (Pappas, Kiefer, & Levstik, 1999; Wells, 1986). Thus, according to Wells, children engaging in oral texts from an epistemic orientation has them viewing the role of language quite differently. It introduces them to literate thinking because it fosters a reflection upon and reformulations of meanings, thereby making this primarily silent and covert "mental ability" explicit to them.

In this chapter, we examine cultural practices in kindergarten and first-grade classrooms where children display their early understandings of reading and writing, which, like oral language use, have roots that reach back into infancy. Early literacy begins when children encounter books and other written texts in their families and communities and learn that written texts, too, can be used to get things done. Children learn written language by interacting with adults (and older children) in reading and writing situations, by exploring print on their own, and by observing significant adults, especially their parents, actually using written language for their communicative ends. The term *emergent literacy* is used to emphasize the continuities in literacy development and to characterize young children's early efforts to read and write, using their own inventions or approximations of adult written forms (Sulzby & Teale, 1991; Teale & Sulzby, 1986).

All young children develop early concepts and skills basic to learning to read and write because our larger culture, in which their particular communities are embedded, is a literate one. Individual children's emergent literacy knowledge may differ as a result of the manner and the extent to which written language has been shared with them in their family and community social practices. Unfortunately, much of the instruction in the primary grades still does not acknowledge either this area of literacy development or the kinds of transitions or routes children make on the path to conventional literacy.

The teacher-researchers here, however, have striven to support their students' efforts to learn conventional literacy by acknowledging and appreciating their students' developing emergent literacy understandings. They have attempted to build on their students' literate approximations as they participate in various literacy events. Moreover, in doing so, these teachers have provided opportunities for them to engage with texts epistemically – for them to see the provisional nature of written language by encouraging students' revision and consideration of alternative interpretations of texts.

Summary

Although all of the teacher-researchers have confronted difficulties in taking on collaborative styles of teaching, their overall efforts have been extremely successful (see Pappas & Zecker [in press a, in press b] for a fuller picture of this work). New borderlands of teaching–learning cultural practices have been created to support their young students' literate understandings. It could be that these teachers would have adopted these approaches no matter where they taught or no matter who their students were. However, because these teacher-researchers have chosen to teach children of color in urban classrooms, and are critically challenging the all-too-common deficit premise that so many hold regarding the children they teach, the following vignettes illustrate that the nature of this literate development is also politically significant. More is said on this issue in the last section of the chapter.

Three Vignettes: Examples of Literacy Cultural Practices in the Borderlands

Only snapshots of the cultural literacy cultural practices of three teacher-researchers' classrooms are possible here. The focus in Sonia's bilingual kindergarten is on geographic topics; Anne is sharing ABC books with a group of first-grade children; and Pam is conferencing with a first-grade writer, Julissa. For each, brief descriptions of the teacher-researchers' inquiries are provided, along with classroom discourse samples to illustrate the collaborative interactions that were constructed to support students' literacy learning. (See Appendix A at the end of the chapter for transcription conventions for all the classroom discourse examples.)

Sonia's Bilingual Kindergarten – Becoming Literate in Geography Lessons

Sonia White Soltero is an Argentinean who had 22 full-day kindergarten students during the year of her inquiry – all of whom are Spanish-speaking children who are Mexican or first-generation Mexican-American, with 1 child having a Colombian background, and 4 having Puerto Rican heritage. Sonia set up as her inquiry goal to study the rich linguistic and intellectual resources she had informally observed in her students. By explicitly pursuing the "funds of knowledge" (Moll, 1992) of her students and their families/communities, she hoped to use this information as a springboard on which to co-construct new meanings in the classroom.

She studied what happened when she read aloud to children and when children wrote, but she also created other new routines to explore topics that her children seemed to be especially interested in and which were relevant to her overall kindergarten curricular objectives. This occurred, for example, during a thematic unit on travel. Because many children in the class were from immigrant families from Mexico and were used to traveling to visit their relatives there, Sonia included "geography lessons" having to do with Mexico. She often elicited her students as ethnographers or informants to gather information from their families about these travel experiences, which were then shared in class discussions.

Example 9.1 consists of a discussion that utilized a map and globe as artifacts to study travel. In terms of Wells's ideas described in the previous section, all three – the discussion itself, the map, and the globe – are conceived of as texts. The example begins by Sonia pointing out the United States and Mexico on a large map that has been put up on one of the walls. Student initiations are frequent as they bring up topics, such as "the stealing of Mexico," "wetbacks," and other issues of immigration that are extremely relevant in the everyday lives of these children. What is important to note here is that Sonia believes that her students' contributions represent important knowledge to consider and learn about. Frequently, her responses are: "How do you know?" "Who told you?" "Why?" She often provides "oooooooh's" or "aaaaaaah's" to their ideas, which are phatic utterances (Halliday & Hasan, 1976) that communicate to students "yes, please continue, I'm listening and interested." Her comments therefore indicate her acceptance of her students' ideas, as well as nudge these children to further rethink and reconsider them. Thus, Example 9.1 – which is an English translation (see Appendix B for the original Spanish version) illustrates the ways in which the classroom talk was a joint enterprise in which children could engage meanings epistemically.

EXAMPLE 1. Stealing from Mexico and Wetbacks[2]

1 **Sonia:**   Here it says Mexico. This is the United States, this is Mexico. (*pointing to them on the map*)
2 **Esteban:** But yet Mexico is not – is not small, when they stole – the land, it is still big, Mexico.
3 **Sonia:**   Mexico was big before. And who stole the land?
4 **Esteban:** Those from here.
5 **Sonia:**   Ooooh. And who told you?
6 **Esteban:** My dad.
7 **Sonia:**   Your dad. And do you know what part was Mexico's and

---

[2] Fieldnotes, videotape, 02/28/95.

it is not any more? (*She waits, but there is no response.*) What part would that be? This is Mexico. (*pointing on the map*) Which was the part that was Mexico's before?

8 **Esteban:** This was – was – was from here to there. (*pointing toward the map*)

9 **Sonia:** Going down?

10 **Esteban:** (*** ***).

11 **C1:** That one was not, Teacher.

12 **Sonia:** But the United States is up here. These are other countries. (*pointing to countries south of Mexico in the map*)

13 **Cf:** That one, Teacher, that one.

14 **Sonia:** I believe that up here, here, this is the part that your dad told you was Mexico's . . .

15 **Esteban:** Maybe – maybe th – this is a famous place because there is also a – a country that is famous bec – because, there, the Mexicans cannot – cannot go in through – through the line (***).

16 **Sonia:** They cannot go in?

17 **Esteban:** No.

18 **Sonia:** Where?

19 **Esteban:** The – the line is of U – is part of the United States.

20 **Sonia:** Here in the – in the – in the border? Right here, on this border?

21 **Esteban:** Uhum.

22 **Sonia:** They don't let them in?

23 **Esteban:** And <my uncle> was caught last year.

24 **Sonia:** Who knew that?

25 **Esteban:** My daddy told me and also . . .

26 **Sonia:** What did he tell you? (*She waits but there is no response.*) Who knew about that – ooops, let's wait for Vicente and Mariela because they are playing. Esteban's dad told him that there are parts here, in the border with Mexico and the United States, that they do not let the Mexicans in. Why would that be? Why don't they let them in?

27 **Cm1:** Because they don't . . .

28 **Sonia:** Why would that be?

29 **Cm1:** Because . . .

30 **Mariela:** The – they are not from this country.

31 **Sonia:** Because the Mexicans are from Mexico and they are not from the United States?

32	**Cf1:**	#Teacher . . . #
33	**Sonia:**	#But you are here, and you are from Mexico . . . #
34	**Cf1:**	#Teacher . . Teacher . . my dad came to the United States.#
35	**Cm:**	#They let me in, and I am from Chicago.#
36	**Sonia:**	Because you were born in Chicago? And because of that they let you in? Hmmm. Who else was born in Chicago? Who was born in Mexico?
37	**Cs:**	(*raise hands and talk all at once*)
38	**C:**	#I was born in Chicago.#
39	**C:**	#I was born here.#
40	**C:**	#Me too.#
	. . .	(*Sonia names some of the ones born in Chicago and some of the ones born in Mexico. Then she asks some of them who have not volunteered information. Some do not know, and Sonia tells them to ask their mothers. Then Sonia poses another question.*)
41	**Sonia:**	And your mom and dad, where were they born?
42	**Cf:**	In Mexico, my mo – mom and my dad were born in Mexico.
43	**Esteban:**	My uncle is wetback.
44	**Sonia:**	In Wetback? (*Because they were talking about being born in Mexico and reluctant to believe that the children would know the word* mojado *('wetback') in Spanish, Sonia initially responded to the child's comment as if* mojado *were the name of a place in Mexico.*)
45	**Cs:**	(*laughter*)
46	**Cf1:**	Walking . . went walking because a friend of my mom's said that.
47	**Sonia:**	What?
48	**Cf1:**	Tha . . a . . a – that wetback means that they come walking, from there.
49	**Sonia:**	Hmmmm, and they came walking. And why do they call him wetback? (*Sonia waits, but there is no response.*) Because he got wet?
50	**Cs:**	No.
51	**Esteban:**	But my dad says that – he came, I believe . . .
	. . . .	(*Sonia asks Cs not to touch the microphone, to sit down in their chairs, and calls some names specifically because Esteban wants to keep talking.*)

52 **Esteban:** I believe that – I believe that – I believe that he came in a cab from Mexico.
53 **Sonia:** In a cab from Mexico? (*with emphasis, as "Can this be?"*)
54 **Esteban:** Maybe.
55 **Sonia:** In a cab from Mexico? Here is Chicago, up here. They had to cross aaaaall this to get to Mexico. (*pointing on the map*) Would he have gone in a cab?
56 **Cs:** (*** ***)
57 **Esteban:** (***) instead of a cab, maybe he went on a plane.
58 **Sonia:** Hmmmm. Okay, we are talking – Esteban told us that someone had told him that the people that cross by walking are called wetbacks. Does anybody know why? (*waits but there is no response*) What does wetback mean?
59 **Cm:** That they are wet.
60 **Sonia:** That he got wet. Because many people that live in Mexico cross through a river and get wet. But they call them wetbacks, but it is not a nice thing to say. When they call them wetback it is not, it is not something nice, it is something that is not . . .
61 **Cf:** That should not be repeated.
62 **Sonia:** It is an insult. Do you know what an insult is?
63 **Cm1:** Teacher!
64 **Sonia:** What is an insult?
65 **Cm1:** Teacher!
66 **Sonia:** When I tell someone, "You are a dummy," that is an insult.
67 **Cs:** (*laughter*)
68 **Sonia:** If someone tells you, "You are a wetback," what is that?
69 **Cs:** An insult.
70 **Cf:** It is a rude comment.
71 **Sonia:** It is a rude comment, uhum. Okay, here we have the globe, the Earth globe it is called.

Esteban is a critical informant of a Mexican's historical perspective of the land that is part of the United States today. And, with Sonia's help, he, Mariela, and others tell how certain Mexicans now cannot "go in through the line" and are caught if they do so.

In the segment of talk that follows line 40 (not included here), Sonia posed another inquiry for those children who were unsure as to whether they were born in Chicago or in Mexico. Then, as a response to her asking them if they knew where their moms and dads were born (line 41), Esteban states, "My uncle is wetback." This topic is then taken up and examined by others, including Sonia, who tries to have them think more about what the term might mean. At the end of the excerpt, although Esteban has said that his uncle is one, children learn – with Sonia's assistance – that calling someone a "wetback" might be seen as an insult, or a rude comment (line 70), by many, even in the Latino community around their school.

Thus, Sonia has made a concerted effort to encourage her students to bring what they have learned in their community to share in the school classroom. This enables them to interrogate and consider alternative interpretations of the historical and geographical "facts" of the map. Their local cultural knowledge was valued by Sonia, as she and they jointly created new knowledge epistemically.

This first example is perhaps the strongest one included in this chapter because the explicit purpose of Sonia's inquiry was to discover the cultural capital of her students' home and community for use in fashioning her curriculum. However, this seeking out, valuing, and respecting of children's views and capabilities are also evident in the following vignettes. Moreover, the notion of epistemic engagement of texts is present as well.

Anne's First Grade – Becoming Literate by Reading ABC Books

Anne Barry is an Anglo teacher. For her inquiry, she studied one group of 18 first-grade children. Most were Mexican-American children, many of whom were learning English as a second language, 2 were African-American students, 1 was Anglo, and 1 was a first-generation Middle-Eastern child.

Anne had noted over the years that she frequently had one or two students, even by the end of first grade, who did not develop stable understandings of the phonetic principles of written language. Because the reading-aloud routine had been the core of her literacy program for several years, she decided to study how the reading of alphabet books could better foster her students' phonological or phonemic awareness. She knew that this skill had been related to children's learning the letter-sound relationships of printed words (Adams, 1990; Richgels, Poremba, & McGee, 1996). Phonemic awareness is the *conscious* attention of phonemes or units of sound that are normally unconsciously used in spoken words. It is the knowledge that words can be segmented into units of sound, as well as the ability to manipulate those sounds.

Anne had hoped that by reading ABC books her students could explore, play with, and exploit the sounds of words that are presented in these books. Thus, how she read the books, how she fostered student participation, and how she responded to their responses would be critical to her success. Recent research examining how teachers conduct reading-aloud sessions has indicated that although teachers vary in the *style* in which they orchestrate the sharing of books, most teachers control much of the talk, asking most of the questions for which they already know the answers (Dickinson & Keebler, 1989; Martinez & Teale, 1993). In contrast, Anne had worked for several years to make her reading-aloud routine collaborative so that students could spontaneously ask questions and make comments as she read to them. (See Oyler [1996] and Pappas & Barry [1997] for earlier research on Anne's reading-aloud routines.) Thus, these student initiations during her reading of these ABC books were the major focus of her study because they revealed the ongoing understandings of her students' phonemic knowledge.

Excerpts from two read-aloud sessions (Examples 9.2 and 9.3) give a flavor of these interactions. Example 9.2 occurred early in the year when Anne read the classic ABC book, *Alligators All Around: An Alphabet* by Sendak (1962). When Anne reads, she stands so that all of the children, who sit on their chairs (moved from their regular tables) near and around her, can see the book. In this example, many student initiations show connections of the alphabet letters to "sounds" or letters of their names, which was quite frequent in the early read-alouds. Also illustrated is how Anne contingently responded to these efforts (cf. Wells, 1986; Wells & Chang-Wells, 1992). Moreover, there are other student responses that show other kinds of sophisticated knowledge about the phonetic principles of written language.

EXAMPLE 9.2: *Alligators All Around: An Alphabet* (Sendak, 1962)[3]

1 **Anne:**   K KEEPING KANGAROOS
2 **C:**   Karen
3 **C1:**   Kangaroo. My favorite animal.
4 **C:**   Casey

---

[3] Fieldnotes, 10/05/94.

 5 **Anne:**   What about "Casey"?
  . . .
 6 **Anne:**   N NEVER NAPPING
 7 **C1:**   No.
 8 **Anne:**   If you put "N" and "O" together it makes "no."
 9 **Cs:**   And "Y" "E" "S" is "yes"!
  . . .
10 **Anne:**   P PUSHING PEOPLE
11 **C:**   Peter Pan.
12 **C:**   Pinoccio.
13 **C:**   Peanut butter.
14 **C:**   Popeye.
15 **C:**   Penguin.
16 **C:**   Bat.
17 **Anne:**   "Pat," "bat," "bat" is a "B" word.
  . . .
18 **Anne:**   Q QUITE QUARRELSOME
19 **C:**   Queatiful.
20 **Anne:**   (*smiling*) Queatiful.
21 **C1:**   Queen.
22 **C:**   King Kong. "King" starts with "K."
23 **Anne:**   "Quiet" is a "Q" word. . . .
  . . .
24 **Anne:**   RIDING REINDEER
25 **C:**   Robin Hood!
26 **Reyn:**   Reynolda. "R" is for me.
27 **C:**   Riding on a bus!
28 **Peron:** Peter Pan.
29 **Anne:**   Does "P," "Pa" (*emphasizing the "P" sound*), Peter Pan
             start with "R"?
30 **Cs:**   #No.#
31 **Peron:** #(*shrugs his head side to side*)#
32 **Anne:**   Peron, I think of you're thinking of your name.
33 **C:**   Rice-a-roni.
34 **Cs:**   Ricky Lay. (*referring to a large gorilla-like stuffed animal in
             the classroom that children frequently lean on when they read
             in the classroom*)
35 **Anne:**   What comes after "R"? S SHOCKINGLY SPOILED
  . . .
36 **Anne:**   Y

37 **Cs:**   Yak, yak, yak.
38 **Anne:**   In our alphabet book, it is YACKETY-YACKING.
39 **Cs:**   Yak, yak, yak.
40 **Anne:**   The book says "yackety-yacking."
41 **C:**   Hawaii.
42 **Anne:**   You hear "Y" in the middle. Say the word "Ha-wa-ii."
            There is a "Y" sound in the middle of "Hawaii." Oh, this
            is interesting.
43 **C1:**   Yes.
44 **C:**   Why.
45 **Anne:**   The question word.
46 **C:**   Wife.
47 **C:**   White.
48 **C:**   Wire.
49 **Anne:**   No, that would be "yire." You are getting "Y" and "W"
            mixed up. We'll have to do something with this.

On lines 2 and 26, students offered names of the children in the class for
the letters of the book ("K" and "R," respectively). Sometimes they
gave approximations – for example, when a child said a "Casey" name
(line 4) for the same sound that the "K" of "KEEPING KANGAROOS"
represented. A major portion of Anne's response to this particular effort
was inaudible (line 5), but we can see how she approached Peron's "Peter
Pan" for the "R" letter (line 28). In line 29, she got him to rethink that
contribution by reinforcing the "P" sound, but she also gave him credit
for the idea in line 32, telling him that he probably came up with it
because there is an "R" in his name (but not at the beginning). Thus,
because Anne showed that she valued her children's risk taking in their
initiations, they felt comfortable to continue to do so, which then provided
her with opportunities to build on them with more "correct" information
about letter-sound relationships.

   This example shows a range of child initiations that reflected what
they already knew about letter-sound relationships, all of which reflect
their developing phonemic awareness (e.g., the "Peter Pan," "Pinoccio,"
"peanut butter," "Popeye," "penguin" contributions for the "P" letter,
and the wonderful "queatiful" and "queen" for the "Q" letter). Anne
was very excited about the "Hawaii" initiation for "Y" that they
"heard" in the middle of that word (line 41), as well as the other words
children subsequently offered – "why," "wife," "white," and "wire" –
which did not start with a "Y" but did show students' phonemic knowl-

edge because children used what has been called the letter-name strategy. That is, they used the *name* of the letter (the name of "Y" is "wye") in presenting their approximations (Temple, Nathan, Temple, & Burris, 1993). Thus, students' developing ideas about letter-sound relationships observed in this and other ABC book sessions provided useful assessment information for Anne that she could follow up on in other instructional contexts. In addition, over the year, children also made interesting comparisons regarding sound–symbol patterns found in English and Spanish. For example, Casey first asked about the spelling of the word "know," which was formatted very bold in a non-ABC book – "Why did they put a 'k' if it doesn't sound?" Anne responded that she thought that was a very good question and was about to explain more about this pattern in English when other students interrupted to tell Anne, who does not speak Spanish, that this, too, occurs in Spanish, "Like 'h' in Spanish doesn't sound" (Fieldnotes, 12/07/94).

Example 9.3 illustrates other kinds of knowledge that were evoked by the reading of ABC books. In the beginning of the excerpt, children give "R" words ("radio" and "rake") for the upcoming letter to be read. Most of the other student initiations, however, focus on their elaborations of the content of the book, *Pop-Up Animal Alphabet Book* (Cerf, 1994).

EXAMPLE 9.3: *Pop-Up Animal Alphabet Book* (Cerf, 1994)[4]

1 **C:**   Radio.
2 **C:**   Rake.
3 **Anne:** R'S FOR THE RHINO, WHOSE TEMPER IS SHORT.
4 **C:**   What is "temper"?
5 **Anne:** (*** ***) *(gives a short definition that is inaudible)*
6 **C:**   People use horns for medicine.
7 **Anne:** *(nods in affirmation)*
8 **C:**   He can go 30 miles per hour.
9 **Anne:** V'S FOR VARYING HARE, SOMETIMES WHITE, SOME-
      TIMES BROWN.
10 **C:**   *(goes up to the book, which shows a white hare in snow, and
      pulls the tab, which now reveals a brown hare in green grass,
      etc.)*
11 **C1:** It's like a picture.

---

[4] Fieldnotes, 10/12/94.

12 **C2:**   It changes its hair.

13 **C3:**   White is for snow, brown is for spring.

14 **Anne:**   (*nods in comfirmation*) W? WOLVES, WHO FORM PACKS TO HUNT GAME.

15 **Cs:**   Oooooooooo.

16 **C1:**   Like a ghost, like a witch.

17 **C2:**   Wolves eat people and lions and leopards. I saw it on a program.

18 **C3:**   A dog looks like a wolf.

Line 4 has a child asking about "temper," for which Anne provided an explanation (but was inaudible). In lines 6 and 8, children offered other information about the rhino – namely, that the horns are used for medicine and that a rhino can go 30 mph. Similarly, extra information is included as initiations for the varying hare and wolves. For the hare, C2 notes that as the tab is moved in the book, it "changes its hair," and C3 follows up by noting that this change was connected to different seasons – "White is for snow, brown is for spring." In lines 15–18, children imitated the sound that wolves make, which led C1 to make the connection to ghosts and witches (which were topics of books being read during this month of Halloween), as well as other information about wolves – namely, what they eat and what they look like.

These latter initiations frequently represented the kinds of intertextual links in the classroom discourse that children made (Bloome & Egan-Robertson, 1993; Lemke, 1985b). That is, they juxtaposed or tied content from other texts – other ABC books on animal topics or the many information books she also read aloud, songs, movies, TV shows, personal stories from their home and communities, and so forth – to the text being read.

In sum, the reading of ABC books facilitated her students' phonemic awareness, and, as Anne found out, the genre of ABC books is huge, varied, and sophisticated, enabling her students to learn much more than their "ABCs." Again, students' initiations and intertextual responses to these books showed the ways in which they engaged in these ABC texts epistemically as they readily drew on their existing linguistic and content knowledge to create new understandings of them.

Pam's First Grade – Julissa Becoming Literate in Writing

Pamela Wolfer is also an Anglo teacher. Of her 27 first-grade students that year, most were Latina/o children, with 4 African-American and 2

Anglo students. Pam was interested in teaching early literacy "skills" through meaningful writing. Her inquiry developed into how to accomplish this goal by implementing her own version of a process-approach writing workshop as an important feature of her curriculum (Calkins, 1986). It was critical to Pam that children be encouraged to write with their own voice. That is, although their texts would be realized by invented spellings, they would embody the social principle of language or what Bakhtin (1981) called "the socially charged life of the word." In this perspective, then, learning to write involves children figuring out how to manipulate words to accomplish some kind of social work (Dyson, 1993, 1996). It has to do with learning "how to mean" in writing (Christie, 1987; Halliday, 1993).

Using some initial ideas from Fisher (1991), Pam was successful in orchestrating a writing workshop to support her students, many of whom had very limited literacy understandings and were unsure about their abilities to be writers. She made many structural changes in the various subcomponents (subroutines) of the writing workshop (e.g., minilessons, her conferences with individual children while they wrote, author-chair sharetime periods) based on her careful monitoring of her students' ongoing understandings and challenges.

Children were given a very high level of autonomy in their writing because she left them alone to write/draw their books (folded paper stapled together) for most of the period while she met individually with others. They collaborated with each other by socializing and borrowing materials from each other, sharing ideas for stories and texts, and rereading their texts to their peers.

In her conferences, she tried to develop flexible ways of interacting with individual children to scaffold best both the message and medium aspects of her students' writing. Example 9.4 illustrates a conference with Julissa, a Latina child who frequently insisted that she couldn't read or spell. Pam encouraged her use of invented spelling (Bissex, 1980; Temple et al., 1993) to tell her story about her experiences "in the community," which was the current classroom thematic unit.

EXAMPLE 9.4: Julissa's "We boutt Flrs for our mother"[5]

1 **Pam:**   What is the main thing the story is about?
2 **Julissa:** My dad told me to buy food. (*reading from her text*) I
              BOUGHT VEGETABLES AND COOKIES. I BUY SOME

---

[5] Videotape, 03/22/95.

FLOWERS. I BUY SOME MILK. I SAW GENNA AT THE
STORE. I SAW RONNIE. I SAW ALBERTO. I SAW
ELENNA . .

3 **Pam:**   Okay and so that's the end. I loved the beginning.

...   (*At Pam's request, Julissa rereads the first part about the grocery shopping.*)

4 **Pam:**   Who did you buy the flowers for?

5 **Julissa:**   For my mother.

6 **Pam:**   Could you tell us that maybe on this page? On the next page? Could you tell us that?

7 **Julissa:**   (*nods slightly*)

8 **Pam:**   Yeah? Do you think we could add a page here and you can write who you bought the flowers for? And what would you say? How would you write it?

...   (*With Pam's help, Julissa orally creates:* "We bought flowers for our mother." *Pam begins to help Julissa to figure out how to spell this addition to her text. Julissa has written "We" and is beginning to tackle "bought."*)

9 **Pam:**   How do you spell "bought" here? Okay, now you're writing the word "bought," right? (*pointing to Julissa's already spelled version of the word in her text*) This is the word "bought." I want you to write that word right here. (*referring to her new sentence*) That's how you spelled "bought" before. That's how you're going to spell "bought" now. Can you write that down?

10 **Julissa:**   (*writes down the word, using her previous spelling*)

11 **Pam:**   Uhhuh. Okay, let's read it. (*pointing to the two words written so far and then to the next space*)

12 **Julissa:**   WE BOUGHT . . flowers.

13 **Pam:**   Okay. Where did you write "flowers" before?

14 **Julissa:**   (*points to the word in her text*)

15 **Pam:**   Okay. If you wrote it like that before, it's going to be spelled and – you're going to use the same letters you used there.

16 **Julissa:**   (*She adds "flowers" to her sentence:* "We boutt Flrs. . . .")

In the beginning of the conference, when Pam addressed the message or content or her text, Julissa, who was often anxious about her writing, was quite able to answer Pam's question about her story. After telling Pam that it was about the time when her father had told her to buy food, Julissa then spontaneously read her text, which related what she had bought and whom she saw – namely, four classmates who were frequently included in her writing.

After responding favorably to the first part of her text, and having Julissa reread it, Pam then attempted to challenge Julissa to revise it by writing more about the person the flowers were for (lines 7 and 9). In posing the question, "Can you tell us that?," Pam emphasized the audience dimensions of writing (MacGillivray, 1994; Rowe, 1989) and showed how texts can be seen as being tentative and potential for revision. Thus, Julissa is given an opportunity to treat her text epistemically by coming up with a new sentence to add to it, "We bought flowers for our mother." Pam spent the rest of the conference explaining to her that she could easily accomplish the task because she had already provided reasonable invented-spelling approximations for "bought" and "flowers" in her preceding text. With Pam's help, Julissa applied this new strategy to extend the meaning of her text.

Through these conferences and the other writing workshop experiences, Julissa and other students who initially had been very reluctant to be writers became confident in developing the symbolic tools to "mean" in writing (Halliday, 1993). In this classroom community, certain values were assigned in the writing process, within which children's identities as writers were created (MacGillivray, 1994). Pam's ways of interacting – balancing the teaching of skills *and* helping children "come to voice" (Lensmire, 1994) – provided for the learning needs of students with a range of literacy abilities and dispositions.

Collaborative Talk: Discourse for Social Change

In all three vignettes, teachers created with their students social practices in which children could learn that the meanings expressed in texts can be seen as tentative in order to be open for alternative interpretation or revision. That is, children were given many opportunities to engage texts epistemically. In Sonia's classroom, children considered an alternative historical interpretation regarding USA–Mexico boundaries and the related topic of wetbacks. In coming up with their own initiations during Anne's reading of ABC books, children contributed other possibilities of the sound/symbol relations that each book offered, as well as related "extra" intertextual links of other texts they knew. In conferences with Pam, Julissa and other students learned that it is possible to develop strategies to expand and elaborate current text to make it more interesting for their classroom audience. Thus, children's contributions to these and other literacy activities facilitated their learning of literacy skills.

These children were becoming literate in many diverse ways as a result of incorporating their culture in school curricula. In each case, to reiterate Wells's earlier words, this way of becoming literate entailed their being able to "empower action, thinking, and feeling in the context of purposeful social activity." This was accomplished through guided participation in the social and discursive practices of joint activity (Reder, 1994; Wells, 1990). However, that these contexts for learning were *collaborative* in nature needs to be further emphasized, and this requires that the issue of power be reexamined more fully.

Power Relationships in the Borderlands

Although all of the teacher researchers here had different foci in their inquiries, they all had purposefully examined how they might alter the power relationships that typically obtain between teachers and students. As Geertz (1973) has argued, "to rework the pattern of social relationships is to rearrange the coordinates of the experienced world" (p. 28). Thus, there was more going on here than teachers merely finding the right "methods" to improve the literacy learning of students who have been historically oppressed (Bartolome, 1994). They challenged the deficit view that many urban school personnel, as well as the general population, still hold regarding low-SES and ethnic-minority children by forging these collaborative arrangements with their students. Thus, in their endeavors to "rework the pattern of social relationships," children's "experienced world" was different in critical ways – there was an encouragement and appreciation of student "voice" and an acceptance and valuing of children's prior knowledge in literacy learning.

The interactions between students and teachers may reflect the relations of culture and power in the society, "but they also *constitute* these relations and, as such, embody a transformative potential" (Cummins, 1994, p. 299). Therefore, to use Cummins's terminology, the "collaborative microinteractions" between teachers and students in the three vignettes presented in this chapter are extremely significant in that they illustrate how to resist and challenge the historically entrenched "coercive macrointeractions" in the broader society. When teacher-dominated IRE discourse patterns or teacher monologic instruction are radically altered to create interactions that allow for joint participation and strategic assistance, multiple literacies are developed. These new power arrangements that have been invoked at the local school site "begin to rupture the transcendent script" in the culture at large (Gutierrez et al., 1995, p. 469). Power relations are learned and become a part of children's identities as they participate in particular social practices of particular communities. Schools can provide conditions for interaction that expand students' expressions and possibilities to learn new identities – they can construct *borderlands* in which children learn to be literate in powerful ways. I have tried to show how that the talk in the borderlands depicted in the three vignettes is critically important because it allows for and legitimates students' local and culturally varied knowledge in literacy learning. This kind of conversation in the classroom empowers students' diversity, as Barber (1984) has stated:

> Because conversation responds to the endless variety of human experience and respects the initial legitimacy of every human perspective, it is served by many voices rather than by one and achieves a rich ambiguity rather than a narrow clarity. It aims at creating a sense of commonality, not of unity, and the mutualism it aspires to weave into one carpet the threads of a hundred viewpoints. (p. 184)

Becoming literate in the borderlands, then, means exchanging experiences and synthesizing varied world views, and this only occurs in the kinds of collaborative cultural practices that Sonia, Anne, and Pam worked hard to construct in their classrooms.

Further Educational and Research Implications of the Borderlands

The borderlands thesis – the collaborative styles of literacy teaching–learning that are depicted in this chapter – also has important political significance. Bartolome (1994), for example, argues that teachers need to develop a political awareness regarding their relationships with students of color as knowers and active participants in their own learning. For her, this means pursuing a "humanizing" pedagogy that respects and uses the history and perspectives of students as an integral part of educational practice. Too frequently, this does not occur because both pre- and in-service teachers (as well as the university professors working with them) get caught up with the finding of "magic" methods to use with children of diverse cultural background, without also examining the ideology or theoretical underpinnings that inform these methods, or critically evaluating whether or not these methods will replicate the subordinated status of these children. It also means that the "multicultural" education that has been described here incorporates and respects students' cultural experiences *all the time* in literacy teaching–learning and throughout the curriculum (rather than as some kind of "add-on" 1-month study on Black history or short-term use of a "package" of multicultural materials).

The teachers presented in this chapter have evolved this political stance, but it is important to note that their work to fashion collaborative, humanizing pedagogy has not been easy to accomplish. Some of the teachers in our project have had many years of experience in teaching-as-transmission and felt that they had much to overcome; the newer teachers found it difficult to conceive of because they had never observed or directly tried it personally. In many ways, these teachers' efforts, then, have constituted what Cochran-Smith (1991) has termed "learning to teach against the grain." Thus, there is major work to be done in educational and professional development programs to support teachers as agents of reform.

Research agendas can also be more infused with a political stance. For me, creating a collaborative arrangement in research with teachers who were interested in creating culturally responsive pedagogy was a major first step toward such a view, because it meant that traditional relationships regarding power/knowledge between teacher-researchers in schools and myself as a university researcher had to be interrogated and altered. It is by working *with* teachers, not *on* them, that I have realized that issues of power and privilege must be made problematic or an explicit concern at many levels in studying children's literacy development.

The teachers have taught me how important it is to try to take on an ideological point of view that contests the discourses that have functioned historically to maintain a deficit, subordinated view of the intellectual and linguistic capabilities of children of low-SES, culturally diverse backgrounds in research on human development. And, in doing so, as the examples show, these children have demonstrated how much, and the many varied ways in which, they are extremely capable of contributing to their own literacy learning in the borderlands.

References

Adams, M. J. (1990). *Beginning to read: Thinking and learning about print.* Cambridge, MA: MIT Press.

Altricher, H., Posch, O., & Somekh, B. (1993). *Teachers investigate their work: An introduction to the methods of action research.* London: Routledge.

Bakhtin, M. M. (1981). *The dialogic imagination: Four essays by M. M. Bakhtin* (M. Holquist, ed.) (M. Holquist & C. Emerson, trans.) Austin: University of Texas Press.

Barber, B. (1984). *Strong democracy: Participatory politics for a new age.* Berkeley: University of California Press.

Bartolome, L. I. (1994). Beyond the methods fetish: Toward a humanizing pedagogy. *Harvard Educational Review, 64,* 173–94.

Bissex, G. L. (1980). *Gnys at wrk: A child learns to write and read.* Cambridge, MA: Harvard University Press.

Bloome, D., & Egan-Robertson, A. (1993). The social construction of intertextuality in classroom reading and writing lessons. *Reading Research Quarterly, 28,* 305–33.

Calkins, L. M. (1986). *The art of teaching writing.* Portsmouth, NH: Heinemann.

Cazden, C. B. (1988). *Classroom discourse: The language of teaching and learning.* Portsmouth, NH: Heinemann.

Cerf, C. B. (1994). *Pop-up animal alphabet book.* New York: Random House.

Christie, F. (1987). Learning to mean in writing. In N. Stewart-Dore (Ed.), *Writing and reading to learn* (pp. 21–34). Rozelle, Australia: Primary English Teaching Association.

Cochran-Smith, M. (1991). Learning to teach against the grain. *Harvard Educational Review, 61,* 279–310.

Cochran-Smith, M., & Lytle, S. L. (1993). *Inside/outside: Teacher research and knowledge.* New York: Teachers College Press.

Crawford, J. (1992). *Hold your tongue: Bilingualism and the politics of "English only."* Reading, MA: Addison-Wesley.

Cummins, J. (1994). From coercive to collaborative relations of power in the teaching of literacy. In B. M. Ferdman, R.-M. Weber, & A. G. Ramierz (Eds.), *Literacy across languages and cultures* (pp. 295–331). Albany: State University of New York Press.

Delgado-Gaitan, C. (1996). *Protean literacy: Extending the discourse on empowerment.* London: Falmer Press.

Dickinson, D. K., & Keebler, R. (1989). Variations in preschool teachers' storybook reading styles. *Discourse Processes, 12,* 353–76.

Dyson, A. H. (1993). *Social worlds of children learning to write in an urban primary school.* New York: Teachers College Press.

Dyson, A. H. (1996). Cultural constellations and childhood identities: On Greek gods, cartoon heroes, and the social lives of schoolchildren. *Harvard Educational Review, 66,* 471–524.

Edwards, D., & Mercer, N. (1987). *Common knowledge: The development of understanding in the classroom.* London: Routledge.

Erickson, F., & Shultz, J. (1977). When is a context? Some issues and methods in the analysis of social competence. *The Quarterly Newsletter of the Institute for Comparative Human Development, 1,* 5–12.

Fairclough, N. (1992). *Discourse and social change.* Cambridge: Polity Press.

Fisher, B. (1991). *Joyful learning: A whole language kindergarten.* Portsmouth, NH: Heinemann

Foster, M. (1992). Sociolinguistics and the African-American community: Implications for literacy. *Theory into Practice, 32,* 303–11.

Freire, P. (1972). *Cultural action for freedom.* Harmondsworth, England: Penguin Books.

Geertz, C. (1973). *The interpretations of cultures: Selected essays.* New York: Basic Books.

Gitlin, A. D. (1990). Educative research, voice and school change. *Harvard Educational Review, 60,* 443–66.

Green, J. L., & Dixon, C. N. (1994). Talking into being: Discursive and social practices in classrooms. *Linguistics and Education, 5,* 231–9.

Gutierrez, K., Rymes, B., & Larson, J. (1995). Script, counterscript, and underlife in the classroom: James Brown versus *Brown v. Board of Education. Harvard Educational Review, 65,* 445–71.

Halliday, M. A. K. (1978). *Language as social semiotic: The social interpretation of language and meaning.* London: Edward Arnold.

Halliday, M. A. K. (1993). Towards a language-based theory of learning. *Linguistics and Education, 5,* 93–126.

Halliday, M. A. K., & Hasan, R. (1976). *Cohesion in English.* London: Longman.

Halliday, M. A. K., & Hasan, R. (1985). *Language, context, and text: Aspects of language in a social-semiotic perspective.* Victoria, Australia: Deakin University Press.

Kreisberg, S. (1992). *Transforming power: Domination, empowerment, and education.* Albany: State University of New York Press.

Lemke, J. L. (1985a). *Using language in the classroom.* Victoria, Australia: Deakin University Press.

Lemke, J. L. (1985b). Ideology, intertextuality, and the notion of register. In J. D. Benson & W. S. Greaves (Eds.), *Systemic perspectives on discourse: Selected theoretical papers from the 9th international systemic workshop* (Vol. 1, pp. 275–94). Norwood, NJ: Ablex.

Lemke, J. L. (1990). *Talking science: Language, learning, and values.* Norwood, NJ: Ablex.

Lensmire, T. J. (1994). *When children write: Critical re-visions of the writing workshop.* New York: Teachers College Press.

Losey, K. M. (1995). Mexican American students and classroom interaction: An overview and critique. *Review of Educational Research, 65,* 283–318.

MacGillivray, L. (1994). Tacit shared understandings of a first-grade writing community. *JRB: A Journal of Literacy, 26,* 245–66.

Martinez, M., & Teale, W. (1993). Teacher storybook reading style: A comparison of six teachers. *Research in the Teaching of English, 27,* 175–99.

McCollum, P. (1991). Cross-cultural perspectives on classroom discourse and literacy. In E. H. Heibert (Ed.), *Literacy for a diverse society: Perspectives, practices and policies* (pp. 108–21). New York: Teachers College Press.

Moll, L. C. (Ed.). (1990). *Vygotsky and education: Instructional implications and applications of sociohistorical psychology.* Cambridge: Cambridge University Press.

Moll, L. C. (1992). Literacy research in community and classrooms: A sociocultural approach. In R. Beach, J. L. Green, M. L. Kamil, & T. Shanahan (Eds.), *Multidisciplinary perspectives on literacy research* (pp. 211–44). Urbana, IL: National Conference on Research in English.

Moll, L. C, & Gonzalez, N. (1994). Lessons from research with language-minority children. *JRB: A Journal of Literacy, 26,* 439–56.

Newman, D. P., Griffin, P., & Cole, M. (1989). *The construction zone: Working for cognitive change in school.* Cambridge: Cambridge University Press.

O'Connor, M. C., & Michaels, S. (1993). Aligning academic task and participation status through revoicing: Analysis of a classroom discourse strategy. *Anthropology and Education Quarterly, 24,* 318–35.

Oyler, C. J. (1996). *Making room for students in an urban first grade: Sharing authority in room 104.* New York: Teachers College Press.

Pappas, C. C. (1997). Making "collaboration" problematic in collaborative school-university research: Studying with urban teacher researchers to transform literacy curriculum genres. In J. Flood, S. B. Heath, & D. Lapp (Eds.), *A handbook of research on teaching through the communicative and visual arts* (pp. 215–31). New York: Simon & Shuster Macmillan.

Pappas, C. C., & Barry, A. (1997). Scaffolding urban students' initiations: Transactions in reading information books in the reading-aloud curriculum genre. In N. J. Karolides (Ed.), *Reader response in the elementary classroom: Quest and discovery* (pp. 215–36). Mahwah, NJ: Erlbaum.

Pappas, C. C., Kiefer, B. Z., & Levstik, L. S. (1999). *An integrated language perspective in the elementary school: An action approach.* New York: Longman.

Pappas, C. C., & Zecker, L. B. (in press a). *Working with teacher researchers in urban classrooms: Transforming literacy curriculum genres.* Mahwah, NJ: Erlbaum.

Pappas, C. C., & Zecker, L. B. (in press b). *Teacher inquiries in literacy teaching–learning: Learning to collaborate in elementary urban classrooms.* Mahwah, NJ: Erlbaum.

Ramirez, A. (1988). Analyzing speech acts. In J. L. Green & J. O. Harker (Eds.), *Multiple perspective analyses of classroom discourse* (pp. 135–63). Norwood, NJ: Ablex.

Reder, S. (1994). Practice-engagement theory: A sociocultural approach to literacy across languages and cultures. In B. M. Ferdman, R.-M. Weber, & A. G. Ramierz (Eds.), *Literacy across languages and cultures* (pp. 33–74). Albany: State University of New York Press.

Richardson, V. (1994). Conducting research on practice. *Educational Researcher*, 23, 5–10.

Richgels, D. J., Poremba, K. J., & McGee, L. M. (1996). Kindergarteners talk about print: Phonemic awareness in meaningful contexts. *The Reading Teacher*, 49, 632–42.

Rowe, D. R. (1989). Author/audience interaction in the preschool: The role of social interaction in literacy learning. *Journal of Reading Behavior, 21*, 311–49.

Sendak, M. (1962). *Alligators all around: An alphabet*. New York: Harper & Row.

Sulzby, E., & Teale, W. H. (1991). Emergent literacy. In R. Barr, M. L. Kamil, P. Mosenthal, & P. D. Pearson (Eds.), *Handbook of reading research* (Vol. 1, pp. 727–57). White Plains, NY: Longman.

Teale, W. H., & Sulzby, E. (Eds.). (1986). *Emergent literacy: Writing and reading*. Norwood, NJ: Ablex.

Temple, C., Nathan, R., Temple, F., & Burris N. A. (1993). *The beginnings of writing*. Boston: Allyn and Bacon.

Vygotsky, L. S. (1962). *Thought and language*. Cambridge, MA: MIT Press.

Vygotsky, L. S. (1978). *Mind in society: The development of higher psychological processes*. Cambridge: Cambridge University Press.

Wells, G. (1986). *The meaning makers: Children learning language and using language to learn*. Portsmouth, NH: Heinemann.

Wells, G. (1990). Talk about text: Where literacy is learned and taught. *Curriculum Inquiry, 20*, 369–405.

Wells, G. (1993). Reevaluating the IRF sequence: A proposal for the articulation of theories of activity and discourse for the analysis of teaching and learning in the classroom. *Linguistics and Education, 5*, 1–37.

Wells, G. (1994). The complimentary contributions of Halliday and Vygotsky to a "language-based theory of learning." *Linguistics and Education, 6*, 41–90.

Wells, G., & Chang-Wells, G. L. (1992). *Constructing knowledge together: Classrooms as centers of inquiry and literacy*. Portsmouth, NH: Heinemann.

Wertsch, J. V. (1991). *Voices of the mind: A sociocultural approach to mediated action*. Cambridge, MA: Harvard University Press.

Willinsky, J. (1990). *The New Literacy: Redefining reading and writing in the schools*. New York: Routledge.

Young, R. (1992). *Critical theory and classroom talk*. Clevedon, England: Multilingual Matters.

Appendix A:
Conventions of Transcription

Unit:	Usually corresponds to an independent clause with all dependent clauses related to it (complex clause or T-unit). Sometimes includes another independent clause if there is no drop of tone and is added without any pausing. Units here are punctuated as sentences.
Turn:	Includes all of a speaker's utterances/units.
Key for Speakers:	First name is listed for teacher-researcher. C, C1, C2, and so forth are noted for individual children (with "m" or "f" to refer to the gender of a child): C is used if a child's voice cannot be identified; Cn's is used to identify particular children in a particular section of the transcript (so that C1 or C2, etc., is not necessarily the same child throughout the whole transcript). Cs represents many children speaking simultaneously.
–	False starts or abandoned language replaced by new language structures.
..	Small/short pause within unit.
.. ..	Longer pause within unit.
...	Breaking off of a speaker's turn due to the next speaker's turn.
< >	Uncertain words.
(***)	One word that is inaudible or impossible to transcribe.
(*** ***)	Longer stretches of language that are inaudible and impossible to transcribe.
Underscore:	Emphasis.
# #	Overlapping language spoken by two or more speakers at a time.
CAPS	Actual reading of a book.
{ }	Teacher's miscue or modification of a text read.
( )	Identifies what is being referred or gestured to and other nonverbal contextual information.
....	Part of a transcript has been omitted.

Appendix B:
Original Spanish Version of Example 9.1[6]

Sonia:	Aquí dice México. Esto es Estados Unidos, esto es México. (*pointing to them on the map*)

[6] Fieldnotes, videotape, 02/28/95.

Esteban:	Pero de todos modos México no es – no es chiquito, cuando ellos robaron – la tierra, todavía es grande, México.
Sonia:	México era grande antes. ¿Y quién le robó la tierra?
Esteban:	Los de aquí.
Sonia:	Ooooh. ¿Y quién te contó?
Esteban:	Mi papá.
Sonia:	Tu papá. ¿Y tú sabes qué parte era de México que ya no es? (*She waits, but there is no response.*) ¿Qué porte sería esa? Esto es México. (*pointing on the map*) ¿Cuál era la parte que era de México antes?
Esteban:	Esto – era – era – era de aquí pa' allá. (*pointing toward the map*)
Sonia:	¿Para abajo?
Esteban:	(*** ***)
C1:	Aquel no era, Maestra.
Sonia:	Pero Estados Unidos está acá arriba. Esos son otros países. (*pointing to countries south of México in the map*)
Cf:	Aquel, Maestra, aquel.
Sonia:	Yo creo que acá arriba, acá, esta era la parte que tu papá te contó que era de México . . .
Esteban:	A lo mej – a lo mejor – es – este es un lugar famoso porque también hay un – pais que es famoso por – porque ahí los mexicanos no – no pueden pasar a través de – de la línea (***).
Sonia:	¿ No pueden pasar?
Esteban:	No.
Sonia:	¿A dónde?
Esteban:	La – la línea es de Est – es parte de Estados Unidos.
Sonia:	¿Acá en la – en el límite? ¿Justo acá, en esta línea?
Esteban:	Uhum.
Sonia:	¿No los dejan pasar?
Esteban:	Ya <mi tío> lo atraparon el año pasado.
Sonia:	¿Quién sabía eso?
Esteban:	Mi papi me lo contó y también . . .
Sonia:	¿Qué te dijo? (*She waits, but there is no response.*) ¿Quién sabia de eso que – uy, vamos a esperar a Vicente y Mariela porque están jugando. El papá de Esteban le contó a él que hay partes acá, en el límite con México y Estados Unidos, que no dejan entrar a los mexicanos. ¿Por qué sería eso? ¿Por qué no los dejan entrar?
Cm1:	Porque no . . .
Sonia:	¿Por qué será?
Cm1:	Porque . . .
Mariela:	Ell – ellos no son de este país.

Sonia:	¿Porque los mexicanos son de México y no son de Estados Unidos?
Cf1:	#Maestra . . . #
Sonia:	#Pero ustedes están acá, y uestedes son de México . . . #
Cf1:	#Maestra . . Maestra . . mi papá vino a los Estados Unidos.#
Cm1:	#A mí si me dejan entrar, y soy de Chicago.#
Sonia:	¿Porque naciste en Chicago? ¿Y por eso te dejan entrar? Hmmm. ¿Quién mas nació en Chicago? ¿Quién nació en México?
Cs:	(*raise hands and talk all at once*)
C:	#Yo nací en Chicago.#
C:	#Yo nací acá.#
C:	#Yo igual.#
	(*Sonia names some of the ones born in Chicago and some of the ones born in México. Then she asks some of them who have not volunteered information. Some do not know, and Sonia tells them to ask their mothers. Then Sonia poses another question.*)
Sonia:	¿Y sus mamá y papá, dónde nacieron?
Cf:	En México, mi mam – mamá y mi papá nacieron en México.
Esteban:	Mi tio es mojado.
Sonia:	¿En Mojado? (*Since they were talking about being born in México and reluctant to believe the children would know the word* mojado (*'wetback'*) *in Spanish, Sonia initially responded to the child's comment as if* mojado *were the name of a place in México.*)
Cs:	(*laughter*)
Cf1:	Caminando . . se fue caminando porque un amigo de mi mamá lo dijo.
Sonia:	¿Qué?
Cf1:	Que . . e . . e – que mojado quiere decir que se vienen caminando, de allá.
Sonia:	Hmmmm, y se vinieron caminando. ¿Y por qué le dicen mojado? (*waits but there is no response*) ¿Porque se mojó?
Cs:	No.
Esteban:	Pero mi papá dice que – se vino, yo creo . . .
. . . .	(*Sonia asks Cs not to touch the microphone, to sit down in their chairs, and calls some names specifically because Esteban wants to keep talking.*)
Esteban:	Yo creo que – yo creo que – yo creo que se vino en un taxi de México.
Sonia:	¿En un taxi de México? (*with emphasis, as "Can this be?"*)
Esteban:	A lo mejor.
Sonia:	¿En un taxi de México? Aquí está Chicago, acá arriba. Tuvieron

que cruzar tooooodo esto para ir a México. (*pointing on the map*) ¿Se habrá ido en un taxi?

Cs: (*** ***)

Esteban: (***) en lugar de en un taxi, a lo mejor se fue en un avión.

Sonia: Hmmmm. Okay, estamos hablando – Esteban nos contó que alguien le habiía dicho que a la gente que se cruza caminando le dicen mojado. ¿Alguien sabe por qué? (*Sonia waits, but there is no response*) ¿Qué quiere decir mojado?

Cm: Que están mojados.

Sonia: Que se mojó. Porque muchas personas que viven en México cruzan por un río y se mojan. Pero le dicen mojados, pero no es una cosa muy linda que le dicen. Cuando le dicen mojado no es – no es algo lindo, es algo que no . . .

Cf: Que no lo deben repetir.

Sonia: Es un insulto. ¿Saben lo que es un insulto?

Cm1: ¡Maestra!

Sonia: ¿Qué es un insulto?

Cm1: ¡Maestra!

Sonia: Cuando yo le digo a alguien, "Eres un tonto," eso es un insulto.

Cs: (*laughter*)

Sonia: Si alguien te dice, "Eres un mojado." ¿Eso qué es?

Cs: Un insulto.

Cf: Es una grosería.

Sonia: Es una grosería, uhum. Okay, aquí tenemos el globo, el globo terráqueo se llama.

Index

ABC books, 241–7
Ackerman, E., 222
acquisition, 17, 134, 141
actions, 154, 154n2, 155
activities: categories/types of, 16, 38–40, 155; and consciousness, 154, 154n2, 155; definition of, 154; motives for, 154, 155. *See also un-der* Mayan children
activity in context, 12, 26–7, 54–5
activity settings, 17, 99–124; and ac-tivity theory, 100–1; and behavior settings, 100; ecocultural models of, 100, 101–3; and ecological cul-tural models, 100; of European- and Korean-American preschool-ers, 118–22; and socially mediated cognition, 100. *See also* pretend play
activity theory, 100–1, 152–6, 166–7, 174
adolescents, boredom of, 192–4, 195
adult work: Mayan men's vs. women's, 29; primacy of, 16, 32–4, 41, 45, 49, 56; work place ex-periences, 89–90. *See also* work
African-American children, 139, 163, 187
African groups, responsibility in, 180–1
Allport, G., 7
American children: African-American, 139, 163, 187; Asian-American, 187; Mexican-American, 187; planning skills of, 186–7 (*see also* planning skills); play of, 46, 50, 60, 159, 161; social orientation of, 43; toys used by, 138. *See also* American families; European-American children; Korean-American preschoolers; Western children
American culture, 119–20, 121, 122
American families: cultural scripts in, 110; nature/purpose of pretend play in, 109; pretend play in, 107–8, 109, 110, 139–42; quiet/solitary activity settings of, 108; sibling re-lationships in, 112, 113; values/be-liefs in, 111. *See also* American children; European-American children; Korean-American preschoolers
apprenticeship, 179
appropriation of skills, 153–4
Asian-American children, 187
Australian children, 184

Bakhtin, M. M., 247
Bandura, A., 179
Barber, B., 251
Barry, Anne, 241–6, 249
Bartolome, L. I., 229, 251
Bateson, G., 150

261

Delgado-Gaitan, C., 229
development, psychological, definition
 of, 130
Developmentally Appropriate Practice
 (DAP), 114–15
developmental niche, 174
Dhol-Ki-Patti, play in (India), 159–61
discipline/control, 78–80
Dreher, M., 187

ecocultural models, 100, 101–3
ecological cultural models, 100
ecological systems theory, 66–7, 68,
 69, 85, 87, 89
economical structure of children's
 communities, 152–3, 156–7
education: and job conditions, 89–90;
 mathematics curricula, reform of,
 203, 223; multicultural, 252; opportunity education, 141; parents'
 level of, 65–6, 69, 89; progressive
 schools, 143; and self-direction, 89–
 90; transmission-oriented, 231,
 233. *See also* lessons; New Literacy
Edwards, C. P., 9
Elkind, David: *The Hurried Child,*
 191–2
emic approach, 13–14
Engestrom, Y., 217
epistemic text engagement, 230, 231,
 234–5, 249
Estonian study of values/beliefs, 75–
 6, 89; and children's activities, 80–
 5, 88; and parental values/beliefs,
 77–80, 84–5, 86–7
ethnocentric bias, 104
European-American children: activity
 settings of, 118–22; nature/purpose
 of indoor activities of, 119; planning skills/after-school activities
 of, 187, 188; play of, 115–19, 136–
 7, 163–6; preschool programs for,

114; values/beliefs governing play
 of, 120–2, 140. *See also* American
 children; American families
everyday behavior of children, 202–3
exosystem, 89

Family Socialization and Develop-
 ment Competence project, 189
Farver, Jo Ann M., 14, 15, 16, 17
flow, 222
freedom to explore, 78–80
Freire, P., 231
Freud, Sigmund, 150
Fung, H., 141

Gabriele, A. J., 216
Gallimore, R., 101–2
Garvey, C., 130
Gaskins, Suzanne, 6, 14, 15, 16
Gauvain, Mary, 6, 15, 18, 99, 191
Geertz, C., 250
Gitlin, A. D., 232
Gladwin, T., 183
goals, 154, 154n2, 155. *See also* val-
 ues
Göncü, Artin, 12, 13, 14, 15, 17–18,
 161
Goodnow, J. J., 10–11, 183, 184–5
Greensboro (NC), 73, 76, 89. *See
 also* United States study of values/
 beliefs
grounded theory method, 107
Guatemala, play in, 159, 160–1
Guberman, Steven R., 5, 15, 18
guided participation, 178, 188, 190–1,
 193–4
Gutierrez, K., 251

Haas, B., 69–70
Haight, Wendy L., 14–15, 16, 17
Harkness, S., 101
Hayes-Roth, B., 181
Hayes-Roth, F., 181

Whiting, B., 9, 99
Whiting, J. M. H., 8–9
Willinsky, J., 229, 234
within-group variability, 6
Wolfer, Pamela, 246–9
work: definition of, 71; in Estonia/
Russia/South Korea/United States,
81–2; of Mayan children, 38, 50–
3, 55–6. *See also* adult work
work activities, 14, 16, 38, 50–3, 55–
6
WPPSI-R (Wechsler Preschool and
Primary Scale of Intelligence-
Revised), 117–18

Yucatec Mayan culture, 28–32. *See
also* Mayan children

zone of proximal development: defini-
tion/conceptions of, 11, 67, 150,
208, 212; and intersubjectivity,
208, 210, 211; and mathematics
outside of school, 204, 207–8,
211, 212–13; vs. Mayan model, 56;
and opportunities for participation,
222; as scaffolding, 100, 210–11,
212; and semiotic mediation, 208,
210; and situation definition, 208–
10